The Great Battles and Leaders of the Second World War
An Illustrated History

Winston S. Churchill

INTRODUCTION BY JOHN KEEGAN

HOUGHTON MIFFLIN COMPANY
BOSTON • NEW YORK 1995

This compilation of selections from THE SECOND WORLD WAR was edited by Giordano Bruno Guerri, with photo research by Eileen Romano.

Compilation: Copyright ©1995 Arnoldo Mondadori Editore S.p.A., Milan, Italy.

First published in the United States in 1995 by Houghton Mifflin Company.

Introduction ©1985, 1995 John Keegan.

Material in this book has been selected from the following works:

  I.   THE GATHERING STORM (first published: 1948)
       Copyright 1948 by Houghton Mifflin Company
       Copyright © renewed1976 by Lady Spencer Churchill,
       The Honourable Lady Sarah Audley, The Honourable Lady Soames.

  II. THEIR FINEST HOUR (first published: 1949)
       Copyright 1949 by Houghton Mifflin Company
       Copyright © renewed 1976 by Lady Spencer Churchill,
       The Honourable Lady Sarah Audley, The Honourable Lady Soames.

  III. THE GRAND ALLIANCE (first published: 1950)
       Copyright 1950 by Houghton Mifflin Company
       Copyright © renewed 1977 by Lady Spencer Churchill,
       The Honourable Lady Sarah Audley, The Honourable Lady Soames.

  IV. THE HINGE OF FATE (first published: 1950)
       Copyright 1950 by Houghton Mifflin Company
       Copyright © renewed 1978 by The Honourable Lady
       Sarah Audley and The Honourable Lady Soames.

  V. CLOSING THE RING (first published: 1951)
       Copyright 1951 by Houghton Mifflin Company
       Copyright © renewed 1979 by The Honourable Lady
       Sarah Audley and The Honourable Lady Soames.

  VI. TRIUMPH AND TRAGEDY (first published: 1953)
       Copyright 1953 by Houghton Mifflin Company
       Copyright © renewed 1981 by The Honourable Lady
       Sarah Audley and The Honourable Lady Soames.

For information about permission to reproduce selections from this book, write to Permissions, Houghton Mifflin Company, 215 Park Avenue South, New York, New York 10003

Library of Congress Cataloging-in-Publication Data

Churchill, Winston, Sir. 1874-1965.
    [Second World War. Selections]
    The great battles and leaders of the Second World War: an
  Illustrated history/Winston S. Churchill: introduction by John Keegan
         p.   cm.
    Selection from The Second World War.
    ISBN 0-395-75516-6
    1. World War. 1938-1945. 2. Statesman–20th century–Biography.
  3. Generals–20th century–Biography.   I. Title.
D743.C4825 1995
940.53'092'2–dc20
[B]   95-18483
                                    CIP

0-395-75516-6
Printed in Spain by Artes Graficas Toledo
D.L.TO:941-1995

TABLE OF CONTENTS

Introduction

John Keegan

Winston Churchill began to write the first of what were to be the six volumes of *The Second World War* in 1946. It was a work he had expected to postpone to a later stage of his life, since he had looked forward in 1945 to extending his wartime leadership into the peace. The rejection of his party by the electorate was a heavy blow, which might have dulled his urge to write. But resilience was perhaps the most pronounced of his traits of character, and he had already written the history of another great war in which he had been a principal actor. Once committed to the task, he attacked it with an energy, enthusiasm, and power of organisation which would have been remarkable in a professional historian of half his age.

His five-volume history of the First World War, *The World Crisis*, had drawn heavily on the evidence he had submitted to the Dardanelles Committee and on episodic accounts written for newspapers. Its origins were therefore in political debate and in journalism. He set about composing *The Second World War* in an entirely different manner—different, too, from the way in which he had written his great life of Marlborough. Then his technique had been to dictate long passages of narrative, later correcting points of detail in consultation with experts. Now he began by assembling a team of advisers and collecting the documents on which the writing was to be based. The documents were set up in print by the publishers, Cassell, while the advisers worked on the chronologies into which they would fit. Churchill meanwhile prepared himself by dictating recollections of what he had identified as key episodes. They consisted partly of firm impressions and partly of queries to his team about dates, times, places, and personalities. He also wrote copiously to fellow-actors, begging of them their own papers and recollections and inviting their comments on what he proposed to say. When documents, chronologies, corrections, and comments were collated, he began to write. The bulk of the writing, which was completed in 1953, was done by his normal method of dictation; however, long passages of the first volume, which is very much an *apologia pro vita sua*, were composed in his own hand.

Churchill was not, did not aspire to be, and would very probably have despised the label scientific historian. Like Clarendon and Macaulay, he saw history as a branch of moral philosophy. Indeed, he gave his history a Moral. Its phrases have become some of the most famous words he pronounced—"In War: Resolution; In Defeat: Defiance; In Victory: Magnanimity; In Peace: Goodwill." Each of the component volumes was also given a Theme —"How the English-speaking peoples through their unwisdom, carelessness and good nature allowed the wicked to rearm" is that of the first—which the author believed encapsulated the period with which the volume dealt, but which he also organised his material to illus-

August 1944-Winston Churchill follows the action from a window of a house near Florence (Italy).

trate. He justified this method by comparing it to that of Defoe's *Memoirs of a Cavalier*, "in which the author hangs the chronicle and discussion of great military and political events upon the thread of the personal experience of an individual."

The history is, indeed, intensely personal. Explicitly so, because Churchill asks the reader to regard it as a continuation of *The World Crisis*, the two together forming both "an account of another Thirty Years War" and an expression of his "life-effort" on which he was "content to be judged." Implicitly so, because he related many of the major episodes of the war autobiographically. An excellent example is his account of the air fighting on September 15, 1940, which is regarded as the crisis of the Battle of Britain. He was lunching at Chequers and decided, since the weather seemed to favour a German attack, to spend the afternoon at the Headquarters of the R.A.F. No. 11 Group. He and his wife at once drove there, were given seats in the command room from which the British fighters were controlled, and watched the development of the action:

Winston Churchill enters the Admiralty building on September 4, 1939

> Presently the red bulbs showed that the majority of our squadrons were engaged. A subdued hum arose from the floor, where the busy plotters pushed their discs to and fro in accordance with the swiftly-changing situation . . . In a little while all our squadrons were fighting, and some had already begun to return for fuel. . . . I became conscious of the anxiety of the Commander. Hitherto I had watched in silence. I now asked, "What other reserves have we?" "There are none," said Air Marshal Park. In an account which he wrote afterwards he said that at this I "looked grave." Well I might. The odds were great; our margins small; the stakes infinite. . . . Then it appeared that the enemy were going home. No new attack appeared. In another ten minutes the action was ended. We climbed again the stairways that led to the surface, and almost as we emerged the "All Clear" sounded . . . It was 4:30 p.m. before I got back to Chequers, and I immediately went to bed [an unvarying wartime habit]. I did not wake till eight. When I rang my Principal Private Secretary came in with the evening budget of news from all over the world. It was repellent. . . . . "However," he said, as he finished his account, "all is redeemed by the air. We have shot down one hundred and eighty-three for the loss of under forty."

This account is both unique—neither Roosevelt, Stalin, nor Hitler left any first-hand narrative of their involvement in the direction of the war—and acutely revealing. Churchill was fascinated by military operations and followed their progress very closely. But he forbore absolutely to intervene in their control at the hour-by-hour and unit-by-unit level adopted by Hitler. He warned and advised, encouraged and occasionally excoriated. He appointed and removed commanders. But he did not presume to do their jobs. Another chapter conveys the extent of his forbearance. It comes in Volume IV and concerns the fall of Singapore in February 1942. Very properly, Churchill was not merely disheartened but outranged by the failure of the Malaya garrison, under its commander, General Percival, to halt a Japanese invading force which it outnumbered. When it became clear that Percival was about to be defeated, outrage mingled with desperation and disbelief. Breaking a rule, he signalled Wavell, the Supreme Commander, to urge that the newly arrived 18th Division fight "to the bitter end" and that "com-

Close–up of the Prime Minister piloting the airplane that is carrying him to Bermuda in January 1942.

manders and senior officers should die with their troops." In the event, the 18th Division was captured by the Japanese almost intact, and General Percival marched into enemy lines under a white flag. By not one immoderate word does the author convey in his narrative how deeply he—and, he felt, his country—were wounded by this humiliating and disastrous episode.

The restraint shown in the Singapore chapter was determined by another principle which he had adopted: that of "never criticising any measure of war or policy after the event unless I had before expressed publicly or formally my opinion or warning about it." The effect is to invest the whole history with those qualities of magnanimity and good will by which he set such store, and the more so as it deals with personalities. The volumes are not only a chronicle of events. They are a record of meetings, debate, and disagreements with a world of people. Some were friends with whom he was forced to differ. Some were with opponents or future enemies with whom he nevertheless succeeded in making common cause, Stalin foremost among them. The descriptions of his personal relationships with these men alone would assure the permanent value of this history to our understanding of the Second World War.

Gathered here in *The Great Battles and Leaders of the Second World War: An Illustrated History* are selections from the six volumes offering Churchill's narrative on the most significant battles and the key protagonists. Many photographs which have never been published or have not been seen in decades are included.

The Second World War is an extraordinary achievement, extraordinary in its sweep and comprehensiveness, balance and literary effect; extraordinary in the singularity of its point of view; extraordinary as the labour of a man, already old, who still had ahead of him a career large enough to crown most other statesmen's lives; extraordinary as a contribution to the memorabilia of the English–speaking peoples. It is a great history and will continue to be read as long as Churchill and the Second World War are remembered.

PUBLISHER'S NOTE

Winston Churchill (1874–1965) was the elder son of Lord Randolph Churchill and his American wife, Jennie Jerome. In 1908, he married Clementine Ogilvy, who gave him life-long support, and they had four daughters and one son.

Churchill entered the army in 1895 and served in Cuba, India, Egypt, and the Sudan; his first publications were *The Story of the Malakand Field Force* (1898), *The River War* (1899), and *Savrola* (1900), his only novel. On a special commission for the *Morning Post*, he became involved in the Boer War, was taken prisoner, and escaped. His experiences led to the writing of *London to Ladysmith, via Pretoria* and *Ian Hamilton's March*, both published in 1900.

He began his erratic political career in October 1900, when he was elected Conservative M.P. for Oldham. Four years later, however, he joined the Liberal party. In 1906, he became Under-Secretary of State for the colonies and showed his desire for reform in such writings as *My African Journey* (1908). He became President of the Board of Trade in 1908 and Home Secretary in 1910 and, together with Lloyd George, introduced social legislation which helped form much of the basis for modern Britain. Because he foresaw the possibilities of war with Germany after the Agadir crisis, he was made First Lord of the Admiralty in October 1911. He achieved major changes, including that of modernising and preparing the Royal Navy for war, despite unpopularity in the Cabinet because of the cost involved. In May 1915, however, pressurised by the Opposition, he left the Admiralty and served for a time as Lieutenant-Colonel in France. Lloyd George appointed him Minister of Munitions in July 1917 and Secretary of State for War and Air the following year. In 1924, he rejoined the Conservative party and was made Chancellor of the Exchequer by Baldwin. He resigned in January 1931 and, during the 1930s, wrote numerous books, amongst which were *My Early Life* (1930), *Thoughts and Adventures* (1932), and *Great Contemporaries* (1937). Churchill again was asked to take office in September 1939, after the German invasion of Poland and, when Chamberlain was forced to retire because of the Labour party's refusal to serve under him, Churchill became Prime Minister (May 1940–May 1945). From 1945, he spent most of his time writing *The Second World War*; he returned to office in 1951. In 1953, he accepted the garter and also won the Nobel Prize for literature. In April 1955, however, owing to increasing illness, he resigned as Prime Minister, although he continued to write. *A History of the English-speaking Peoples* (1956–8) is his major work of this time. He died at the age of ninety.

The Battles

THE ATTACK ON POLAND

On September 1, 1939, German bombers destroyed Poland's air force. Then, the Wehrmacht launched a land attack. Finally, the Soviet Union intervened from the East.

According to Hitler's plan the German armies were unleashed on September 1, and ahead of them his Air Force struck the Polish squadrons on their airfields. In two days the Polish air power was virtually annihilated. Within a week the German armies had bitten deep into Poland. Resistance everywhere was brave but vain. All the Polish armies on the frontiers, except the Posen group, whose flanks were deeply turned, were driven backwards. The Lodz group was split in twain by the main thrust of the German Tenth Army; one half withdrew eastwards to Radom, the other was forced north-westward; and through this gap darted two Panzer divisions, making straight for Warsaw. Farther north the German Fourth Army reached and crossed Vistula, and turned along it in their march on Warsaw. Only the Polish northern group

was able to inflict a check upon the German Third Army. They were soon outflanked and fell back to the river Narew, where alone a fairly strong defensive system had been prepared in advance. Such were the results of the first week of the Blitzkrieg.

The second week was marked by bitter fighting, and by its end the Polish Army, nominally of about two million men, ceased to exist as an organised force. In the south the Fourteenth German Army drove on to reach the river San. North of them the four Polish divisions which had retreated to Radom were there encircled and destroyed. The two armoured divisions of the Tenth Army reached the outskirts of Warsaw, but having no infantry with them could not make headway against the desperate resistance organised by the townsfolk. North-east of Warsaw the Third Army encircled the capital from the

The Polish cavalry fought valiantly, but was not in a position to offer much resistance to German armoured forces.

Top: Polish snipers are taken prisoner.

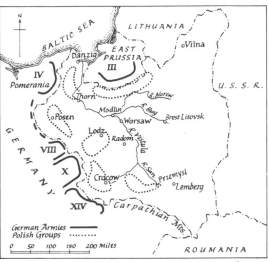

THE GERMAN AND POLISH CONCENTRATIONS Sept. 1st 1939

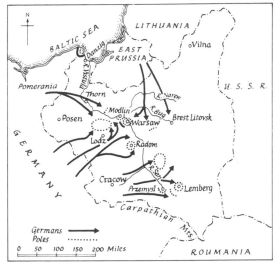

THE INNER PINCERS CLOSE Sept. 13th

THE OUTER PINCERS CLOSE · THE RUSSIANS ADVANCE Sept. 17th

A German motorcyclist and a German infantryman seen **through the breach in a defensive structure near Warsaw.** **The war against Poland was very short, a sample of the Blitzkrieg that German generals had envisaged.**

The crew of a German bomber listens to instructions before take-off on an action against the Polish rear.

east, and its left column reached Brest-Litovsk, a hundred miles behind the battle-front.

It was within the claws of the Warsaw pincers that the Polish Army fought and died. Their Posen group had been joined by divisions from the Thorn and Lodz groups, forced towards them by the German onslaught. It now numbered twelve divisions, and across its southern flank the German Tenth Army was streaming towards Warsaw, protected only by the relatively weak Eighth Army. Although already virtually surrounded, the Polish commander of the Posen group, General Kutrzea, resolved to strike south against the flank of the main German drive. This audacious Polish counter-attack, called the Battle of the River Bzura, created a crisis which drew in not only the German Eighth Army but a part of the Tenth, deflected from their Warsaw objective, and even a corps of the Fourth Army from the north. Under the assault of all these powerful

In an already occupied town, two German soldiers read the notice announcing

Poland's general mobilisation.

14

bodies, and overwhelmed by unresisted air bombardment, the Posen group maintained its ever-glorious struggle for ten days. It was blotted out on September 19.

In the meantime the outer pincers had met and closed. The Fourteenth Army reached the outskirts of Lemberg on September 12, and, striking north, joined hands on the 17th with the troops of the Third Army, which had passed through Brest-Litovsk. There was now no loophole of escape save for straggling and daring individuals. On the 20th the Germans announced that the Battle of the Vistula was "one of the greatest battles of extermination of all time".

It was now the turn of the Soviets. What they now call "Democracy" came into action. On September 17 the Russian armies swarmed across the almost undefended Polish eastern frontier and rolled westward on a broad front. On the 18th they occupied Vilna, and met their German collaborators at Brest-Litovsk. Here in the previous war the Bolsheviks, in breach of their solemn agreements with the Western Allies, had made their separate peace with the Kaiser's Germany and had bowed to its harsh terms. Now in Brest-Litovsk it was with Hitler's Germany that the Russian Communists grinned and shook hands. The ruin of Poland and its entire subjugation proceeded apace. Warsaw and Modlin still remained unconquered. The resistance of Warsaw, largely arising from the surge of its citizens, was magnificent and forlorn. After many days of violent bombardment from the air and by heavy artillery, much of which was rapidly transported across the great lateral highways from the idle Western Front, the Warsaw radio ceased to play the Polish National Anthem, and Hitler entered the ruins of the city. Modlin, a fortress twenty miles down the Vistula, had taken in the remnants of the Thorn group, and fought on until the 28th. Thus in one month all was over, and a nation of thirty-five millions fell into the merciless grip of those who sought not only conquest, but enslavement and indeed extinction for vast numbers.

We had seen a perfect specimen of the modern Blitzkrieg; the close interaction on the battlefield of Army and Air Force; the violent bombardment of all communications and of any town that seemed an attractive target; the arming of an active Fifth Column; the free use of spies and parachutists; and above all the irresistible forward thrusts of great masses of armour. The Poles were not to be the last to endure this ordeal.

October 5, 1939: invading German troops march through the center of Warsaw, deserted by Polish citizens. Warsaw fell on September 27, less than a month into the war.

THE INVASION OF FRANCE

In May 1940, after a lapse of several months in combat, Hitler attacked France: he outflanked enemy defensive lines by invading Belgium and the Netherlands.

During the night of May 9-10, heralded by widespread air attacks against airfields, communications, headquarters, and magazines, all the German forces in the Bock and Rundstedt Army Groups sprang forward towards France across the frontiers of Belgium, Holland, and Luxembourg. Complete tactical surprise was achieved in nearly every case. Out of the darkness came suddenly innumerable parties of well-armed, ardent storm troops, often with light artillery, and long before daybreak a hundred and fifty miles of front were aflame. Holland and Belgium, assaulted without the slightest pretext or warning, cried aloud for help. The Dutch had trusted to their water-line; all the sluices not seized or betrayed were opened, and the Dutch frontier guards fired upon the invaders. The Belgians

succeeded in destroying the bridges of the Meuse, but the Germans captured intact two across the Albert Canal.

By Plan D, the First Allied Army Group, under General Billotte, with its small but very fine British army, was, from the moment when the Germans violated the frontier, to advance east into Belgium. It was intended to forestall the enemy and stand on the line Meuse-Louvain-Antwerp. In front of that line, along the Meuse and the Albert Canal, lay the main Belgian forces. Should these stem the first German onrush the Army Group would support them. It seemed more probable that the Belgians would be at once thrown back on to the Allied line. And this, in fact, happened. It was assumed that in this case the Belgian resistance would give a short breathing-space, during which the French and British could

May 1940: Adolf Hitler poses with a group of paratroop pioneers, whom he has just decorated with the Iron Cross for taking the fort at Eben Emael.

Top: in Belgium, a German soldier tests a captured French light armoured vehicle.

organise their new position. Except on the critical front of the French Ninth Army, this was accomplished. On the extreme left or seaward flank the Seventh French Army was to seize the islands commanding the mouth of the Scheldt, and, if possible, to assist the Dutch by an advance towards Breda. It was thought that on our southern flank the Ardennes constituted an impassable barrier, and south of that again began the regular fortified Maginot Line, stretching out to the Rhine and along the Rhine to Switzerland. All therefore seemed to depend upon the forward left-handed counter-stroke of the Allied Northern Armies. This again hung upon the speed with which Belgium could be occupied. Everything had been worked out in this way with the utmost detail, and only a signal was necessary to hurl forward the Allied force of well over a million men. At 5.30 a.m. on May 10 Lord Gort received a message from General Georges ordering "Alertes 1, 2, and 3"; namely, instant readiness to move into Belgium. At 6.45 a.m. General Gamelin ordered the execu-

tion of Plan D, and the long-prepared scheme of the French High Command, to which the British had subordinated themselves, came at once into action.

At the signal the Northern Armies sprang to the rescue of Belgium and poured forward along all the roads amid the cheers of the inhabitants. The first phase of Plan D was completed by May 12. The French held the left bank of the Meuse to Huy, and their light forces beyond the river were falling back before increasing enemy pressure. The armoured divisions of the French First Army reached the line Huy-Hannut-Tirlemont. The Belgians, having lost the Albert Canal, were falling back to the line of the river Gette and taking up their prescribed position from Antwerp to

A group of German infantrymen jumping over an entrenchment. The German Army routed Belgian, Dutch, and French defences with ease.

French front, May 1940: while a German pioneer shelters in a pit, an explosion damages the wire entanglement in front of the bulwarks of a fort along the Maginot Line.

Lysander reconnaissance aircraft lined up in a British air base. Airmen are loading supplies to be parachuted to retreating troops in France.

Louvain. They still held Liége and Namur. The French Seventh Army had occupied the islands of Walcheren and South Beveland, and were engaged with mechanised units of the German Eighteenth Army on the line Herenthals-Bergen-op-Zoom. So rapid had been the advance of the French Seventh Army that it had already outrun its ammunition supplies. The superiority in quality though not in numbers of the British Air Force was already apparent. Thus up till the night of the 12th there was no reason to suppose that the operations were not going well.

However, during the 13th Lord Gort's headquarters became aware of the weight of the German thrust on the front of the French Ninth Army. By nightfall the enemy had established themselves on the west bank of the Meuse, on either side of Dinant and Sedan. The French G.Q.G (Grand-Quartier-Général) were not yet certain whether the main German effort was directed through Luxembourg against the left of the Maginot Line or through Maastricht towards Brussels. Along the whole front Louvain-Namur-Dinant to Sedan an intense, heavy battle had developed, but under conditions which General Gamelin had not contemplated, for at Dinant the French Ninth Army had no time to install themselves before the enemy was upon them.

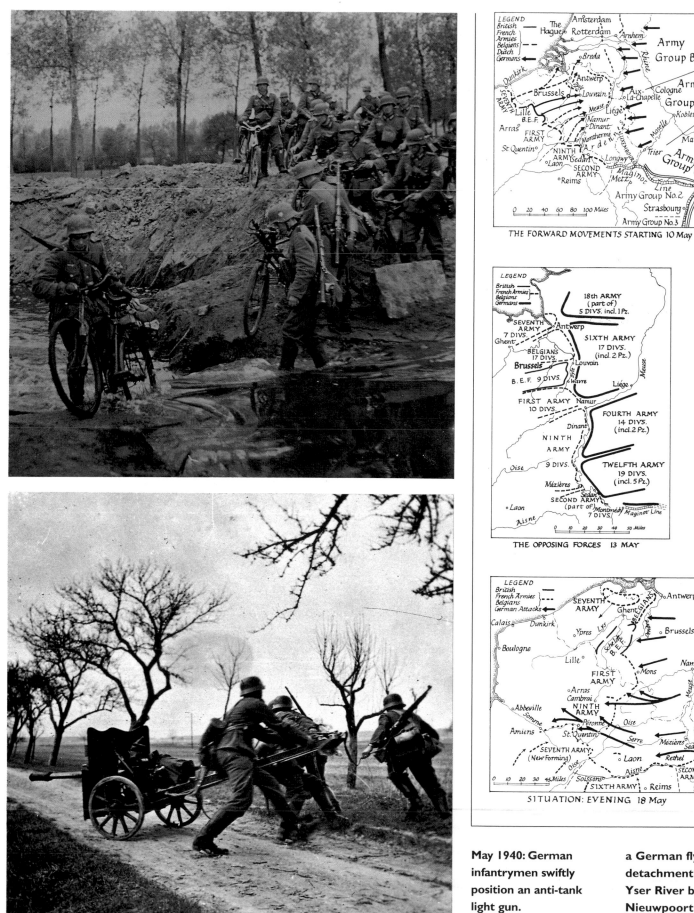

THE FORWARD MOVEMENTS STARTING 10 May

THE OPPOSING FORCES 13 MAY

SITUATION: EVENING 18 May

May 1940: German infantrymen swiftly position an anti-tank light gun.
Top: bikers from a German flying detachment wading the Yser River between Nieuwpoort and Diksmuide.

GIACOMELLI

A patrol of German pioneers advancing down a Flemish watercourse.

Right: a German anti-aircraft-artillery soldier during a British air-raid.

Top: German infantrymen work their way onto the opposite bank of a river by grasping the parapet of a shelled bridge.

During the 14th the bad news began to come in. At first all was vague. At 7 p.m. I read to the Cabinet a message received from M. Reynaud stating that the Germans had broken through at Sedan, that the French were unable to resist the combination of tanks and dive-bombing, and asking for ten more squadrons of fighters to re-establish the line. Other messages received by the Chiefs of Staff gave similar information, and added that both Generals Gamelin and Georges took a serious view of the situation and that General Gamelin was surprised at the rapidity of the enemy's advance. In fact, Kleist's Group, with its immense mass of armour, heavy and light, had completely scattered or destroyed the French troops on their immediate front, and could now move forward at a pace never before known in war. At almost all points where the armies had come in contact the weight and fury of the German attack was overpowering. They crossed the Meuse in the Dinant sector with two more armoured divisions. To the north the fighting on the front of the French First Army had been most severe. The Ist and IInd British Corps were still in position from Wavre to Louvain, where our 3rd Division, under General Montgomery, had had sharp fighting. Farther north the Belgians were retiring to the Antwerp defences. The French Seventh Army, on the seaward flank, was recoiling even quicker than it had advanced.

From the moment of the invasion we began Operation "Royal Marine", the launching of the fluvial mines into the Rhine, and in the first week of the battle nearly 1,700 were "streamed". They produced immediate results. Practically all river traffic between Karlsruhe and Mainz was suspended, and extensive damage was done to the Karlsruhe barrage and a number of pontoon bridges. The success of this device was however lost in the deluge of disaster.

All the British air squadrons fought continuously, their principal effort being against the pontoon bridges in the Sedan area. Several of these were destroyed and others damaged in desperate and devoted attacks. The losses in the low-level attacks on the bridges from the German anti-aircraft artillery were cruel. In one case, of six aircraft only one returned from the successful task. On this day alone we lost a total of sixty-seven machines, and, being engaged principally with the enemy's anti-aircraft forces, accounted for only fifty-three German aircraft. That night there remained in France of the Royal Air Force only 206 serviceable aircraft out of 474.

About half-past seven on the morning of the 15th I was woken up with the news that M. Reynaud was on the telephone at my bedside. He spoke in English, and evidently under stress. "We have been defeated." As I did not immediately respond he said again: "We are beaten; we have lost the battle." I said: "Surely it can't have happened so soon?" But he replied: "The front is broken near Sedan; they are pouring through in great

The sea-front in Ostend (Belgium) damaged by air attacks. A soldier sits on a bridge cluttered with furniture.

numbers with tanks and armoured cars"—or words to that effect.

On this day the French Ninth Army, Corap's, was in a state of complete dissolution, and its remnants were divided up between General Giraud, of the Seventh French Army, who took over from Corap in the north, and the headquarters of the Sixth French Army, which was forming in the south. A gap of some fifty miles had in fact been punched in the French line, through which the vast mass of enemy armour was pouring. By the evening of the 15th German armoured cars were reported to be in Liart and Montcornet, the latter sixty miles behind the original front. The French First Army was also pierced on a 5,000-yards front south of Limal. Farther north all attacks on the British were repulsed. The German attack and the retirement of the French division on their right compelled the making of a British defensive flank facing south. The French Seventh Army had retreated into the Antwerp defences west of the Scheldt, and was being driven out of the islands of Walcheren and South Beveland.

On this day also the struggle in Holland came to an end. Owing to the capitulation of the Dutch High Command at 11 a.m., only very few Dutch troops could be evacuated.

On the 16th the German spearheads stood along the line La Capelle-Vervins-Marle-Laon, and the vanguards of the German XIVth Corps were in support at Montcornet and Neufchâtel-sur-Aisne. The fall of Laon confirmed the penetration of over sixty miles inward upon us from the frontier near Sedan. Under this threat and the ever-increasing pressure on their own front, the First French Army and the British Expeditionary Force were ordered to withdraw in three stages to the Scheldt.

Servicemen from a Dutch detachment taken prisoner by German paratroopers march with raised hands through a devastated town.

Hitler between two German officers in front of the Eiffel Tower.

DUNKIRK

At the end of May, the French and the British were besieged at Dunkirk. Churchill organised a dramatic rescue operation.

By May 23 the Ist and IInd Corps of the B.E.F., withdrawn by stages from Belgium, were back again on the frontier defences north and east of Lille, which they had built for themselves during the winter. The German scythe-cut round our southern flank had reached the sea, and we had to shield ourselves from this. As the facts forced themselves upon Gort and his headquarters, troops had successively been sent to positions along the canal line La Bassée-Béthune-Aire-St. Omer Watten. These, with elements of the French XVIth Corps, touched the sea at the Gravelines water-line. The British IIIrd Corps was responsible in the main for this curled-in flank facing south. There was no continuous line, but only a series of defended "stops" at the main crossings, some of which, like St. Omer and Watten, had already fallen to the enemy. The indispensable roads northwards from Cassel were threatened. Gort's reserve consisted only of the two British divisions, the 5th and 50th, which had, as we have seen, just been so narrowly extricated from their southerly counter-attack made at Arras in forlorn fulfilment of the Weygand plan. At this date the total frontage of the B.E.F. was about ninety miles, everywhere in close contact with the enemy.

To the south of the B.E.F. lay the First French Army, having two divisions in the frontier defences and the remainder, comprising eleven divisions in no good shape, cramped in the area north and east of Douai. This army was under attack from the south-east claw of the German encirclement. On our left the Belgian Army was being driven back from the Lys canal at many places, and with their retirement northwards a gap was developing north of Menin.

May 31, 1940: troops from the British Expeditionary Force crowd beneath the bulwarks of a ship docked in Dunkirk for embarkation.

Top: troops from the Expeditionary Force rest during a lull in combat in Belgium.

In the evening of the 25th Lord Gort took a vital decision. His orders still were to pursue the Weygand plan of a southerly attack towards Cambrai, in which the 5th and 50th Divisions, in conjunction with the French, were to be employed. The promised French attack northwards from the Somme showed no sign of reality. The last defenders of Boulogne had been evacuated. Calais still held out. Gort now abandoned the Weygand plan. There was in his view no longer hope of a march to the south and to the Somme. Moreover, at the same time the crumbling of the Belgian defence and the gap opening to the north created a new peril, dominating in itself. A captured order of the German Sixth Army showed that one corps was to march north-westwards towards Ypres and another corps westwards towards Wytschaete.

Armoured vehicles from the British Expeditionary Force, on their way to the front line, are cheered by the residents of a Belgian city.

On the way back: infantry and tanks retreat towards Dunkirk.

25

Near the port of Brest, troops from a detachment of the British Expeditionary Force wait to embark following the evacuation order.

How could the Belgians withstand this double thrust? Confident in his military virtue, and convinced of the complete breakdown of all control, either by the British and French Governments or by the French Supreme Command, Gort resolved to abandon the attack to the southward, to plug the gap which a Belgian capitulation was about to open in the north, and to march to the sea. At this moment here was the only hope of saving anything from destruction or surrender. At 6 p.m. he ordered the 5th and 50th Divisions to join the IInd British Corps to fill the impending Belgian gap. He informed General Blanchard, who had succeeded Billotte in command of the First Army Group, of his action; and this officer, acknowledging the force of events, gave orders at 11.30 p.m. for a withdrawal on the 26th to a line behind the Lys canal west of Lille, with a view to forming a bridgehead around Dunkirk.

Early on May 26 Gort and Blanchard drew up their plan for withdrawal to the coast. As the First French Army had farther to go, the first movements of the B.E.F. on the night of the 26th-27th were to be preparatory, and rearguards of the British Ist and IInd Corps remained on the frontier defences till the night of the 27th-28th. In all this Lord Gort had acted upon his own responsibility. But by now we at home, with a somewhat different angle of information, had already reached the same conclusions. On the 26th a telegram from the War Office approved his conduct, and authorised him "to operate towards the coast forthwith in conjunction with the French and Belgian armies". The emergency gathering on a vast scale of naval vessels of all kinds and sizes was already in full swing.

The reader must now look at the diagram which shows the areas held on the night of the 25th-26th by the British divisions.

On the western flank of the corridor to the

sea the position remained largely unchanged during the 26th. The localities held by the 48th and 44th Divisions came under relatively little pressure. The 2nd Division however had heavy fighting on the Aire and La Bassée canals, and they held their ground. Farther to the east a strong German attack developed around Carvin, jointly defended by British and French troops. The situation was restored by the counter-attack of two battalions of the 50th Division, which were in bivouac close by. On the left of the British line the 5th Division, with the 143rd Brigade of the 48th Division under command, had travelled through the night, and at dawn took over the defence of the Ypres-Comines canal to close the gap which had opened between the British and Belgian armies. They were only just in time. Soon after they arrived the enemy attacked, and the fighting was heavy all day. Three battalions of the 1st Division in reserve were drawn in. The 50th Division, after bivouacking south of Lille, moved northwards to prolong the flank of the 5th Division around Ypres. The Belgian Army, heavily attacked throughout the day and with their right flank driven in, reported that they had no forces with which to regain touch with the British, and that they were unable to fall back to the line of the Yser canal in conformity with the British movement.

Meanwhile the organisation of the bridgeheads around Dunkirk was proceeding. The French were to hold from Gravelines to Bergues, and the British thence along the canal by Furnes to Nieuport and the sea. The various groups and parties of all arms which were arriving from both directions were woven into this line. Confirming the orders of the 26th, Lord Gort received from the War Office a telegram, dispatched at 1 p.m. on the 27th, telling him that his task henceforward was "to evacuate the maximum force possible". I had informed M. Reynaud the day before that the policy was to evacuate the British Expeditionary Force, and had requested him to issue corresponding orders. Such was the breakdown in communications that at 2 p.m. on the 27th the commander of the First French Army issued an order to his corps: "La bataille sera livrée sans

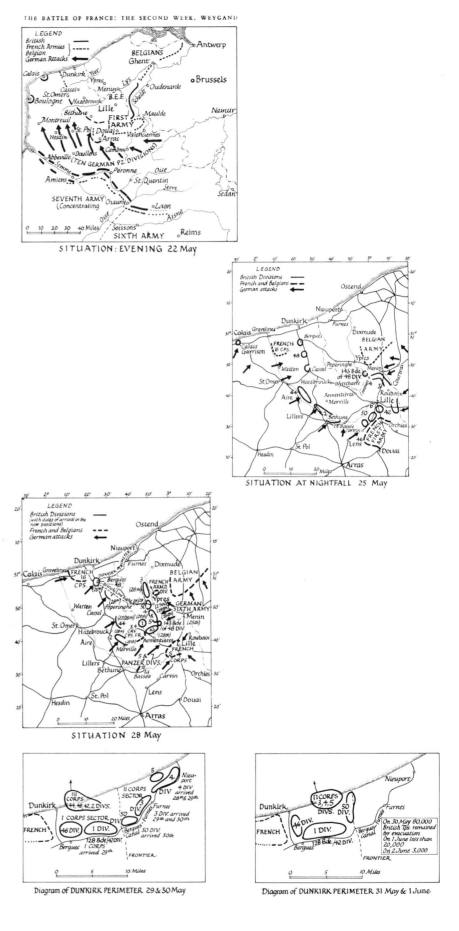

THE BATTLE OF FRANCE: THE SECOND WEEK. WEYGAND

SITUATION: EVENING 22 May

SITUATION AT NIGHTFALL 25 May

SITUATION 28 May

Diagram of DUNKIRK PERIMETER 29 & 30 May

Diagram of DUNKIRK PERIMETER 31 May & 1 June

In the North Sea, off the coast of Dunkirk, a group of soldiers try to save themselves on the wreck of a half-sunken vessel and on the wing of a German airplane.

esprit de recul sur la position de la Lys."

Four British divisions and the whole of the First French Army were now in dire peril of being cut off around Lille. The two arms of the German encircling movement strove to close the pincers upon them. Although we had not in those days the admirable map rooms of more coherent periods, and although no control of the battle from London was possible, I had for three days past been harrowed by the position of the mass of Allied troops around Lille, including our four fine divisions. This however was one of those rare but decisive moments when mechanical transport exercises its rights. When Gort gave the order all these four divisions came back with surprising rapidity almost in a night. Meanwhile, by fierce battles on either side of the corridor, the rest of the British Army kept the path open to the sea. The pincer-claws, which were delayed by the 2nd Division, and checked for three days by the 5th Division, eventually met on the night of May 29 in manner similar to the great Russian operation round Stalingrad in 1942. The trap had taken two and a half days to close, and in that time four British divisions and a great part of the First French Army, except the Vth Corps, which was lost, withdrew in good order through the gap, in spite of the French having

only horse transport, and the main road to Dunkirk being already cut and the secondary roads filled with retiring troops, long trains of transport, and many thousands of refugees.

All this day of the 28th the escape of the British Army hung in the balance. On the front from Comines to Ypres and thence to the sea, facing east and attempting to fill the Belgian gap, General Brooke and his IInd Corps fought a magnificent battle. For two days past the 5th Division had held Comines against all attacks, but as the Belgians withdrew northwards, and then capitulated, the gap widened beyond repair. The protection of the flank of the B.E.F. was now their task. First the 50th Division came in to prolong the line; then the 4th and 3rd Divisions, newly withdrawn from east of Lille, hastened in motor transport to extend the wall of the vital corridor that led to Dunkirk. The German thrust between the British and Belgian Armies was not to be prevented, but its fatal consequence, an inward turn across the Yser, which would have brought the enemy on to the beaches behind our fighting troops, was foreseen and everywhere forestalled.

The Germans sustained a bloody repulse. Orders were given to the British artillery, both field and medium, to fire off all their ammuni-

An image of the rout: from aboard a transport ship, some rescued troops observe the fires caused by air raids. In the distance, a British hospital ship.

French in Lille fought on gradually contracting fronts against increasing pressure, until on the evening of the 31st, short of food and with their ammunition exhausted, they were forced to surrender. About fifty thousand men thus fell into German hands. These Frenchmen, under the gallant leadership of General Molinié, had for four critical days contained no less than seven German divisions which otherwise could have joined in the assaults on the Dunkirk perimeter. This was a splendid contribution to the escape of their more fortunate comrades and of the B.E.F.

Meanwhile ashore around Dunkirk the occupation of the perimeter was effected with precision. The troops arrived out of chaos and were formed in order along the defences, which even in two days had grown. Those men who were in best shape turned about to form the line. Divisions like the 2nd and 5th, which had suffered most, were held in reserve on the beaches and were then embarked early. In the first instance there were to be three corps on the front, but by the 29th, with the French taking a greater share in the defences, two sufficed. The enemy had closely followed the withdrawal, and hard fighting was incessant, especially on the flanks near Nieuport and Bergues. As the evacuation went on the steady decrease in the number of troops, both British and French, was accompanied by a corresponding contraction of the defence. On the beaches, among the sand dunes, for three, four, or five days scores of thousands of men dwelt under unrelenting air attack. Hitler's belief that the German Air Force would render escape impossible, and that therefore he should keep his armoured formations for the final stroke of the campaign, was

tion at the enemy, and the tremendous fire did much to quell the German assault. All the time, only about four miles behind Brooke's struggling front, vast masses of transport and troops poured back into the developing bridgehead of Dunkirk, and were fitted with skilful improvisation into its defences. Moreover, within the perimeter itself the main east-west road was at one time completely blocked by vehicles, and a one-way track was cleared only by bulldozers hurling them into the ditches on either side.

In the afternoon of the 28th Gort ordered a general withdrawal to the bridgehead, which now ran Gravelines-Bergues-Furnes-Nieuport. On this front the British divisions stood from right to left, and from Bergues to the sea by Nieuport, in the following order: 46th, 42nd, 1st, 50th, 3rd, and 4th. By the 29th a large part of the B.E.F. had arrived within the perimeter, and by this time the naval measures for evacuation were beginning to attain their full effect. On May 30 G.H.Q. reported that all British divisions, or the remains of them, had come in.

More than half the First French Army found their way to Dunkirk, where the great majority were safely embarked. But the line of retreat of at least five divisions was cut by the German pincers movement west of Lille. On the 28th they attempted to break out westwards, but in vain; the enemy closed in upon them from all sides. All through the next three days the a mistaken but not unreasonable view.

Three factors falsified his expectations. First, the incessant air-bombing of the masses of troops along the seashore did them very little harm. The bombs plunged into the soft sand, which muffled their explosions. In the early stages, after a crashing air raid, the troops were astonished to find that hardly anybody had been killed or wounded. Everywhere there had been explosions, but scarcely anyone was the worse. A rocky shore would have produced far more deadly results. Presently the soldiers regarded the air attacks with contempt. They crouched in the sand dunes with composure and growing hope. Before them lay the grey but not unfriendly sea. Beyond, the rescuing ships and—Home.

The second factor which Hitler had not foreseen was the slaughter of his airmen. British and German air quality was put directly to the test. By intense effort Fighter Command maintained successive patrols over the scene, and fought the enemy at long odds. Hour after hour they bit into the German fighter and bomber squadrons, taking a heavy toll, scattering them and driving them away. Day after day this went on, till the glorious victory of the Royal Air Force was gained. Wherever German aircraft were encountered, sometimes in forties and fifties, they were instantly attacked, often by single squadrons or less, and shot down in scores, which presently added up into hundreds. The whole Metropolitan Air Force, our last sacred reserve, was used. Sometimes the fighter pilots made four sorties a day. A clear result was obtained. The superior enemy were beaten or killed, and for all their bravery mastered, or even cowed. This was a decisive clash. Unhappily, the troops on the beaches saw very little of this epic conflict in the air, often miles away or above the clouds. They knew nothing of the loss inflicted on the enemy. All they felt was the bombs scourging the beaches, cast by the foes who had got through, but did not perhaps return. There was even a bitter anger in the Army against the Air Force, and some of the troops landing at Dover or at Thames ports in their ignorance insulted men in Air Force uniform. They should have clasped their hands; but how could they know? In Parliament I took pains to spread the truth.

But all the aid of the sand and all the prowess in the air would have been vain without the sea. The instructions given ten or twelve days before had, under the pressure and emotion of events, borne amazing fruit. Perfect discipline prevailed ashore and afloat. The sea was calm. To and fro between the shore and the ships plied the little boats, gathering the men from the beaches as they waded out or picking them from the water, with total indifference to the air bombardment, which often claimed its victims. Their numbers alone defied air attack. The Mosquito Armada as a whole was unsinkable. In the midst of our defeat glory came to the Island people, united and unconquerable; and the tale of the Dunkirk beaches will shine in whatever records are preserved of our affairs.

A Lockheed Hudson reconnaissance plane flies over the ships that have arrived from England and are moored off the Dunkirk coast in order to rescue the remaining troops.

May 28, 1940: Embarkation of the British Expeditionary Force aboard merchant ships.

THE BATTLE OF BRITAIN

Between the autumn of 1940 and the spring of 1941, Hitler tried to wear down the enemy with bombing attacks, but the resistance of the British Air Force upset his plans.

London, October 16, 1940: a policeman next to a delayed-action bomb parachuted into the city centre by the Germans and defused by the British.

Two employees at a British ammunitions factory weigh bombs.

Top: German airmen "decorate" a bomb destined for England.

Our fate now depended upon victory in the air. The German leaders had recognised that all their plans for the invasion of Britain depended on winning air supremacy above the Channel and the chosen landing places on our south coast. The preparation of the embarkation ports, the assembly of the transports, the minesweeping of the passages, and the laying of the new minefields were impossible without protection from British air attack. For the actual crossing and landings, complete mastery of the air over the transports and the beaches was the decisive condition. The result, therefore, turned upon the destruction of the Royal Air Force and the system of airfields between London and the sea. We now know that Hitler said to Admiral Raeder on July 31: "If after eight days of intensive air war the Luftwaffe has not achieved considerable destruction of the enemy's air force, harbours, and naval forces, the operation will have to be put off till May, 1941." This was the battle that had now to be fought.

In the fighting between August 24 and September 6, the scales had tilted against Fighter Command. During these crucial days the Germans had continuously applied powerful forces against the airfields of South and Southeast England. Their object was to break down the day fighter defence of the capital, which they were impatient to attack. Far more important to us than the protection of London from terror-bombing was the functioning and articulation of these airfields and the squadrons working from them. In the life-and-death struggle of the two air forces, this was a decisive phase. We never thought of the struggle in terms of the defence of London or any other place, but only who

won in the air. There was much anxiety at Fighter Headquarters at Stanmore, and particularly at the headquarters of Number Eleven Fighter Group at Uxbridge. Extensive damage had been done to five of the group's forward airfields, and also to the six sector stations. Manston and Lympne on the Kentish coast were on several occasions and for days unfit for operating fighter aircraft. Biggin Hill Sector Station, to the south of London, was so severely damaged that for a week only one fighter squadron could operate from it. If the enemy had persisted in heavy attacks against the adjacent sectors and damaged their operations rooms or telephone communications, the whole intricate organisation of Fighter Command might have been broken down. This would have meant not merely the maltreatment of London, but the loss to us of the

perfected control of our own air in the decisive area. They were getting terribly knocked about, and their runways were ruined by craters. It was therefore with a sense of relief that Fighter Command felt the German attack turn on to London on September 7, and concluded that the enemy had changed his plan. Goering should certainly have per-

Two British anti-aircraft-artillery observers at their checkpoint on the roof of a building on the outskirts of London.

Close-up of a German NCO, decorated with the Iron Cross, in the cockpit of his bomber just before take-off on a mission to Britain.

severed against the airfields, on whose organisation and combination the whole fighting power of our air force at this moment depended. By departing from the classical principles of war, as well as from the hitherto accepted dictates of humanity, he made a foolish mistake.

This same period (August 24 to September 6) had seriously drained the strength of Fighter Command as a whole. The Command had lost in this fortnight 103 pilots killed and 128 seriously wounded, while 466 Spitfires and Hurricanes had been destroyed or seriously damaged. Out of a total pilot strength of about a thousand, nearly a quarter had been lost. Their places could only be filled by 260 new, ardent, but inexperienced pilots drawn from training units, in many cases before their full courses were complete. The night attacks on London for ten days after September 7 struck at the London docks and railway centres, and killed and wounded many civilians, but they were in effect for us a breathing space of which we had the utmost need.

We must take September 15 as the culminating date. On this day the Luftwaffe, after

Captive barrage balloons in the sky over London.

A different aspect of the British defence: a detachment of bikers assigned to patrol the countryside to watch for and fight paratroopers.

A room of the British anti-aircraft control centre: the operators are at their positions ready to intercept signals.

A group of farmers and WACs of the Royal Air Force looking at a German bomber that was forced to make an emergency landing.

In the aftermath of the bombing of London: amidst the rubble of a room at Holland House, in Kensington, some patrons look at the books still ranged on the shelves.

A bus smashes into a crater in the ground caused by a bomb.

two heavy attacks on the 14th, made its greatest concentrated effort in a resumed daylight attack on London.

Although post-war information has shown that the enemy's losses on this day were only fifty-six, September 15 was the crux of the Battle of Britain. That same night our Bomber Command attacked in strength the shipping in the ports from Boulogne to Antwerp. At Antwerp particularly heavy losses were inflicted. On September 17, as we now know, the Fuehrer decided to postpone "Sea Lion" indefinitely. It was not till October 12 that the invasion was formally called off till the following spring. In July, 1941, it was postponed again by Hitler till the spring of 1942, "by which time the Russian campaign will be completed". This was a vain but an important imagining. On February 13, 1942, Admiral Raeder had his final interview on "Sea Lion" and got Hitler to agree to a complete "stand-down." Thus perished "Operation Sea Lion". And September 15 may stand as the date of its demise.

A rescue team saves a woman injured in the collapse of her house.

Coventry, an industrial city 30 kilometres from Birmingham, was almost entirely razed by German air raids.

WAR AGAINST GREECE

On October 28, 1940, Mussolini attacked Greece without previously warning Hitler. It would be an unfortunate war. Meanwhile, on November 11, 1940, the British inflicted severe wreckage onto the Italian fleet in the port of Taranto.

A fresh though not entirely unexpected outrage by Mussolini, with baffling problems and far-reaching consequences to all our harassed affairs, now broke upon the Mediterranean scene.

The Duce took the final decision to attack Greece on October 15, 1940. That morning a meeting of the Italian war leaders was held in the Palazzo Venezia. He opened the proceedings in the following words:

The object of this meeting is to define the course of action—in general terms—which I have decided to initiate against Greece. In the first instance, this action will have aims of both a maritime and territorial character. The territorial aims will be based on the possession of the whole coast of Southern Albania...and the Ionian islands— Zante, Cephalonia, and Corfu—and the occupation of Salonika. When we have attained these objectives we shall have improved our position *vis-à-vis* England in the Mediterranean. In the second instance...the complete occupation of Greece, in order to put her out of action and to assure that in all circumstances she will remain in our politic-economic sphere.

Having thus defined the question, I have laid down the date—which in my opinion must not be postponed even for an hour—and that is for the 26th of this month. This is an action which I have matured at length for months, before our entry into the war and before the beginning of the conflict...I would add that I foresee no complications in the north. Yugoslavia has every interest to keep quiet...I also exclude complications from the side of Turkey, particularly since Germany has established herself in Roumania and since Bulgaria has increased her strength. The latter can play a part in our game, and I shall take the necessary steps so as not to miss the present unique opportunity for achieving her aspirations in Macedonia and for an outlet to the sea...

On October 19 Mussolini wrote to Hitler telling him of the decision to which he had come. Hitler was then on his journey to Hendaye and Montoire. The letter (the text of which has not come to light) seems to have followed him round. When it finally reached him he at once proposed to Mussolini a meeting to discuss the general political situation in Europe. This meeting took place in Florence on October 28. That morning the Italian attack on Greece had begun.

It seems however that Hitler did not choose to make an issue of the Greek adventure. He said politely that Germany was in accord with the Italian action in Greece, and then proceeded to tell the tale of his meetings with Franco and Pétain. There can be no doubt that he did not like what had been done by his associate. A few

A Greek soldier presents arms. The Greek army proved far more combative and efficient than expected.

Top: Italian troops, accompanied by a civilian, carry a casualty to the rear.

weeks later, after the Italian attack was checked, he wrote to Mussolini in his letter of November 20: "When I asked you to receive me at Florence I began the journey with the hope of being able to expound my views *before* the threatened action against Greece had been taken, about which I had heard only in general terms." In the main however he accepted the decision of his ally.

Before dawn on October 28 the Italian Minister in Athens presented an ultimatum to General Metaxas, the Premier of Greece. Mussolini demanded that the whole of Greece should be opened to Italian troops. At the same time the Italian army in Albania invaded Greece at various points. The Greek Government, whose forces were by no means unready on the frontier, rejected the ultimatum. They also invoked the guarantee given by Mr. Chamberlain on April 13, 1939. This

we were bound to honour. By the advice of the War Cabinet, and from his own heart, His Majesty replied to the King of Hellenes: "Your cause is our cause; we shall be fighting against a common foe." I responded to the appeal of General Metaxas: "We will give you all the help in our power. We will fight a common foe and we will share a united victory." This undertaking was during a long story made good.

The Italian invasion of Greece from Albania was another heavy rebuff to Mussolini. The first assault was repulsed with heavy loss, and the Greeks immediately counter-attacked. In the northern (Macedonian) sector the Greeks advanced into Albania, capturing Koritza on November 22. In the central sector of the northern Pindus an Italian Alpini division was annihilated. In the coastal zone, where the Italians had at first succeeded in making deep

Hailed by the applause of the population, an old Greek motorised artillery unit heads for the front along the streets of Athens.

In this Italian propaganda photograph, a formation of SM-79 bombers flies over Athens after an attack on a base in Tatoi, during the first days of the war (the caption reads, "Enemy Greece"). Contrary to all expectations, the Greeks advanced into Albania and the Italians were driven back to the coastal area. The Greek army, led by General Papagos, proved to be better trained for mountain warfare than the Italians.
For several months, 16 Greek divisions managed to check 27 Italian divisions: it was a momentous setback for Mussolini's prestige. Hitler had to come to his aid by invading Yugoslavia.

penetrations, they hastily retreated from the Kalamas river. The Greek army, under General Papagos, showed superior skill in mountain warfare, out-manœuvering and outflanking their enemy. By the end of the year their prowess had forced the Italians thirty miles behind the Albanian frontier along the whole front. For several months twenty-seven Italian divisions were pinned in Albania by sixteen Greek divisions. The remarkable Greek resistance did much to hearten the other Balkan countries and Mussolini's prestige sank low.

GRECIA NEMICA

Close-up of Lieutenant Colonel Galeazzo Ciano, commander of the bomber squadron *La Disperata*, right before taking off on a mission to Greece.

Mussolini, who loved to pilot aircraft himself, followed the campaign in Greece with both avidity and apprehension, and even went to the front to encourage the troops.

A Greek soldier , armed with three Garand guns and bayonets, rides a donkey.

The winter of 1940–41 sorely tried the Italian army and proved that its matériel was inadequate. In this photograph, a squad from the Julia Alpine division is retreating in a blizzard.

An Alpine soldier unloads a burden of poles from his mule, mired down in mud.

Top: an Italian warship in the navigable canal of the port of Taranto, shortly before the British air raid.

The battleship *Cavour*, torpedoed by British aircraft.

The *Littorio*, pride of the Italian navy, alongside a tugboat after enemy attack.

The Italian Fleet had not reacted in any way against our occupation of Crete, but Admiral Cunningham had for some time been anxious to strike a blow at them with his now augmented naval air forces as they lay in their main base at Taranto. The attack was delivered on November 11 as the climax of a well-concerted series of operations, during which Malta received troops, and further naval reinforcements, including the battleship *Barham*, two cruisers, and three destroyers, reached Alexandria. Taranto lies in the heel of Italy three hundred and twenty miles from Malta. Its magnificent harbour was heavily defended against all modern forms of attack. The arrival at Malta of some fast reconnaissance machines enabled us to discern our prey. The British plan was to fly two waves of aircraft from the *Illustrious*, the first of twelve and the second of nine, of which eleven were to carry torpedoes, and the rest either bombs or flares. The *Illustrious* released her aircraft shortly after dark from a point about a hundred and seventy miles from Taranto. For an hour the battle raged amid fire and destruction among the Italian ships. Despite the heavy flak only two of our aircraft were shot down. The rest flew safely back to the *Illustrious*.

By this single stroke the balance of naval power in the Mediterranean was decisively altered. The air photographs showed that three battleships, one of them the new *Littorio*, had been torpedoed, and in addition one cruiser was reported hit and much damage inflicted on the dockyard. Half the Italian battle fleet was disabled for at least six months, and the Fleet Air Arm could rejoice at having seized by their gallant exploit one of the rare opportunities presented to them.

An ironic touch is imparted to this event by the fact that on this very day the Italian Air Force at the express wish of Mussolini had taken part in the air attack on Great Britain. An Italian bomber force, escorted by about sixty fighters, attempted to bomb Allied convoys in the Medway. They were intercepted by our fighters, eight bombers and five fighters being shot down. This was their first and last intervention in our domestic affairs. They might have found better employment defending their fleet at Taranto.

THE BATTLE OF THE ATLANTIC

In the spring of 1941, even before the United States entered the war, the Atlantic was the theatre of a crucial battle between British convoys and German submarines.

Amid the torrent of violent events one anxiety reigned supreme. Battles might be won or lost, enterprises might succeed or miscarry, territories might be gained or quitted, but dominating all our power to carry on the war, or even keep ourselves alive, lay our mastery of the ocean routes and the free approach and entry to our ports. From any port or inlet along this enormous front the hostile U-boats, constantly improving in speed, endurance, and radius, could sally forth to destroy our sea-borne food and trade. Their numbers grew steadily. In the first quarter of 1941 production of new craft was at the rate of ten a month—soon afterwards increased to eighteen a month. These included the so-called 500-ton and 740-ton types, the first with a cruising range of 11,000 miles and the latter of 15,000 miles.

To the U-boat scourge was now added air attack far out on the ocean by long-range aircraft. Of these the Focke-Wulf 200, known as the Condor, was the most formidable, though happily at the beginning there were few of them. They could start from Brest or Bordeaux, fly right round the British Island, refuel in Norway, and then make a return journey next day. On their way they would see far below them the very large convoys of forty or fifty ships to which scarcity of escort had forced us to resort, moving inwards or outwards on their voyages. They could attack these convoys, or individual ships, with destructive bombs, or they could signal the positions to which the waiting U-boats should be directed in order

Top: a sentinel on the look-out with binoculars on a German submarine.

Survivors from a German submarine sunk by the escort units of a convoy swim towards an enemy ship in order to be rescued.

March 1941: a German Focke-Wulf Condor reconnaissance bomber flies over the Atlantic.

A flight of British Beaufighters circles over a German convoy. Two ships, from which smoke is rising, have already been hit.

to make interceptions.

The U-boats now began to use new methods, which became known as "wolf-pack" tactics. These consisted of attacks from different directions by several U-boats working together. Attacks were at this time usually made by night, the U-boats operating on the surface at full speed unless detected in the approach.

Under these conditions only the destroyers could rapidly overhaul them.

These tactics, which formed the keynote of the conflict for the next year or more, presented us with two problems. First, how to defend our convoys against this high-speed night attack, in which the Asdic was virtually impotent. The solution lay not only in the multi-

A British shipyard: the keel of a new vessel has just been laid down. The British industrial effort, like the German effort, was enormous throughout the war.

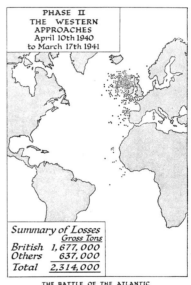

PHASE I
From the Outbreak of War to the Invasion of Norway
September 3rd 1939
to April 9th 1940

Summary of Losses
Gross Tons

	Gross Tons
British	339,000
Others	349,000
Total	688,000

THE BATTLE OF THE ATLANTIC
MERCHANT SHIPS SUNK BY U-BOAT IN THE ATLANTIC

PHASE II
THE WESTERN APPROACHES
April 10th 1940
to March 17th 1941

Summary of Losses
Gross Tons

	Gross Tons
British	1,677,000
Others	637,000
Total	2,314,000

THE BATTLE OF THE ATLANTIC
MERCHANT SHIPS SUNK BY U-BOAT IN THE ATLANTIC

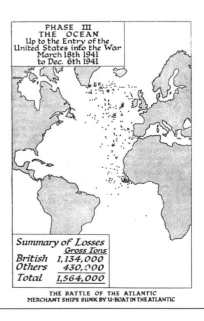

PHASE III
THE OCEAN
Up to the Entry of the United States into the War
March 18th 1941
to Dec. 6th 1941

Summary of Losses
Gross Tons

	Gross Tons
British	1,134,000
Others	430,000
Total	1,564,000

THE BATTLE OF THE ATLANTIC
MERCHANT SHIPS SUNK BY U-BOAT IN THE ATLANTIC

Bismarck shipwreck survivors are rescued by one of the attacking ships. The sinking of the Bismarck, in May 1941, was a heavy blow for the German navy.

Adolf Hitler salutes the warship Bismarck.

plication of fast escorts, but still more in the development of effective Radar. Moreover, a prompt answer here was imperative or our losses would soon become unbearable. The small scale of the earlier onslaughts of the U-boats, against which we had been relatively successful, had created an undue sense of security. Now, when the full fury of the storm broke, we lacked the scientific equipment equal to our needs. We addressed ourselves vigorously to this problem, and by the unsparing efforts of the scientists, supported by the solid team-work of sailors and airmen, good progress was made. The results came slowly, and meanwhile grave anxiety and heavy losses continued.

The second need was to exploit the vulnerability to air attack of the surfaced U-boat. Only when we could afford to court attack in the knowledge that we were masters would the long-drawn battle be won. For this we needed an air weapon which would kill, and also time to train both our sea and air forces in its use. When eventually both these problems were solved the U-boat was once more driven back to the submerged attack, in which it could be dealt with by the older and well-tried methods. This vital relief was not achieved for another two years.

Meanwhile the new "wolf-pack" tactics, inspired by Admiral Doenitz, the head of the U-boat service, and himself a U-boat captain of the previous war, were vigorously applied by the redoubtable Prien and the other tiptop U-boat commanders. Swift retribution followed. On March 8 Prien's U.47 was sunk with himself and all hands by the destroyer *Wolverine*, and nine days later U.99 and U.100 were sunk while engaged in a combined attack on a convoy. Both were commanded by outstanding officers, and the elimination of these three able men had a marked

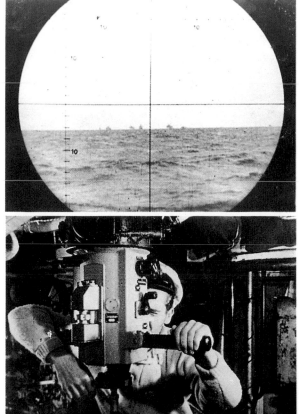

effect on the progress of the struggle. Few U-boat commanders who followed them were their equals in ruthless ability and daring. Five U-boats were sunk in March in the Western Approaches, and though we suffered grievous losses, amounting to 243,000 tons, by U-boat, and a further 113,000 tons by air attack, the first round in the Battle of the Atlantic may be said to have ended in a draw.

Left: in the double photograph, the commander of a German submarine observes a British convoy through a periscope.

Bottom: the aircraft carrier *Ark Royal*, sails alongside the cruisers *Sheffield* and *Renown*, during the hunt for the *Bismarck*.

THE ATTACK ON THE USSR

On June 22, 1941, Hitler attacked the Soviet Union and easily penetrated the Russian plains. But the opening of the vast new front proved fatal for the German Army.

Hitler's invasion of Russia altered the values and relationships of the war. The Soviet prejudices had blinded them to many of the steps which comprehension and prudence would have dictated for their own safety. On the other hand, by indifference to the fate of others they had gained time, and when their hour of trial struck on June 22, 1941, they were far stronger than Hitler imagined. Perhaps not only he but his generals had been misled by their poor performance against the Finns. Nevertheless it was the Russians who were taken by surprise, and tremendous initial disasters fell upon them. It will not be possible in this account to do more than place before the reader the salient features of the new colossal struggle of armies and populations which now began.

The German line of battle was drawn up along the whole frontier from the Baltic to the Black Sea. The Northern Army Group, under von Leeb, with twenty-nine divisions, including three armoured and three motorised, was to advance from East Prussia upon Leningrad. The Central Army Group, under von Bock, consisting of fifty divisions, including nine armoured and six motorised, was to move from Northern Poland on Smolensk. The Southern Army Group of von Rundstedt, with forty-one divisions, including five armoured and three motorised, was to drive from Southern Poland to the lower Dnieper. A further twenty-six divisions were held, or would shortly be available, as the General Reserve. Over two thousand seven hundred aircraft supported the attack. In the north twelve Finnish divisions were to advance on Leningrad to support the main attack. In the south eleven divisions of the Roumanian Army were to stand on the defensive along the

A post of the Russian artillery, in the Karelian forest, overcome by a German unit in a night action.

September 1941: German infantry advancing on Leningrad under Russian artillery fire.

Top: a group of Russian POWs.

A Mongolian soldier taken prisoner in eastern Karelia. Soviet losses in World War II are estimated to have been scores of millions.

river Pruth, and six to join in the advance of Army Group South. In all one hundred and sixty-four divisions rolled eastward.

The invaders, according to the best accounts available, were confronted by a hundred and nineteen Russian divisions and at least five thousand aircraft. Sixty-seven more divisions were available in Finland, the Caucasus, and in Central Russia. Although nearly in equal numbers to the German armies, the Russians were at once swept back by deep-plunging armoured thrusts, and their Air Force suffered severe losses. Other countries had been surprised and overrun. Only vast Russia had the supreme advantage of Depth; and this was once again to prove her salvation. In the first month the Germans bit and tore their way three hundred miles into Russia. Smolensk was taken after stern fighting in which the Russians had counterattacked heavily. But Leningrad was not attained, and Kiev was still in Russian hands.

It was already late autumn. On October 2 the Central Army Group of von Bock renewed its advance on Moscow, with its two armies moving direct on the capital from the south-west and a Panzer group swinging wide on either flank. Orel on October 8 and a week later Kalinin on the Moscow-Leningrad road were taken. With his flanks thus endangered and under strong pressure

AFI

THE GERMAN ATTACK ON RUSSIA

The German attack on the USSR between June and December 1941.

Two German soldiers crossing anti-tank trenches.

September 1941: Adolf Hitler is greeted by a group of soldiers upon his arrival for an inspection at an airport on the central Russian front.

A German soldier is shot by an enemy fusillade as he exits a bunker in Karelia.

A Finnish infantryman advances through the smoking ruins of a village in the Leningrad region.

Close-up of German motorcyclist being greeted by the residents of a Soviet town.

from the central German advance, Marshal Timoshenko withdrew his forces to a line forty miles west of Moscow, where he again stood to fight. The Russian position at this moment was grave in the extreme. The Soviet Government, the Diplomatic Corps, and all industry that could be removed were evacuated from the city over five hundred miles farther east to Kuibyshev. On October 19 Stalin proclaimed a state of siege in the capital and issued an Order of the Day: "Moscow will be defended to the last." His commands were faithfully obeyed. Although Guderian's armoured group from Orel advanced as far as Tula, although Moscow was now three parts surrounded and there was some air bombardment, the end of October brought a marked stiffening in Russian resistance and a definite check to the German advance.

CYRENAICA

In Cyrenaica, at the beginning of 1942, Rommel's skill, the armament edge, and the efficiency of the Afrika Korps led to a short-term Italian-German supremacy.

Rommel had again proved himself a master of desert tactics, and, outwitting our commanders, regained the greater part of Cyrenaica. This retreat of nearly three hundred miles ruined our hopes and lost us Benghazi and all the stores General Auchinleck had been gathering for his hoped-for offensive in the middle of February. Rommel must have been astounded by the overwhelming success of the three small columns with which he started the attack, and he supported them with whatever troops he could muster. General Ritchie reassembled the crippled XIIIth Corps and other forces which had been sent forward in the neighbourhood of Gazala and Tobruk. Here pursuers and pursued gasped and glared at each other until the end of May, when Rommel was able to strike again.

This extraordinary reversal of fortune and the severe military disaster arose from the basic facts that the enemy had gained virtually free passage across the Mediterranean to reinforce and nourish his armour, and had brought a large part of his Air Force back from Russia. But the tactical events on the spot have never been explained. The decisive day was January 25, when the enemy broke through to Msus. Thereafter confusion and changes of plan left the initiative to Rommel. The Guards Brigade could not understand why they were not allowed to make a stand, but the orders to retreat were reiterated and imperative. The 4th British-Indian Division was given no useful part to play.

Only later has it come to light from enemy records that the enemy tank strength was superior to ours. The Afrika Korps had 120

A wrecked British motor vehicle on the side of a coastal road in Cyrenaica.

Top: in an Italian air base in Cyrenaica, a tank advances amidst the wrecks of bombers.

tanks in action and the Italians 80 or more against the 150 of the 1st Armoured Division. Nevertheless the ineffective use made of the division remains unexplained. We are told in Auchinleck's dispatch, "being newly arrived from the United Kingdom, it was inexperienced in desert fighting", and as a general comment, "Not only were all our tanks outgunned by the German tanks but our cruiser tanks were mechanically inferior under battle conditions. The inferior armament and mechanical unreliability of our tanks was aggravated by the great shortage of anti-tank weapons, compared with the Germans."

All these statements require careful scrutiny. The 1st Armoured Division was one of the finest we had. It consisted largely of men who had more than two years' training, and repre-

January 1941: tanks get ready to attack the British in the Antelat region. There were 200 Italian-German tanks in action against 150 British tanks.

sented as high a standard of efficiency as any to found in our Regular forces. They had landed in Egypt in November. Before they left England every effort had been made, in accordance with all the latest information and experience, to make their vehicles desert-worthy. After the usual overhaul in the Cairo workshops this division moved across the desert to Antelat, which it reached on January 6. In order to preserve the tracks, its tanks were carried on special transporters across the whole desert, and arrived at Antelat unworn and in good order. Yet, without having been deeply committed into action this fine division lost over a hundred of its tanks. The very considerable petrol supplies which had been brought forward were abandoned in its precipitate retreat, and many of its tanks were left behind because they ran out of fuel.

The Guards Brigade, withdrawing under orders, found large petrol supplies, which they had to destroy as the enemy were near. As however they found numbers of our tanks abandoned in the desert, they brought on as much petrol as they could and manned these tanks themselves. One company of the Coldstream alone collected six, which they drove to safety, and other units collected more. In fact, some companies emerged actually stronger than they set out, having acquired a few tanks to work with their motorised infantry in the German fashion. When we remember the cost, time, and labour the creation of an entity like an armoured division,

A Macchi 202 fighter from the Incocca-Tende-Scaglia ("Notch-Draw-Shoot") squadron is ready for take-off on an airfield in Sirtica.

A squadron of Australian Gladiator fighters flies over the air base immediately after take-off, before a new raid on Bardia's defences.

In a Libyan port, British POWs are embarking, on their way to concentration camps in Italy.

Indian soldiers taken prisoner during the advance on Benghazi and Bardia.

January 1942: an Italian artilleryman adjusts the fuse of a shell before loading the piece.

with all its experts and trained men, involves, the effort required to transport it round the Cape, the many preparations made to bring it into battle, it is indeed grievous to see the result squandered through such mismanagement. Still more are these reflections painful when our failure is contrasted with what the Germans accomplished, although over four hundred miles from their base at Tripoli.

U-BOATS

In 1942, even after the United States had entered the war, German submarines continued to wreak havoc along the American and British Atlantic coasts.

Top: anchored XXI U-boats. These brand-new submarines were never used in World War II, because Germany surrendered before it had a chance to deploy them.

A squadron of German torpedo boats sailing towards its base in a Norwegian port. Torpedo boats were mostly engaged in the hunt for Allied submarines.

Side: a U-boat captured in the Atlantic by a Hudson plane is moored in a British port, waiting to be inspected by experts.

Two Australian units attack and destroy a German submarine. Allied naval forces were completely engaged in the combat against U-boats, especially in 1942.

We had greeted the entry of the United States into the war with relief and an uprising of spirit. Henceforth our load would be shared by a partner of almost unlimited resources and we might hope that in the war at sea the U-boats would soon be brought under control. With American help our Atlantic life-line would become secure, although losses must be expected until the full power of our Ally was engaged. Thus preserved, we could prosecute the war against Hitler in Europe and in the Middle East. The Far East would for the time be the darkest scene.

But the year 1942 was to provide many rude shocks and prove in the Atlantic the toughest of the whole war. By the end of 1941 the U-boat fleet had grown to nearly two hundred and fifty, of which Admiral Doenitz could report nearly a hundred operational, with a monthly addition of fifteen. At first our joint defences, although much stronger than when we stood alone, proved unequal to the new

giacomelli

A United States convoy advances through the tropical seas, zigzagging to evade the attacks of German submarines.

A U-boat on the high seas, its crew partially on deck during a pause in the hunt for enemy ships.

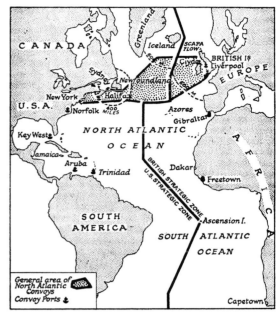

ATLANTIC OCEAN: DEFENCE ORGANIZATION, 1942

An air attack on a U-boat: the plane has dropped depth charges; after thirty minutes, the damaged submarine must emerge, and it is then bombed.

THE U-BOAT PARADISE
December 7th, 1941–
July 31st, 1942

Summary of Losses
Gross Tons
British   1,144,000
Others   2,106,000
Total   3,250,000

THE BATTLE OF THE ATLANTIC
MERCHANT SHIPS SUNK BY U-BOAT IN THE ATLANTIC

THE CRISIS OF THE
U-BOAT WAR
August 1st, 1942–
May 21st, 1943

Summary of Losses
Gross Tons
British   1,974,000
Others   1,786,000
Total   3,760,000

THE BATTLE OF THE ATLANTIC
MERCHANT SHIPS SUNK BY U-BOAT IN THE ATLANTIC

assault upon what had now become a much larger target. For six or seven months the U-boats ravaged American waters almost uncontrolled, and in fact almost brought us to the disaster of an indefinite prolongation of the war. Had we been forced to suspend, or even seriously to restrict for a time, the movement of shipping in the Atlantic all our joint plans would have been arrested.

On December 12 at a conference with the Fuehrer it was resolved to carry the U-boat war into American coastal waters. As many U-boats and several of the best German commanders had been transferred to the Mediterranean, and as by Hitler's order Doenitz was also compelled to maintain a strong group in Norwegian and Arctic waters, only six U-boats of the larger 740-ton type were at first dispatched. These left the Biscay ports between December 18 and 30, with orders to penetrate the northern end of the coastal route between Newfoundland and New York, near the assembly ports of the homeward-bound convoys. Their success was immediate. By the end of January thirty-one ships, of nearly 200,000 tons, had been sunk off the United States and Canadian coast. Soon the attack spread southward off Hampton Roads and Cape Hatteras, and thence to the coast of Florida. This great sea highway teemed with defenceless American and Allied shipping. Along it the precious tanker fleet moved in unbroken procession to and from the oil ports of Venezuela and the Gulf of Mexico. The interruption of this traffic would affect our whole war economy and all fighting plans.

In the Caribbean Sea, amid a wealth of targets, the U-boats chose to prey chiefly on the tankers. Neutrals of all kinds were assailed equally with Allied ships. Week by week the scale of this massacre grew. In February the U-boat losses in the Atlantic rose to seventy-one ships, of 384,000 tons, all but two of which were sunk in the American zone. This was the highest rate of loss which we had so far suffered throughout the war. It was soon to be surpassed.

All this destruction, far exceeding anything known in this war, though not reaching the catastrophic figures of the worst period of 1917, was caused by no more than twelve to fifteen boats working in the area at one time. The protection afforded by the United States Navy was for several months hopelessly inadequate. It is surprising indeed that during two years of the advance of total war towards the American continent more provision had not been made against this deadly onslaught. Under the President's policy of "all aid to Britain short of war" much had been done for us. We had acquired the fifty old destroyers and the ten American Revenue cutters. In exchange we had given the invaluable West Indian bases. But the vessels were now sadly missed by our Ally. After Pearl Harbour the Pacific pressed heavily on the United States Navy. Still, with all the information they had about the protective measures we had adopted, both before and during the struggle, it is remarkable that no plans had been made for coastal convoys and for multiplying small craft.

Neither had the Coastal Air Defence been developed. The American Army Air Force, which controlled almost all military shore-based aircraft, had no training in anti-submarine warfare, whereas the Navy, equipped with float-planes and amphibians, had not the means to carry it out. Thus it happened that in these crucial months an effective American defence system was only achieved with painful, halting steps. Meanwhile the United States and all the Allied nations suffered grievous losses in ships, cargoes, and lives. These losses might have been far greater had the Germans sent their heavy surface ships raiding into the Atlantic. Hitler was however obsessed with the idea that we intended to invade Northern Norway at an early date. With his powerful one-track mind he sacrificed the glittering chances in the Atlantic and concentrated every available surface ship and many a precious U-boat in Norwegian waters. "Norway," he said, "is the zone of destiny in this war." It was indeed, as the reader is aware, most important, but at this time the German opportunity lay in the Atlantic. In vain the admirals argued for a naval offensive. Their Fuehrer remained adamant, and his strategic decision was strengthened by the shortage of oil fuel.

Already in January he had sent the *Tirpitz*, his only battleship, but the strongest in the world, to Trondheim.

THE BATTLE OF MIDWAY

After Japan established supremacy in the Pacific, the United States reorganized and with the battle of Midway, in June 1942, turned the course of the war.

Top: a Japanese plane dives after being hit at Midway.

Japanese youths from the Naval Academy learn how to use a sextant.

During the last week of May the main strength of the Japanese Navy began to move from their bases. The first to go was the Aleutian diversionary force, which was to attack Dutch Harbour on June 3 and draw the American fleet in that direction. Thereafter landing forces were to seize the islands of Attu, Kiska, and Adak, farther to the westward. Nagumo with his group of four carriers would strike at Midway the following day, and on June 5 the landing force would arrive and capture the island. No serious opposition was expected. Yamamoto with his battle fleet would meanwhile lie well back to the westward, outside the range of air search, ready to strike when the expected American counter-attack developed.

This was the second supreme moment for Pearl Harbour. The carriers *Enterprise* and *Hornet* arrived from the south on May 26. The *Yorktown* appeared next day, with damage calculated to take three months to repair, but by a decision worthy of the crisis within forty-eight hours she was made taut and fit for battle and was rearmed with a new air group. She sailed again on the 30th to join Admiral Spruance, who had left two days before with the other two carriers. Admiral Fletcher remained in tactical command of the combined force. At Midway the airfield was crammed with bombers, and the ground forces for the defence of the island were at the highest "Alert". Early information of the approach of the enemy was imperative, and continuous air search began on May 30. United States submarines kept their watch west and north of Midway. Four days passed in acute suspense. At 9 a.m. on June 3 a Catalina flying-boat on patrol more than seven hundred miles west of Midway sighted a group of eleven enemy ships.

The bombing and torpedo attacks which followed were unsuccessful, except for a torpedo hit on a tanker, but the battle had begun, and all uncertainty about the enemy's intentions was dispelled. Admiral Fletcher through his Intelligence sources had good reason to believe that the enemy carriers would approach Midway from the north-west, and he was not put off by the reports received of the first sighting, which he correctly judged to be only a group of transports. He turned his carriers to reach his chosen position about two hundred miles north of Midway by dawn on the 4th, ready to pounce on Nagumo's flank if and when he appeared.

June 4 broke clear and bright, and at 5.34 a.m. a patrol from Midway at last broadcast the long-awaited signal reporting the approach of the Japanese aircraft-carriers. Reports began to

arrive thick and fast. Many planes were seen heading for Midway, and battleships were sighted supporting the carriers. At 6.30 a.m. the Japanese attack came in hard and strong. It met a fierce resistance, and probably one-third of the attackers never returned. Much damage was done and many casualties suffered, but the airfield remained serviceable. There had been time to launch a counter-attack at Nagumo's fleet. His crushing superiority in fighters took heavy toll, and the results of this gallant stroke, on which great hopes were set, were disappointing. The distraction caused by their onslaught seems however to have clouded the judgment of the Japanese commander, who was also told by his airmen that a second strike at Midway would be necessary. He had retained on board a sufficient number of aircraft to deal with any American carriers which might appear, but he was not expecting them, and his search had been under-powered and at first fruitless. Now he decided to break up the formations which had been held in readiness for this purpose and to rearm them for another stroke at Midway. In any case it was necessary to clear his flight decks to recover the aircraft returning from the first attack. This decision exposed him to a deadly peril, and

although Nagumo later heard of an American force, including one carrier, to the eastward, it was too late. He was condemned to receive the full weight of the American attack with his flight decks encumbered with useless bombers, refuelling and rearming.

Admirals Fletcher and Spruance by their earlier cool judgment were well placed to intervene at this crucial moment. They had intercepted the news streaming in during the early morning, and at 7 a.m. the *Enterprise* and *Hornet* began to launch a strike with all the planes they had, except for those needed for their own defence. The *Yorktown*, whose aircraft had been carrying out the morning search, was delayed while they were recovered, but her striking force was in the air soon after 9 a.m., by which time the first waves from the other two carriers were approaching their prey. The weather near the enemy was cloudy, and the dive-bombers failed at first to find their target. The *Hornet*'s group, unaware that the enemy had turned away, never found them and missed the battle. Owing to this mischance the first attacks were made by torpedo bombers alone from all three carriers, and, although pressed home with fierce courage, were unsuccessful in the face of the overwhelming opposi-

A U.S. bomber attacks and strikes a Japanese ship at Wewak Harbour, a base in New Guinea, in the southwest Pacific Ocean.

An Australian vessel is struck by Japanese aircraft at Port Moresby, in New Guinea. A boat headis towards the hull to rescue the survivors.

tion. Of forty-one torpedo bombers which attacked only six returned. Their devotion brought its reward. While all Japanese eyes and all available fighter strength were turned on them, the thirty-seven dive-bombers from the *Enterprise* and *Yorktown* arrived on the scene. Almost unopposed, their bombs crashed into Nagumo's flagship, the *Agaki*, and her sister the *Kaga*, and about the same time another wave of seventeen bombers from the *Yorktown* struck the *Soryu*. In a few minutes the decks of all three ships were a shambles, littered with blazing and exploding aircraft. Tremendous fires broke out below, and it was soon clear that all three ships were doomed. Admiral Nagumo could but shift his flag to a cruiser and watch three-quarters of his fine command burn.

It was past noon by the time the Americans had recovered their aircraft. They had lost over sixty, but the prize they had gained was great. Of the enemy carriers only the *Hiryu* remained, and she at once resolved to strike a blow for the banner of the Rising Sun. As the American pilots were telling their tale on board the *Yorktown* after their return news came that an attack was approaching. The enemy, reported to be about forty strong, pressed it home with vigour, and although heavily mauled by fighters and gunfire they scored three bomb hits on the *Yorktown*. Severely damaged but with her fires under control, she carried on, until two hours later the *Hiryu* struck again, this time with torpedoes. This attack ultimately proved fatal. Although the ship remained

A kamikaze (indicated by the arrow) crashes onto the British aircraft carrier *Indomitable*, escorted by a destroyer. Kamikazes, Japan's desperate suicidal weapon, caused serious damage to the Allies.

A pilot illustrates his winning encounter with a Japanese Zero to General Martin F. Scallion (second from right).

afloat for two days she was sunk by a Japanese submarine.

The *Yorktown* was avenged even while she still floated. The *Hiryu* was marked at 2.45 p.m., and within the hour twenty-four dive-bombers from the *Enterprise* were winging their way towards her. At 5 p.m. they struck, and in a few minutes she too was a flaming wreck, though she did not sink until the following morning. The last of Nagumo's four fleet carriers had been smashed, and with them

were lost all their highly trained air crews. These could never be replaced. So ended the battle of June 4, rightly regarded as the turning-point of the war in the Pacific.

This memorable American victory was of cardinal importance, not only to the United States, but to the whole Allied cause. The moral effect was tremendous and instantaneous. At one strike the dominant position of Japan in the Pacific was reversed. The glaring ascendancy of the enemy, which had frustrated our combined endeavours throughout the Far East for six months, was gone for ever. From this moment all our thoughts turned with sober confidence to the offensive. No longer did we think in terms of where the Japanese might strike the next blow, but where we could best strike at him to win back the vast territories that he had overrun in his headlong rush.

The road would be long and hard, and massive preparations were still needed to win victory in the East, but the issue was not in doubt; nor need the demands from the Pacific bear too heavily on the great effort the United States was preparing to exert in Europe.

A Japanese ship tries to evade an American air attack.

A Japanese freighter is sunk off the coast of Guadalcanal (in the Solomon Islands) while carrying supplies to garrison forces.

Another Japanese transport catches fire in front of the northwestern coast of Guadalcanal.

A post of marines with a 74 mm gun not far from the seashore at Guadalcanal.

Aerial view of two Midway islands transformed into airstrips.

MALTA AND THE CONVOYS

In 1942, a raging battle developed around Malta, which was of the utmost importance for the convoys that were supplying the troops in northern Africa.

Top: the port of Malta in 1942.

The escort of a British convoy, composed of cruisers and aircraft carriers, arrives in Malta.

The interrelation between Malta and the Desert operations was never so plain as in 1942, and the heroic defence of the island in that year formed the keystone of the prolonged struggle for the maintenance of our position in Egypt and the Middle East. In the bitter land fighting in the Western Desert the outcome of each phase was measured by a hand's-breadth, and frequently depended on the rate at which supplies could reach the combatants by sea. For ourselves this meant the two or three months' voyage round the Cape, subject to all the perils of the U-boats, and the employment of enormous quan-

tities of high-class shipping. For the enemy there was only the two or three days' passage across the Mediterranean from Italy, involving the use of a moderate number of smaller ships. But athwart the route to Tripoli lay the island fortress Malta. We have seen in an earlier volume how the island had been converted into a veritable hornets' nest, and how in the last days of 1941 the Germans had been compelled to make a supreme, and partially successful, effort to curb its action.

In 1942 the air attack on Malta mounted formidably and the plight of the island became desperate. In January, while Rommel's counter-

BOMBE SU MALTA

Aerial view of Valletta. The units and installations that were damaged in the last air raid are marked. In the foreground is an Italian plane. (The caption reads, "Bombs on Malta").

Members of an anti-air-craft-artillery post with their Bofors and ammunitions.

An anti-aircraft-artillery post ready to open fire with an automatic Bofors.

offensive prospered, Kesselring struck chiefly at the Malta airfields. Under German pressure, the Italian Navy used battleships to support their Tripoli convoys. The Mediterranean Fleet, stricken as has been described, could offer only a limited challenge to these movements. Our submarines and air forces from Malta continued however to take their toll.

In February Admiral Raeder, whose repute at that time stood high, sought to convince Hitler of the importance of decisive victory in the Mediterranean. On February 13, the day after the successful passage up the Channel by the German battle-cruisers, he had found the Fuehrer in a receptive mood, and his representations had at last met with some success. The intervention of the Germans in North Africa and the Mediterranean, which had begun as a

Valletta: after an air raid, civilians stand in line to receive a ration of milk.

An old tunnel on Malta, transformed into an air-raid shelter for civilians.

Valletta: after an air raid, civilians stand in line to receive a ration of milk.

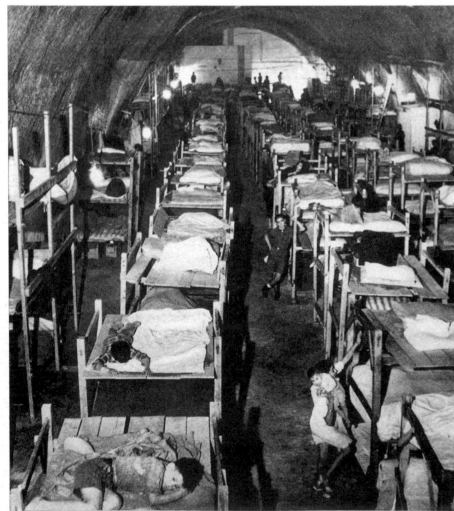

An old tunnel on Malta, transformed into an air-raid shelter for civilians.

purely defensive measure to save their weak ally from defeat, was now viewed in a new light as an aggressive means of destroying British power in the Middle East. Raeder dwelt on events in Asia and the irruption of Japanese power into the Indian Ocean. In the course of his statement he said, "Suez and Basra are the western pillars of the British position in the East. Should these positions collapse under the weight of concerted Axis pressure the consequences for the British Empire would be disastrous." Hitler was impressed, and, having hitherto paid little attention to the unfruitful task of helping the Italians, he now consented to press forward his vast plan for the conquest of the whole of the Middle East. Admiral Raeder insisted that Malta was the key, and urged the immediate preparation of transports for its storm.

Hitler and his military advisers did not relish the plan of seaborne assault. The Fuehrer had only recently given orders for the final cancellation of the long-term plans for the invasion of England, which had dragged on since 1940. The slaughter of his cherished airborne troops in Crete a year before was a deterrent factor. It was however agreed at this time that

Servicemen and civilians amidst the rubble in a Valletta neighborhood after a heavy Italian-German air attack.

Malta should be captured and that German forces should participate. Hitler had reservations, and continued to hope that the attacks of the Luftwaffe would bring about capitulation, or at least paralyse the defence and its activities.

We tried to run supplies through to Malta from the east. Four ships were successful in January, but the February convoy of three ships met disaster by air attack. In March the cruiser *Naiad*, wearing Admiral Vian's flag, was sunk by a U-boat. By May the island would be in danger of famine.

The Admiralty were ready to face all risks to carry in supplies. On March 20 four merchant ships left Alexandria, with a strong escort supported by four light cruisers and a flotilla. Admiral Vian, now in the *Cleopatra*, again commanded. By the morning of the 22nd the air attacks had started and heavy Italian warships were approaching. Presently the *Euryalus*

sighted four ships to the northward, and the British admiral at once turned to attack, while the convoy headed away to the south-west under cover of smoke. The enemy cruisers retired, but only to return two hours later, supported by the battleship *Littorio* and what appeared to be two more cruisers. For the next two hours the British ships, Vian's squadron, fought a bold and successful action at these fantastic odds to protect the convoy, which meanwhile was under heavy attack from German bombers. Thanks to the effective smoke cover and the fierce defence by the close escort and the merchant ships themselves, not a ship was damaged. In the evening the enemy turned away. Four light cruisers with eleven destroyers, in stormy weather, had held at bay one of the most powerful battleships afloat, supported by two heavy cruisers, one light cruiser, and ten destroyers. Although the *Cleopatra* and three destroyers had been hit, all

At an air base on Malta, a torpedo is secured to a torpedo bomber ready for take-off.

remained in vigorous action to the end.

The convoy had to make for Malta by itself. Admiral Vian could not refuel there, and so could protect it no farther. Little of its precious cargoes reached the defenders of Malta. The heavy air attacks were renewed as the ships approached the island. The *Clan Campbell* and then the *Breconshire* were sunk when there was only eight miles to go. The two remaining ships reached harbour only to be sunk there while being unloaded. Of 26,000 tons of supplies carried in the four ships only about 5,000 were landed. Malta got no

more for another three months.

This decided us not to send any more convoys until we could reinforce the island with fighter aircraft. During March the *Eagle* had flown in thirty-four, but this was not nearly enough. Admiral Vian's action had convinced the Germans that the Italian Navy did not mean to fight and that they must rely on their own resources. From the beginning of April Kesselring's air attacks on Malta did very great damage to the dockyard and the ships in the harbour. Naval vessels could no longer use the

island as a base, and before the end of the month all that could move were withdrawn.

The Royal Air Force stayed to fight for its life and for that of all the island. In those critical weeks we often had only a handful of serviceable fighters. Our men were pressed to the limit of endurance to prevent their own annihilation and to keep up the constant flow of aircraft that used Malta as a staging base to Egypt. While the air crews fought and the ground crews toiled to service and refuel for the next engagement, the soldiers repaired the stricken airfields. Malta won through only by the narrowest margin, and at home we were very anxious.

During April and May 126 aircraft were safely delivered to the Malta garrison from the *Wasp* and *Eagle*, with salutary results. The bombing attacks, which had reached their peak in April, now began to slacken, largely as a result of great air battles on May 9 and 10, when sixty Spitfires which had just arrived went into action with destructive effect. Daylight raiding was brought to an abrupt end. In June the stage was at last set for another large-scale attempt to relieve the island, and

this time it was intended to pass convoys through from the east and west simultaneously. Six ships entered the Mediterranean from the west on the night of June 11, escorted by the A.A. cruiser *Cairo* and nine destroyers. In support was Admiral Curteis with the battleship *Malaya*, the carriers *Eagle* and *Argus*, two cruisers, and eight destroyers. Off Sardinia on the 14th the heavy air attacks began, one merchant ship being sunk and the cruiser *Liverpool* damaged and put out of action. That evening the heavy coverings forces withdrew as the convoy approached the Narrows, but next morning when south of Pantelleria an attack developed by two Italian cruisers, supported by destroyers and numerous aircraft. The British ships were outranged, and in the ensuing action the destroyer *Bedouin* was sunk and another heavily damaged before the enemy were driven off, not without loss. Repeated air attacks continued throughout the day, and three more merchant ships were lost. The two surviving ships of the battered convoy reached Malta that night.

The eastern convoy of eleven ships was even

less fortunate. Admiral Vian, who again commanded, now had at his disposal much more powerful covering forces of cruisers and destroyers than when he had driven off the enemy in March, but he lacked the support of any battleship or aircraft-carrier, and it was to be expected that the main strength of the Italian Fleet would be deployed against him. After sailing on the 11th the convoy met heavy and continuous air attack on the 14th, when south of Crete. That evening Vian learned that the enemy fleet, including two *Littorio* class battleships, had left Taranto presumably to intercept him. It was hoped that the British submarines and the land-based air attacks from Cyrenaica and Malta would cripple the enemy during his approach. One Italian cruiser was

hit, and later sunk. But this was not enough. The enemy held on to the south-eastward, and our interception by an overwhelming force on the morning of the 15th seemed inevitable. The convoy and its escort had to return to Egypt, having lost the cruiser *Hermione* by U-boat, as well as three destroyers and two merchant ships by air attack. The Royal Air Force losses were also considerable. On the Italian side one heavy cruiser was sunk and a battleship damaged, but the approach to Malta from the eastward remained sealed, and no convoy again attempted this passage until November.

Thus in spite of our greatest efforts only two supply ships out of seventeen got through, and the crisis in the island continued.

Servicemen and civilians stand before the ruins of the opera house in Valletta.

A monument to Queen Victoria is intact amidst the devastation of a Valletta neighborhood.

EL ALAMEIN

The battle of El Alamein began in May 1942 and proved crucial for the conquest of northern Africa. Rommel was more powerful initially, but in November he was defeated.

General Montgomery had at his immediate disposal three armoured and the equivalent of seven infantry divisions. The concentration of so large a force demanded a number of ingenious deceptive measures and precautions. It was especially necessary that enemy aircraft should be prevented from overlooking the preparations. All this was attended by great success and the attack came as a complete surprise.

In the full moon of October 23 nearly a thousand guns opened upon the enemy batteries for twenty minutes, and then turned on to their infantry positions. Under this concentration of fire, deepened by bombing from the air, the XXXth (General Leese) and XIIIth Corps (General Horrocks) advanced. Attacking on a front of four divisions, the whole XXXth Corps sought to cut two corridors through the enemy's fortifications. Behind them the two armoured divisions of the Xth Corps (General Lumsden) followed to exploit success. Strong advances were made under heavy fire, and by dawn deep inroads had been made. The engineers had cleared the mines behind the leading troops. But the minefield system had not been pierced in its depth, and there was no early prospect of our armour breaking through. Farther south the 1st South African Division fought their way forward to protect the southern flank of the bulge, and the 4th Indian Division launched raids from the Ruweisat Ridge, while the 7th Armoured and 44th Divisions of the XIIIth Corps broke into the enemy defences opposite to them. This achieved its object of inducing the

Attacking British soldiers during the fourth British offensive (October 23, 1942).

Top: improvised tombs for two British casualties.

African-Italian troops after surrender.

enemy to retain his two armoured divisions for three days behind this part of the front while the main battle developed in the north.

So far however no hole had been blown in the enemy's deep system of minefields and defences. In the small hours of the 25th Montgomery held a conference of his senior commanders, at which he ordered the armour to press forward again before dawn in accordance with his original instructions. During the day more ground was indeed gained, after hard fighting; but the feature known as Kidney Ridge became the focus of an intense struggle with the enemy's 15th Panzer and Ariete armoured divisions, which made a series of violent counter-attacks. On the front of the XIIIth Corps the attack was pressed no farther, in order to keep the 7th Armoured Division intact for the climax.

There had been serious derangements in the enemy's command. Rommel had gone to hospital in Germany at the end of September, and his place was taken by General Stumme. Within twenty-four hours of the start of the battle Stumme died of a heart attack. Rommel, at Hitler's request, left hospital and resumed his command late on the 25th.

Hard fighting continued on October 26 all along the deep bulge so far forced into the enemy line, and especially again at Kidney Ridge. The enemy Air Force, which had been quiescent on the previous two days, now made its definite challenge to our air superiority. There were many combats, ending mostly in our favour. The efforts of the XIIIth Corps had delayed but could not prevent the movement of the German armour to what they now knew

General Erwin Rommel talking with General Boettcher (the commander of an armoured division) during an inspection in the Tobruk sector.

was the decisive sector of their front. This movement however was severely smitten by our Air Force.

At this moment a new and fruitful thrust was made by the 9th Australian Division, under General Morshead. They struck northwards from the bulge towards the sea. Montgomery was prompt to exploit this notable success. He held back the New Zealanders from their westward drive and ordered the Australians to continue their advance towards the north. This threatened the retreat of part of the German infantry division on the northern flank. At the same time he now felt that the momentum of his main attack was beginning to falter in the midst of the minefields and strongly posted anti-tank guns. He therefore regathered his forces and reserves for a renewed and revived assault.

All through the 27th and the 28th a fierce conflict raged for Kidney Ridge against the repeated attacks of the 15th and 21st Panzer Divisions, now arrived from the southern sector.

Montgomery now made his plans and dispositions for the decisive break-through (Operation "Supercharge"). He took out of the line the 2nd New Zealand and the 1st British Armoured Divisions, the latter being in special need of reorganisation after its notable share in the repulse of the German armour at Kidney

General Bernard Montgomery (with glasses) and General Willie Wendel during the battle of El Alamein.

Ridge. The British 7th Armoured and 51st Divisions and a brigade of the 44th were brought together and the whole welded into a new reserve. The break-through was to be led by the 2nd New Zealand Division, the 151st and 152nd British Infantry Brigades, and the 9th British Armoured Brigade.

Meanwhile, in Alexander's words,

> On the night of October 28 and again on October 30 the Australians attacked northwards towards the coast, succeeding finally in isolating in the pocket thus formed the four [German] battalions remaining there. The enemy appear to have been firmly convinced that we intended to strike up the road and railway, and he reacted to our thrust most vigorously. He moved up his 21st Armoured Division from its position west of our salient, added to it his 90th Light Division, which was guarding the northern flank of the salient, and used both in furious attacks to relieve his encircled troops. Into the position vacated by the 21st Armoured Division he put the Trieste Division, his last uncommitted reserve formation. While he was thus fully extended and was eking out his last remaining fresh formations in an attempt to extricate one regiment, we were able to carry out, undisturbed, the reorganisation of our forces for Operation "Supercharge".

The magnificent forward drive of the Australians, achieved by ceaseless bitter fighting, had swung the whole battle in our favour. At 1 a.m. on November 2 "Supercharge" began. Under a barrage of 300 guns the British brigades attached to the New Zealand Division broke through the defended zone, and the 9th British Armoured Brigade drove on ahead. They found however that a new line of defence strong in anti-tank weapons was facing them along the Rahman track. In a long engagement the brigade suffered severely, but the corridor behind was held open and the 1st British Armoured Division moved forward through it. Then came the last clash of armour in the battle. All the remaining enemy tanks attacked our salient on each flank, and were repulsed. Here was the final decision; but even next day,

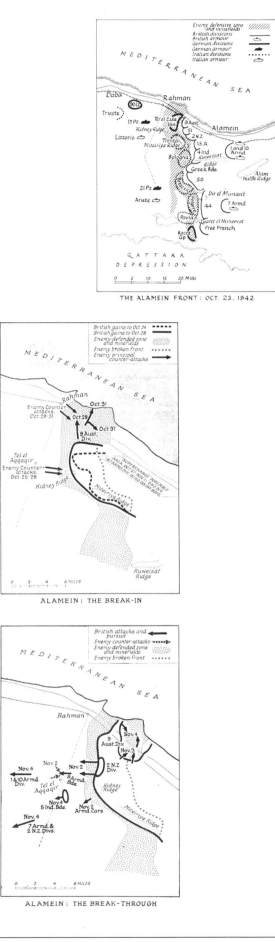

THE ALAMEIN FRONT: OCT. 23, 1942

ALAMEIN: THE BREAK-IN

ALAMEIN: THE BREAK-THROUGH

An Italian Bersaglieri unit, in retreat at El Alamein, tows anti-tank artillery pieces.

the 3rd, when our air reports indicated that the enemy's retirement had begun, his covering rearguard on the Rahman track still held the main body of our armour at bay. An order came from Hitler forbidding any retreat, but the issue was no longer in German hands. Only one more hole had to be punched. Very early on November 4, five miles south of Tel el Aggagir, the 5th Indian Brigade launched a quickly mounted attack which was completely successful. The battle was now won, and the way finally cleared for our armour to pursue across the open desert.

Rommel was now in full retreat, but there was transport and petrol for only a part of his force, and the Germans, though they had fought valiantly, gave themselves priority in vehicles. Many thousands of men from six Italian divisions were left stranded in the desert, with little food or water, and no future but to be rounded up into prison camps. The battlefield was strewn with masses of destroyed

or useless tanks, guns, and vehicles. According to their own records, the German armoured divisions, which had started the battle with 240 serviceable tanks, on November 5 mustered only thirty-eight. The German Air Force had given up the hopeless task of combating our superior Air, which now operated almost unhindered, attacking with all its resources the great columns of men and vehicles struggling westward. Rommel has himself paid notable tribute to the great part played by the Royal Air Force. His army had been decisively beaten; his lieutenant, General von Thoma, was in our hands, with nine Italian generals.

There seemed good hopes of turning the enemy's disaster into annihilation. The New Zealand Division was directed on Fuka, but when they reached it on November 5 the enemy had already passed. There was still a chance that they might be cut off at Mersa Matruh, upon which the 1st and 7th British Armoured Divisions had been thrust. By

German motorised
troops and armoured
vehicles withdraw from
the lines at El Alamein
(November).

Close-up of an artillery
piece fired to prevent
a night attack.

nightfall on the 6th they were nearing their
objective, while the enemy were still trying to
escape from the closing trap. But then rain
came and forward petrol was scarce.
Throughout the 7th our pursuit was halted.
The twenty-four-hour respite prevented complete encirclement. Nevertheless four German
divisions and eight Italian divisions had ceased
to exist as fighting formations.

An Afrika Korps casualty next to his destroyed artillery piece.

A column of Italian-German POWs marches toward the rear.

A British soldier halts before a crowd of Italian-German signs.

British anti-aircraft batteries in Tobruk.

THE CAUCASUS AND STALINGRAD

In the summer of 1942, the Germans launched a significant offensive to conquer Stalingrad and the Caucasus, but at the end of the year they were defeated and surrounded.

In order to free the way for the south-easterly drive to the Caucasus Rostov had to be taken and the Russians cleared from within the bend of the Lower Don. The first thrusts, on May 28, were from north of Kursk and Byelgorod. By July 7 the former had reached the outskirts of Rostov, but could not capture it. The long defensive flank from Orel to Voronezh was left to be guarded largely by Hungarians, while the German 4th Panzer Army drove down the western bank of the Don. A later thrust broke through the Russian defences before Izyum and joined the southerly drive. Finally, a third attack from Stalino swept round to reach the Lower Don above Rostov. All this went very much according to plan, though not quite so swiftly as had been hoped. Russian resistance was strong, but the several penetrations of their line by armoured and motorised troops enforced a general withdrawal, much harassed by the enemy, to behind the river Don.

After three weeks the first phase was virtually over and Hitler issued his orders for the next. The Southern Army Group was now divided into Army Group A, commanded by List, and Army Group B, under Bock. Hitler's directive of July 23 gave them their tasks. Army Group A was to capture the entire eastern shore of the Black Sea. After the capture of the Maikop oilfields a mobile force was to take Grozny. "Subsequently the Baku area is to be captured by an advance along the Caspian Sea." Army Group B, having established a defensive flank along the river Don, was to advance on Stalingrad, "smash the enemy forces being assembled there, and occupy the city". Mobile forces were to proceed down the Volga to Astrakhan.

Local operations by the Central Army Group were to take place in order to prevent the Russians withdrawing troops from that front, and in the north Leningrad was to be captured in early September. For this purpose Hitler ordered five divisions of the Eleventh Army, released by the capture of Sebastopol, to join the Northern Army Group, an improvident weakening of his major attack. They arrived in time not to

On the southern front: on the Kerc peninsula, a German officer is about to order an assault.

Top: Roumanian troops on a dray drawn by a camel behind the Stalingrad front.

Two Soviet soldiers surrender in a town on the Kerc peninsula.

A German wagoneer tries to free the horses pulling a supply cart mired down in a pool caused by a thaw.

Wreckage and casualties of a Soviet column on the battlefield at Kharkov-Izium.

Soviet WACs taken prisoner in the Stalingrad region are sent to a camp on a freight car.

A Luftwaffe patrol mops up amidst the rubble in Stalingrad (October 1942). The soldier in the foreground is holding an automatic pistol.

attack, but to defend a German line sagging under Russian assault.

The drive of the German Army Group A to reach the Caucasus had been led by Kleist's First Panzer Army of fifteen divisions. Once across the Don they made much headway against little opposition. They reached Maikop on August 9, to find the oilfields thoroughly destroyed. Another column took Mozdok on August 25, but was held on the river Terek and failed to reach the Grozny oilfields. Those of Baku, the greatest of them all, were still three hundred miles away. On the shore of the Black Sea Novorossisk was taken on September 10, and the Russian Black Sea Fleet, which had sheltered there when Sebastopol fell, sailed to Tuapse, where they remained. Hitler's orders to seize the whole of the Black Sea littoral could not be carried out. In the centre the Germans reached the foothills of the Caucasus, but no farther. Russian resistance, reinforced by fresh troops sent down by railway along the western shore of the Caspian, was everywhere firm. Kleist, weakened by diversions for the Stalingrad effort, struggled on till November. He took

A German flag waves above the devastation of a building in downtown Stalingrad, after a long battle for control of the city.

A trench amidst the rubble of a Stalingrad residential area. In the foreground is an injured serviceman; in the background, "Sergeant Pavlov's house," named after a patrol that resisted throughout the siege, on Sergeant Pavlov's orders.

THE GERMAN CAMPAIGN IN RUSSIA. 1942

RUSSIAN COUNTER-ATTACKS AT STALINGRAD

Nalchik on November 2. Winter conditions then intervened. His bolt was shot.

On the front of German Army Group B worse than failure befell. The lure of Stalingrad fascinated Hitler; its very name was a challenge. The city was important as a centre of industry, and also as a strong point on the defensive flank protecting his main thrust to the Caucasus. It became a magnet drawing to itself the supreme effort of the German Army and Air Force.

The deflection southward of the Fourth Panzer Army to help Army Group A to cross the Don also had serious consequences. It delayed the drive on Stalingrad, and by the time this army turned east again the Russian forces that had withdrawn across the river were reorganising. Resistance grew daily stiffer. It was not till September 15 that, after heavy fighting between the Don and the Volga, the outskirts of Stalingrad were reached. The battering-ram attacks of the next month made some progress at the cost of terrible slaughter. Nothing could overcome the Russians, fighting with passionate devotion amid the ruins of their city.

The German generals, long uneasy, had good cause for their anxiety. After three months of fighting the main objectives of the campaign, the Caucasus, Stalingrad, and Leningrad, were still in Russian hands. Casualties had been very heavy and replacements insufficient. Hitler, instead of sending fresh contingents forward to replace losses, was forming them into new and untrained divisions. In military opinion it was high time to call a halt, but "the Carpet-eater" would not listen. At the end of September Halder, Hitler's Chief of Staff, finally resisted his master, and was dismissed. Hitler scourged his armies on.

By the middle of October the German position had markedly worsened. The frontage of Army Group B stretched over seven hundred miles. General Paulus's Sixth Army had expended its efforts at Stalingrad, and now lay exhausted with its flanks thinly protected by allies of dubious quality. Winter was near, when the Russians would surely make their counter-stroke. If the Don front could not be held the safety of the armies on the Caucasus front would be undermined. But Hitler would not countenance any suggestion of withdrawal. On November 19 the Russians delivered their long and valiantly prepared encircling assault, striking both north and south of Stalingrad upon the weakly defended German flanks. Four days later the Russian pincers met and the Sixth German Army was trapped between the Don and the Volga. Paulus proposed to break out. Hitler ordered him to hold his ground. As the days passed his army was compressed into an ever-lessening space. On December 12, in bitter weather, the Germans made a desperate effort to break through the Russian cordon and relieve their besieged Sixth Army. They failed. Thereafter, though Paulus and his army held out for seven more terrible weeks, their doom was certain.

THE BATTLE OF TUNIS

With the victory in Tunisia, in May 1943, the Allies gained complete control of northern Africa and were thus able to organise the invasion of southern Italy.

The main attack of the First Army began on April 22. On the right, south of Goubellat, the IXth Corps advanced with the 46th Infantry and the 1st and 6th Armoured Divisions; north of them was the Vth Corps, the 1st, 4th, and 78th Divisions, moving astride the Medjerda river towards Massicault. Five days of hard fighting failed to break the enemy's resistance, but his losses were heavy, and important ground was gained which was to prove of value a week later. South of the British sector the French XIXth Corps occupied the Djebel Fkirine, while in the north the U.S. IInd Corps, attacking on the 23rd, made steady progress towards Mateur. Despite the physical difficulties of the ground the Americans kept up unremitting pressure, and gradually forced the Germans back.

It was clear that yet one more heavy punch would be needed before the enemy would break. A final attack by the Eighth Army on April 24 had proved that the Enfidaville position was too strong to be overcome without heavy loss. As we have seen, General Alexander transferred to the First Army three of their veteran divisions who had fought in the Desert since the earliest days. On May 6 the culminating attack was launched. The IXth Corps made the principal assault, on a narrow front on either side of the Medjez-Tunis road. The leading infantry, the 4th British and the 4th Indian Divisions, were closely followed by the 6th and 7th Armoured Divisions. On their left the Vth Corps protected the flank of the advance. The Allied Air Forces again put forth a supreme effort, with 2,500 sorties in the day. The Axis Air Force had been gradually worn down over many weeks, and at this crisis was able to make only

Top: a British patrol during mopping-up operations amidst heaps of rubble in a street in Bizerta.

American troops advance along the walls of the ancient Gafsa fortress.

sixty sorties in reply. The climax was at hand. The relentless blockade by sea and air was fully established. Enemy movement over the sea was at a standstill, their air effort ended.

The IXth Corps made a clean break in the enemy front. The two armoured divisions passed through the infantry and reached Massicault, half-way to Tunis. Next day, May 7, they pressed on, and the 7th Armoured Division entered Tunis, and then swerved north to join hands with the United States forces. Resistance on the main American front had cracked at the same time, and their 9th Infantry Division reached Bizerta. Three German divisions were thus trapped between the Allied troops, and surrendered on May 9.

No one could doubt the magnitude of the victory of Tunis. It held its own with

A detachment of Bersaglieri from the Trieste division in action near Djebel Garci.

Order of the day signed by General Alexander, commander of the Eighteenth Army group.

Tunis, May 20, 1943: contingents of African-French troops and American troops march past Generals Eisenhower, Alexander, and Anderson during the victory parade.

Stalingrad. Nearly a quarter of a million prisoners were taken. Very heavy loss of life had been inflicted on the enemy. One-third of their supply ships had been sunk. Africa was clear of our foes. One continent had been redeemed. In London there was, for the first time in the war, a real lifting of spirits. Parliament received the Ministers with regard and enthusiasm, and recorded its thanks in the warmest terms to the commanders. I had asked that the bells of all the churches should be rung. I was sorry not to hear their chimes, but I had more important work to do on the other side of the Atlantic.

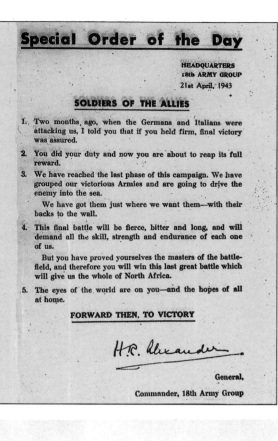

Special Order of the Day

HEADQUARTERS
18th ARMY GROUP
21st April, 1943

SOLDIERS OF THE ALLIES

1. Two months ago, when the Germans and Italians were attacking us, I told you that if you held firm, final victory was assured.

2. You did your duty and now you are about to reap its full reward.

3. We have reached the last phase of this campaign. We have grouped our victorious Armies and are going to drive the enemy into the sea.

   We have got them just where we want them—with their backs to the wall.

4. This final battle will be fierce, bitter and long, and will demand all the skill, strength and endurance of each one of us.

   But you have proved yourselves the masters of the battlefield, and therefore you will win this last great battle which will give us the whole of North Africa.

5. The eyes of the world are on you—and the hopes of all at home.

FORWARD THEN, TO VICTORY

H.R. Alexander

General,
Commander, 18th Army Group

Aerial view of the concentration camps where thousands of POWs were gathered after Axis forces surrendered.

THE LANDING IN SICILY

After trying to decide between Sardinia, Salerno, and Sicily, the Allies chose to land in the latter, and rapidly conquered it in July and August 1943. The invasion of Italy had begun.

In the channel between Tunisia and Sicily lay the small island of Pantelleria, which served as an enemy base for aircraft and E-boats. In January 1941 we had planned to assault and capture it, but the opportunity passed and it remained a thorn in our side throughout the hardest period of the siege of Malta. Now it became necessary not only to subdue it, but to use it ourselves for our fighter aircraft. Attacks by air and sea began immediately after the fall of Tunis. Bombardment continued until June 8, when unconditional surrender was demanded. This being refused, a landing from the sea was carried out on June 11, supported by heavy naval and air bombardment. Much had been made beforehand of the magnitude and perils of this enterprise. It was entirely successful, with no casualties,

except, according to sailor's stories, one soldier bitten by a mule. Over 11,000 prisoners fell into our hands. During the next two days the neighbouring islands of Lampedusa and Linosa also capitulated. No enemy outpost now remained south of Sicily.

Intense air attack upon Sicily began on July 3 with the bombing of airfields both there and in Sardinia, which made many unusable. The enemy fighters were thrown on to the defensive, and their long-range bombers forced to withdraw their bases to the Italian mainland. Four of the five train ferries operating across the Straits of Messina were sunk. By the time our convoys were approaching the island air superiority was firmly established, and Axis warships and aircraft made no serious effort to interfere with

Top: a group of civilians cheer the Allied forces that conquered a Sicilian city.

April 1943: at the Pentagon, a group of U.S. officers is briefed on the measures necessary for a swift conquest of the fortified island of Pantelleria.

The light cruiser *Boise* protects the troops of the Seventh Army as they land on the beach at Gela.

the seaborne assault. By our cover plans the enemy were kept in doubt until the last moment where our stroke would fall. Our naval movements and military preparations in Egypt suggested an expedition to Greece. Since the fall of Tunis they had sent more planes to the Mediterranean, but the additional squadrons had gone, not to Sicily, but to the Eastern Mediterranean, North-West Italy, and Sardinia. In the critical period while the convoys were approaching their target General Eisenhower established his headquarters in Malta, where communications were excellent. Here he was joined by General Alexander and Admiral Cunningham. Air Marshal Tedder remained near Carthage to control the combined air operations.

July 10 was the appointed day. On the morning of July 9 the great armadas from east and west were converging south of Malta, and it was time for all to steam for the beaches of Sicily. Admiral Cunningham says in his dispatch: "The only incidents which occurred to mar the precision of this remarkable concentration were the loss by U-boat attack of three ships in convoy. The passage of the convoys was covered most effectively; the majority were not sighted by enemy aircraft."

Meanwhile Allied Forces were harrying the enemy communications and airfields in Southern Italy and the port of Naples. On July

On the seashore near Gela, a detachment boards a landing craft in order to be transported to a different sector of the bridgehead.

19 a strong force of American bombers attacked the railway yards and airport at Rome. Havoc was wrought, and the shock was severe. In Sicily itself the Americans were advancing steadily under the spirited leadership of General Patton. Their 3rd Infantry and 2nd Armoured Divisions were given the task of reducing the western end, where only Italians now remained, while their IInd Corps, comprising the 1st and 45th Divisions, was directed to gain the northern coast and then to thrust eastward along the two main roads towards Messina. Palermo was taken on July 22, and by the end of the month the Americans had reached the line Nicosia-S. Stefano. Their 3rd Division, its task in Western Sicily completed, had been brought in to support the coastal drive, while the 9th Division was brought over from Africa, where like our 78th, it had been in reserve.

The field was thus disposed for the final battles. These were certain to be severe, since, apart from what remained of the Italian garrison, more than three German divisions were now in action, under a well-tried German commander, General Hube. But the speedy collapse of Italy became probable. There was a marked change of feeling in our circles in Whitehall, and we decided on the bolder plan of a direct attack on the west coast of Italy to seize Naples. Washington agreed, but insisted that no more forces could be provided than those agreed upon at the "Trident" Conference. The Americans held that none of the operations elsewhere, especially "Overlord", should be prejudiced by more vigorous action in the Mediterranean. This reservation was to cause keen anxiety during the landing at Salerno.

General Eisenhower and his principal com-

After disembarking from a pontoon, Lieutenant General George S. Patton (middle, center) is photographed as he arrives ashore.

In the region around Licata, soldiers lead donkeys from the pontoons. Donkeys were used to transport matériel to inaccessible areas.

Ready and positioned in improvised ditches, British and Indian infantrymen wait for the order to advance on Messina.

A patrol from a Canadian detachment rides mules during their advance through Sicily.

After the occupation of Palermo, infantrymen advance along cliffs damaged by the bombing.

manders now agreed that Italy should be the next and immediate target. They still preferred to land first on the toe, because they were short of landing-craft and planes, but for the first time they too began to favour the direct attack on Naples. This was so far from our newly won air bases in Sicily that it would much reduce the fighter cover for the landing. None the less Naples soon became the centre of all thoughts. The chance of quickly crushing Italy seemed to justify delaying operations against Burma, and the Admiralty stopped the assault shipping for India from leaving the Mediterranean.

On July 22 the British Chiefs of Staff urged their American colleagues to plan the direct attack on Naples on the assumption that extra shipping and aircraft-carriers would be available. The Americans took a different view.

An Allied serviceman with a razor helps a fellow soldier groom himself during a pause in the fighting.

A Sicilian offers a pitcher of wine to two American soldiers.

While agreeing to the attack, they adhered to their original decision that no reinforcements from America should be sent to General Eisenhower for this or any other purpose. He should do the best he could with what he had. Moreover, they insisted that three of his heavy bomber groups should be withdrawn to Britain. Conflict thus arose. The American Chiefs of Staff did not believe that the conquest of Italy would threaten Germany, and they also feared that the Germans would withdraw and that we should find ourselves hitting the air. They did not think there was much to be gained by bombing Southern Germany from airfields in Southern Italy, and they wanted all efforts against Germany to be concentrated on the shortest route across the English Channel, although nothing could happen there for ten months.

The British Chiefs of Staff pointed out that the Washington Conference had expressly stated that the elimination of Italy from the war was one of the prime Allied objects. The attack on Naples, now given the code-name

of "Avalanche", was the best means of accomplishing this, and the collapse of Italy would increase enormously the chances of the cross-Channel invasion being not only successful but decisive. Portal, Chief of the Air Staff, emphasised that the full-scale attack on German industry, particularly on factories producing fighters, could only be effective with the help of the Italian airfields. Their possession would therefore be a great contribution to a successful invasion of France. The Americans remained unmoved. However, most of the forces to be employed in "Avalanche" were British, and we resolved to do everything in our power to ensure its success. To overcome the weakness in long-range fighters the Admiralty allotted four

escort carriers and a light fleet carrier to support the landing, and the Air Ministry gave General Eisenhower three of our bomber squadrons which had been due for early withdrawal.

While these somewhat sharp discussions were in progress the scene was completely transformed by the fall of Mussolini on July 25. The argument for invading Italy seemed overwhelming. As will be seen, the Germans reacted very quickly, and our invasion, and particularly the attack on Naples, was not greatly eased. "Avalanche" only just succeeded, and it was fortunate that we had provided additional British sea- and air-power. The

risks would have been further reduced if the extra shipping which we considered essential to accelerate the build-up after landing there had been accorded. In this we could not carry American opinion with us, and before the operation began many American ships were withdrawn, and some of the British assault shipping was also released to India.

The brilliant capture of Centuripe by our newly arrived 78th Division marked the last phase. Catania fell on the 5th, and thereafter the whole British line swung forward to the southern and western slopes of Mount Etna. The U.S. 1st Division took Troina on August 6 after a stiff fight, and their 9th Division,

In Brolo (near Messina), a sergeant of the Second American Corps poses like the statue on a memorial to the casualties of World War I.

111

Infantrymen and a tank of the vanguard forces advance through the rubble at Melilli (near Syracuse).

After laying down his arms, an Italian soldier accompanied by a girl heads home with his backpack.

passing through the 1st, entered Cesaro on the 8th. Along the north coast the U.S. 45th Division, followed by their 3rd Division, reached Cape Orlando on August 10, with the aid of two small but skilful outflanking amphibious operations. After the capture of Randazzo on the 13th the enemy broke contact all along the front, and, under cover of their strong anti-aircraft defences of the Messina Straits, escaped during the following nights to the mainland. Our armies raced for Messina. Enemy demolitions on the coastal road from Catania slowed up the Eighth Army, and by a narrow margin the prize fell to the Americans, who entered the town on August 16.

So ended a successful and skilful campaign of thirty-eight days. The enemy, once they had recovered from the initial surprise, had fought stubbornly. The difficulties of the ground were great. The roads were narrow, and cross-country movement was often impossible except for men on foot. On the Eighth Army front the towering mass of Mount Etna blocked the way, and enabled the enemy to watch our moves. As they lay on the low ground of the Catania plain malaria ran riot among our men. Nevertheless, once we were safely ashore and our Air Forces were operating from captured airfields the issue was never in doubt. The enemy, according to General Marshall's report, lost 167,000 men, of whom 37,000 were Germans. The Allies lost 31,158 killed, wounded, and missing.

THE LANDING AT SALERNO

In order to work their way up the Italian peninsula faster, the Allies decided on a second landing at Salerno on the very day of the armistice (September 8, 1943). Here they encountered a stout Italian-German resistance.

O n the night of September 8 Alexander sent me his "Zip" message. As the Allied armada approached the Salerno beaches that evening they heard the announcement from the British broadcast of the Italian surrender. To men keyed up for battle the news came as a shock, which for the moment relaxed the tension and had an unfortunate psychological effect. Many thought that on the morrow their task would be a walkover. Officers at once strove to correct any such impression, pointing out that whatever the Italians might do there would certainly be strong resistance from German forces. There was a sense of anticlimax. Nevertheless, as Admiral Cunningham remarked, to have withheld the existence of the armistice would have been a breach of faith with the Italian people.

Covered by a strong British fleet, the assault convoys entered the Gulf of Salerno with only minor air attack. The enemy was aware of their approach, but he could not tell until the last moment where the blow would fall.

The landing of the Fifth Army, commanded by General Clark, began before dawn. The assault was delivered by the VIth U.S. Corps and the British Xth Corps, with British Commandos and U.S. Rangers on the northern flank. The convoys had been sighted at sea, and General Eisenhower's broadcast of the previous evening caused the German troops in the neighbourhood to act immediately. Disarming the Italians, they took over the whole defence themselves, and made good use of the advantage which modern weapons give to the defence in the early stages of a landing. Our men were met by well-aimed fire as they waded ashore, and they suffered heavily. It was difficult to provide proper

Top: a woman searches through the rubble of her home in Boiano (near Campobasso).

Two motorboats shuttle between ships and a pier in the port of Salerno, where the ships are anchored.

The command of a detachment from the Eighth Army analyses the situation using a map of Italy.

In a church in Benevento, an American soldier looks at a statue of St. Joseph that escaped destruction.

An American Red Cross soldier offers a drink to a wounded German.

The wreck of a German ME-109 fighter is loaded on a freight car in the port of Salerno.

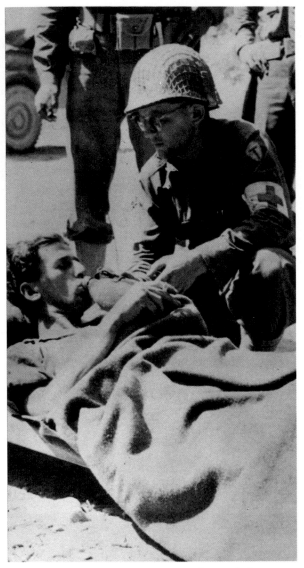

air cover for them, as many of our fighters were operating at extreme range from Sicily, but these were reinforced by carrier-borne aircraft.

Once across the beaches the VIth U.S. Corps made good progress, and by the night of the 11th had advanced as much as ten miles, with their right flank bent back to the sea. The British corps met stiffer opposition. They succeeded in taking Salerno and Battipaglia. The Montecorvino airfield also fell into our hands, but as it remained under enemy fire it could not provide the sorely needed refuelling ground for our fighters. The Germans reacted very quickly. Their troops opposing the Eighth Army, which was toiling its way up the toe of Italy, were brought at all speed to the new battle. From the north came the greater part of three divisions, from the east a regiment of parachutists. Our own reinforcement was much slower, as ship-

Near Salerno, a balloon is taken ashore for later use in the anti-aircraft barrage against German air raids.

ping, especially small craft, was scarce. The German Air Force, though weakened by their losses in Sicily, made an intense effort, and their new radio-controlled and glider bombs caused losses to our shipping. All the resources of the Allied Air were turned on to hamper the approach of enemy reinforcements and blast their concentrations. Warships steamed into Salerno Bay to give the support of their heaviest guns. The Eighth Army was spurred on by Montgomery to gain contact with the hard-pressed Fifth. All this helped, and in the opinion of a highly placed German officer the eclipse of the Luftwaffe and the lack of any defence against naval bombardment were decisive.

Once the Battle of Salerno had been won Naples and the Foggia airfields lay before us. The British Xth Corps, with the United States VIth Corps on their right, drove back the enemy's rearguards around Vesuvius, marched past the ruins of Pompeii and Herculaneum, and entered Naples. An immense effort was now concentrated upon opening the harbour, which had been subjected to every form of

destruction at experienced hands. Nevertheless this work, in which the Americans excelled, was so effective that within a fortnight 5,000 tons of supplies a day could be handled. The two airfields near the city were soon brought into use, and gave welcome relief to our fighter squadrons, hitherto acting from improvised landing strips. Meanwhile on the east coast the 1st Airborne Division had patrolled as far as Gioja and Bari by September 15. The 78th Division and an armoured brigade landed behind them, and, with the Vth Corps headquarters, joined the Eighth Army. Six Royal Air Force squadrons began to act from the Gioja airfield at the same time. The enemy evacuated the Foggia airfields on September 25. Termoli was taken by Commandos landed from the sea, who, with the help of reinforcements, held out against fierce counter-attacks.

A pause was now enforced upon both our armies. North of Naples the Fifth Army met strong resistance along the river Volturno, which needed time and supplies to overcome. In the Eighth Army's advance up the toe of Italy General Montgomery had deliberately

Not far from Acerno (near Salerno), a group of German POWs is taken over by an American Military Police NCO while MPs with Thompson guns keep the group under surveillance.

In a town near Salerno, the mayor, accompanied by some soldiers, salutes the Allied troops from the town hall balcony.

taken every administrative risk in order to reach the Salerno battlefield. His base had now to be moved from the toe at Reggio to the heel at Taranto and Bari. Until this was accomplished the Eighth Army had reached the end of its tether. Moreover, the capture of Foggia enabled a start to be made in occupying its airfields with heavy bombers. This was a massive task, requiring the carriage of many thousand tons of stores, and could be effected only by degrees. In mid-October the Germans had nineteen divisions in Italy, and the Allies the equivalent of thirteen. Large reinforcements and much consolidation were required to hold our rapid and brilliant conquests. All this put a strain on our shipping.

September had been indeed a fruitful month. Anglo-American inter-Service co-operation by land, sea, and air had reached a new record. The commander of the German Tenth Army in Italy has since stated that the harmonious co-opera-

tion between our Army, Air, and Naval forces under one supreme command was regarded by the Germans with envy. The Italian Fleet was in our hands; their Air Force and Army, though prevented by the Germans from joining us in useful numbers, were no longer ranged against us. The enemy had been defeated in pitched battle and our armies had bitten three hundred miles off Italy's boot. Behind them lay captured airfields and ports, ample, when developed, for our needs. Sardinia, so long thrust forward in Staff argument as the alternative to the assault on Italy, fell into our hands for nothing, as a mere bonus, on September 19, and Corsica was taken by French troops a fortnight later. The Italian enterprise, to launch which we had struggled so hard, had been vindicated beyond the hopes even of its most ardent and persistent advocates.

THE BATTLE OF ANZIO

On January 22, 1944, the Allies landed at Anzio, near Rome. Before they could advance towards the capital, though, they encountered fierce Italian-German resistance.

The VIth Corps, under the American General Lucas, had landed on the Anzio beaches at 2 a.m. on the 22nd, the 3rd United States Division south of the town, and the 1st British Division north of it. There was very little opposition and practically no casualties. By midnight 36,000 men and over 3,000 vehicles were ashore. "We appear," signalled Alexander, who was on the spot, "to have got almost complete surprise. I have stressed the importance of strong-hitting mobile patrols being boldly pushed out to gain contact with the enemy, but so far have not received reports of their activities." I was in full agreement with this, and replied: "Thank you all for your messages. Am very glad you are pegging out claims rather than digging in beach-heads."

But now came disaster, and the ruin in its prime purpose of the enterprise. General Lucas confined himself to occupying his beach-head and having equipment and vehicles brought ashore. General Penney, commanding the British 1st Division, was anxious to push inland. His reserve brigade was however held back with the corps. Minor probing attacks towards Cisterna and Campoleone occupied the 22nd and 23rd. No general attempt to advance was made by the commander of the expedition. By the evening of the 23rd the

Top: aerial view, from an RAF reconnaissance plane, of the area opposite the port of Anzio.

Salerno: a contingent of troops ready to leave for the new bridgehead at Anzio.

whole of the two divisions and their attached troops, including two British Commandos, the United States Rangers, and parachutists, had been landed, with masses of impedimenta. The defences of the beach-head were growing, but the opportunity for which great exertions had been made was gone.

Kesselring reacted quickly to his critical situation. The bulk of his reserves were already committed against us on the Cassino front, but he pulled in whatever units were available, and in forty-eight hours the equivalent of about two divisions was assembled to resist our further advance.

On the 25th Alexander reported that the beach-head was reasonably secure. The 3rd United States Division was four miles from Cisterna and the British 1st Division two miles from Campoleone, and contact was continuous along the entire front. On the 27th serious

news arrived. Neither place had been taken. The Guards Brigade had beaten off a counter-attack of infantry and tanks and had gone forward, but they were still about a mile and a half short of Campoleone, and the Americans were still south of Cisterna. Alexander said that neither he nor General Clark was satisfied with the speed of the advance, and that Clark was going to the beach-head at once.

While the fighting at Cassino was at its zenith, on January 30 the VIth Corps at Anzio made its first attack in strength. Some ground was gained, but the 3rd U.S. Division failed to take Cisterna and the 1st British Division Campoleone. More than four divisions were already ashore in the beach-head. But the Germans, despite our air action against their communications, had reinforced quickly and strongly. Elements of eight divisions faced us in positions which they had now had time to for-

In the port of Salerno, the landing craft that will be used to transport the troops of the Sixth Corps to the Anzio sector are being loaded.

121

A convoy of troops from the Sixth Army Corps, under General Lucas' command, comes into view of the Anzio coast.

tify. Galling artillery fire harassed the crowded lodgments we had gained, and our shipping lying off the beaches suffered damage from air attacks by night. On February 2 Alexander again visited the battle-front, and sent me a full report. German resistance had increased, and was especially strong opposite the 3rd U.S. Division at Cisterna and the 1st British Division at Campoleone. No further offensive was possible until these points were captured. The 3rd Division had fought hard for Cisterna during the last two or three days. The men were tired and were still about a mile from the town. A brigade of the 1st Division was holding Campoleone railway station, but they were in a very long and narrow salient and were being shot at "by everything from three sides". Alexander concluded: "We shall presently be in a position to carry out a properly co-ordinated

thrust in full strength to achieve our object of cutting the enemy's main line of supply, for which I have ordered plans to be prepared."

Before effect could be given to Alexander's orders the enemy launched a counter-attack on February 3 which drove in the salient of the 1st British Division and was clearly only a prelude to harder things to come. In the words of General Wilson's report, "the perimeter was sealed off and our forces therein are not capable of advancing."

By the seventh day 12,350 vehicles had been landed, including 356 tanks; by the fourteenth day 21,940 vehicles, including 380 tanks. This represented a total of 315 L.S.T. shipments. It was interesting to notice that, apart from 4,000 trucks which went to and fro in the ships, nearly 18,000 vehicles were landed in the Anzio beach-head by the fourteenth day in order to

serve a total force of 70,000 men, including of course the drivers and those who did the repair and maintenance of the vehicles.

The expected major effort to drive us back into the sea at Anzio opened on February 16, when the enemy employed over four divisions, supported by 450 guns, in a direct thrust southwards from Campoleone. Hitler's special order of the day was read out to the troops before the attack. He demanded that our beach-head "abscess" be eliminated in three days. The attack fell at an awkward moment, as the 45th U.S. and 56th British Divisions, transferred from the Cassino front, were just relieving our gallant 1st Division, who soon found themselves in full action again. A deep, dangerous wedge was driven into our line, which was forced back here to the original

beach-head. The artillery fire, which had embarrassed all the occupants of the beach-head since they landed, reached a new intensity. All hung in the balance. No further retreat was possible. Even a short advance would have given the enemy the power to use not merely their long-range guns in harassing fire upon the landing stages and shipping, but to put down a proper field artillery barrage upon all intakes or departures. I had no illusions about the issue. It was life or death.

But fortune, hitherto baffling, rewarded the desperate valour of the British and American armies. Before Hitler's stipulated three days the German attack was stopped. Then their own salient was counter-attacked in flank and cut out under fire from all our artillery and bombardment by every aircraft we could fly. The

A formation of Mitchell B-25 bombers takes off from an air base of the Twelfth Air Division.

AMERICAN SOLDIERS!

Remember those happy days when you stepped out with your best girl "going places and doing things"?

No matter

whether you two were enjoying a nice juicy steak at some tony restaurant or watching a thrilling movie with your favourite stars performing, or dancing to the lilt of a swing band

you were happy.

WHAT IS LEFT OF ALL THIS?

Nothing! Nothing but days and nights of he heaviest fighting and for many of you

NOTHING BUT A PLAIN WOODEN CROSS IN FOREIGN SOIL!

Propaganda dropped by Italian and German aircraft over the Anzio bridgehead to demoralise American troops.

American airmen write witty phrases on bombs destined for the Germans.

Two Allied soldiers shoot against attacking Italian-German forces from the window of a farm in the Anzio sector.

An Allied infantry reserve contingent, and a motor vehicle towing a Bofors anti-aircraft automatic artillery piece, pass through the rubble in a street of Anzio. On a wall, a Fascist slogan is still legible: "While for others the Mediterranean is only a way, for us Italians it is life".

fighting was intense, losses on both sides were heavy, but the deadly battle was won.

One more attempt was made by Hitler—for his was the will-power at work—at the end of February. The 3rd U.S. Division, on the eastern flank, was attacked by three German divisions. These were weakened and shaken by their previous failure. The Americans held stubbornly, and the attack was broken in a day, when the Germans had suffered more than 2,500 casualties. On March 1 Kesselring accepted his failure. He had frustrated the Anzio expedition. He could not destroy it.

Such is the story of the struggle of Anzio; a story of high opportunity and shattered hopes, of skilful inception on our part and swift recovery by the enemy, of valour shared by both. We now know that early in January the German High Command had intended to transfer five of their best divisions from Italy to North-West Europe. Kesselring protested that in such an event he could no longer carry

out his orders to fight south of Rome and he would have to withdraw. Just as the argument was at its height the Anzio landing took place. The High Command dropped the idea, and instead of the Italian front contributing forces to North-West Europe the reverse took place. Hitler was enraged at the failure of his Fourteenth Army to drive the Allies into the sea. After their offensive of February 16 he ordered a selected group of twenty officers of all arms and ranks fighting in Italy to report to him personally about conditions at the front. This was the first and only time that this happened during the war. "He would have done much better," comments General Westphal, "to visit the front himself and been convinced of Allied superiority in planes and guns."

Anzio residents aboard an Allied ship wave to those who stayed behind on the shore, while the ship sets sail for a port behind the front.

A group of cheering British infantrymen by a road sign: though they are still at Anzio, Rome is very close.

ROMA Km.57.6

CASSINO

The battle of Cassino lasted from November 1943 through May 1944. The ancient abbey was destroyed, but the troops that had landed at Anzio were able to join forces with those coming from the south.

The Xth British Corps having drawn to its front most of the enemy reinforcements, it was decided to attack farther north so as to seize the high ground above Cassino and envelop the position from that side. Good progress was made. The IInd U.S. Corps crossed the river Rapido above Cassino town, with the French Corps on their right keeping abreast of them, and took Monte Castellone and Colle Majola. Thence they attacked southwards against Monastery Hill; but the Germans had reinforced and held on fanatically. By early February the IInd Corps had expended its strength. General Alexander decided that fresh troops would be needed to restore impetus to the assault. He had already ordered a New Zealand Corps to be formed, under General Freyberg, composed of three divisions brought over from the Eighth Army on the Adriatic. Indeed, that army, which had attempted to pin the enemy on their front by offensive action, had had to send no fewer than five divisions to sustain the heavy fighting on the west coast, and for the next few months had to remain on the defensive.

The second major attack at Cassino began on February 15 with the bombing of the monastery. The height on which the monastery stood surveyed the junction of the

Top: a German defender armed with a Panzerfaust.

After climbing over Mount Trocchio, soldiers from the Fifth Army found themselves in the Liri Valley, heading towards Cassino.

A unit of Moroccan troops camped near Cassino. The intervention of the French corps (four divisions, mostly Moroccans), who were trained in mountain warfare, proved decisive.

Bottom left: the men of a Moroccan detachment leave their lorries to march to their posts in the Cassino sector.

Bottom right: Green Devils from the First German Paratroop Division counter-attack amidst the rubble in Cassino.

rivers Rapido and Liri and was the pivot of the whole German defence. It had already proved itself a formidable, strongly defended obstacle. Its steep sides, swept by fire, were crowned by the famous building, which several times in previous wars had been pillaged, destroyed, and rebuilt. There is controversy about whether it should have been destroyed once again. The monastery did not contain German troops, but the enemy fortifications were hardly separate from the building itself. The monastery dominated the whole battlefield, and naturally General Freyberg, the Corps Commander concerned, wished to have it heavily bombarded from the air before he launched the infantry attack. The Army Commander, General Mark Clark, unwillingly sought and obtained permission from General Alexander, who accepted the responsibility. On February 15 therefore, after the monks had been given full warning, over 450 tons of bombs were dropped, and heavy damage was done. The great outer walls and gateway still stood. The result was not good. The Germans had now every excuse for making whatever use they could of the rubble of the ruins, and this gave them even better opportunities for defence than when the building was intact.

It fell to the 4th Indian Division, which had recently relieved the Americans on the ridges north of the monastery, to make the attack. On two successive nights they tried in vain to seize a knoll that lay between their position and Monastery Hill. On the night of February 18 a third attempt was made. The fighting was desperate, and all our men who reached the knoll were killed. Later that night a brigade by-passed the knoll and moved directly at the monastery, only to encounter a concealed ravine heavily mined and covered by enemy machine-guns at shortest range. Here they lost heavily and were stopped. While this fierce conflict was raging on the heights above them the New Zealand Division succeeded in crossing the river Rapido just below Cassino town; but they were counter-attacked by tanks before their bridgehead was secure and forced back again. The direct attack on Cassino had failed.

At the beginning of March the weather brought about a deadlock. Napoleon's fifth element—mud—bogged down both sides. We could not break the main front at Cassino, and the Germans had equally failed to drive us into the sea at Anzio. In numbers there was little to choose between the combatants. By now we had twenty divisions in Italy, but both Americans and French had had very heavy losses. The enemy had eighteen or nineteen divisions south of Rome, and five more in Northern Italy, but they too were tired and worn.

There could be no hope now of a break-out from the Anzio beach-head and no prospect of an early link-up between our two separated forces until the Cassino front was broken. The prime need therefore was to make the

beach-head really firm, to relieve and reinforce the troops, and to pack in stores to withstand a virtual siege and nourish a subsequent sortie. Time was short, since many of the landing-craft had to leave for "Overlord" in the middle of the month. Their move had so far been rightly postponed, but no further delay was possible. The Navies put all their strength into the effort, with admirable results. The previous average daily tonnage landed had been 3,000; in the first ten days of March this was more than doubled. I followed this process with attention.

On March 12 I asked, "What is the ration strength in the bridgehead at present? How many vehicles have been landed there from the beginning? How many days' reserve supplies of food and ammunition have been built up, and what is the basis of this calculation?"

February 15, 1944: the Allies bomb Montecassino Abbey for the first time. In the photograph, the abbey is surrounded by smoke from explosions and fires.

Heaps of rubble fill a street in Cassino, as seen from a position held by German paratroopers.

General Alexander replied that the ration strength was 90,200 United States and 35,500 British. Nearly 25,000 vehicles of all kinds had been landed. He gave full details of the supplies of food, ammunition, and petrol. The margins were not large, but improving.

A few days later Vesuvius was in violent eruption. For several days traffic from the Naples airfields was partially interrupted, but the work in the ports went on. On March 24 a report to the Naval Commander-in-Chief stated: "The Naples group of ports is now discharging at the rate of twelve million tons a year, while Vesuvius is estimated to be doing thirty millions a day. We can but admire this gesture of the gods."

After a heavy bombardment, in which nearly 1,000 tons of bombs and 1,200 tons of shells were expended, our infantry advanced. "It seemed to me inconceivable," said Alexander, "that any troops should be left alive after eight hours of such terrific hammering." But they were. The 1st German Parachute Division, probably the toughest fighters in all their Army, fought it out amid the heaps of rubble with the New Zealanders and Indians. By nightfall the greater part of the town was in our hands, while the 4th Indian Division, coming down from the north, made equally good progress and next day were two-thirds of the way up Monastery Hill. Then the battle swung against us. Our tanks could not cross the large craters made by the bombardment and follow up the infantry assault. Nearly two days passed before they could help. The enemy filtered in reinforcements. The weather broke in storm and rain. Our attacks gained ground, but the early success was not repeated, and the enemy were not to be overborne in the slogging match.

The struggle in the ruins of Cassino town continued until the 23rd, with hard fighting in attacks and counter-attacks.

Here and at the Anzio bridgehead we had pinned down in Central Italy nearly twenty good German divisions. Many of them might have gone to France.

Before the Gustav Line could be assaulted again with any hope of success our troops had to be rested and regrouped. Most of the Eighth Army had to be brought over from the Adriatic side and two armies concentrated for the next battle, the British Eighth on the Cassino front, the American Fifth on the lower Garigliano. For this General Alexander needed nearly two months.

The regrouping of our forces in Italy was undertaken in great secrecy. Everything possible was done to conceal the movements from the enemy and to mislead him. By the time

Aerial view of Montecassino Abbey, still occupied by German paratroops after heavy Allied air attack and artillery crossfire.

A patrol of German paratroopers take up position in Cassino, at the end of an Allied shelling attack.

British infantrymen search Cassino's conquered buildings for any remaining isolated German soldiers.

Two British soldiers, armed with a Bren machine gun, put up a poster with a caricature of Hitler.

tance. Our attack came unexpectedly. The Germans were carrying out reliefs opposite the British front, and one of their Army Commanders had planned to go on leave.

The great offensive began at 11 p.m. that night, when the artillery of both our armies, 2,000 guns, opened a violent fire, reinforced at dawn by the full weight of the tactical air force. North of Cassino the Polish Corps tried to surround the monastery on the ridges that had been the scene of our previous failures, but they were held and thrown back. The British XIIIth Corps, with the 4th British and 8th Indian Divisions leading, succeeded in forming small bridgeheads over the Rapido river, but had to fight hard to hold them. On the Fifth Army front the French soon advanced to Monte Faito, but on the seaward flank the IInd U.S. Corps ran into stiff opposition and struggled for every yard of ground. After thirty-six hours of heavy fighting the enemy began to weaken. The French Corps took Monte Majo, and General Juin pushed his motorised division swiftly up the river Garigliano to capture Sant' Ambrogio and Sant' Apollinare, thus clearing all the west bank of the river. The XIIIth Corps bit more deeply into the strong enemy defences across the Rapido, and on May 14, with the 78th Division coming up to reinforce, began to make good progress. The French thrust forward again up the Ausente valley and took Ausonia, and General Juin launched his Goums across the trackless mountains westwards from Ausonia. The American Corps succeeded in capturing Santa Maria Infante, for which they had been fighting for so long. The two German divisions which on this flank had had to support the attack of six divisions of the Fifth Army had suffered crippling losses, and all the German right flank south of the Liri was breaking.

Despite the collapse of their seaward flank the enemy north of the Liri hung on desperately to the last elements of the Gustav Line. But gradually they were overborne. On the 15th the XIIIth Corps reached the Cassino-Pignataro road, and General Leese brought up the Canadian Corps to be ready to exploit

they were completed General Clark, of the Fifth Army, had over seven divisions, four of them French, on the front from the sea to the river Liri; thence the Eighth Army, now under General Leese, continued the line through Cassino into the mountains with the equivalent of nearly twelve. Six divisions had been packed into the Anzio beach-head ready to sally forth at the best moment; the equivalent of only three remained in the Adriatic sector. In all the Allies mustered over twenty-eight divisions.

Opposed to them were twenty-three German divisions, but our deception arrangements, which included the threat of a landing at Civitavecchia, the seaport of Rome, had puzzled Kesselring so well that they were widely spread. Between Cassino and the sea, where our main blows were to fall, there were only four, and reserves were scattered and at a dis-

his success. Next day the 78th Division broke through the defences in a north-westerly drive which reached Route 6, and on the 17th the Poles attacked north of the monastery. This time they succeeded, and occupied the ridges north-west of it which overlooked the highway.

On the morning of May 18 Cassino town was finally cleared by the 4th British Division, and the Poles triumphantly hoisted their red and white standard over the ruins of the monastery. They greatly distinguished themselves in this first major engagement in Italy. Later, under their thrustful General Anders, himself a survivor from Russian imprisonment, they were to win many laurels during the long advance to the river Po. The XIIIth

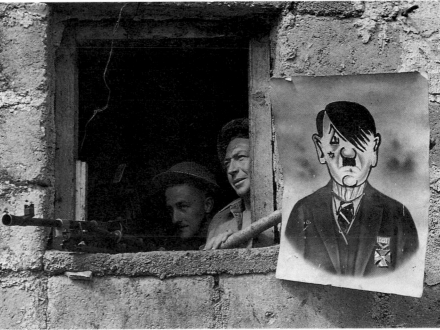

135

Two German soldiers who surrendered to the Sixth American Army Corps in the Anzio sector.

to Piedimonte, but it was now certain that the Germans would soon be forced into a general retreat.

The minds of our commanders were therefore focused on two points: the timing and direction of the Anzio break-out, and the possibility of a final German stand south of Rome, based on the Alban Hills and Valmontone on the high-road.

General Truscott quickly took advantage of the breach he had made at Cisterna. Under General Clark's orders, he dispatched three divisions, one of them armoured, to Velletri and the Alban Hills, but only one, the 3rd U.S. Division, towards Valmontone, where they would cut the most important escape route of the enemy farther south. This was not in accord with Alexander's instructions, which put Valmontone as the primary objective.

But the Hermann Goering Division and elements of others, delayed though they were by damaging attacks from the air, got to Valmontone first. The single American division sent by General Clark was stopped short of it and the escape road remained open. That was very unfortunate.

The enemy in the south were in full retreat, and the Allied Air did its utmost to impede movement and break up concentrations. Obstinate rearguards frequently checked our pursuing forces, and their retirement did not degenerate into a rout. The IInd U.S. Corps moved on Priverno, the French to Ceccano, while the Canadian Corps and British XIIIth Corps advanced up the valley to Frosinone and the Xth Corps up the road to Avezzano. The three American divisions dispatched from the Anzio breach towards Velletri and the Alban Hills, later reinforced by a fourth, the 36th, had met very stiff resistance, and for three days could make no ground. They got ready to renew the attack on Valmontone, which Kesselring had been reinforcing with any troops he could find that were fit to fight. However, a brilliant stroke by the 36th U.S. Division must have disconcerted him. They had been fighting hard at the south-west corner of the Alban Hills. On the night of May 30 they found that the Germans had left a com-

Corps had also advanced all along their front, reaching the outskirts of Aquino, with the Canadian Corps driving forward to the south of them. On the other bank of the Liri the French had reached Esperia and were pushing on towards Pico. The U.S. Corps had taken Formia, and they too were getting on splendidly. Kesselring had been sending down reinforcements as fast as he could muster them, but they were arriving piecemeal, only to be thrown into the battle to check the mounting flood of the Allied advance. The Eighth Army had yet to break the Adolf Hitler Line, running from Pontecorvo to Aquina and thence

Rome, June 1944: a motorised patrol from the 88th Infantry Division drives past the Colosseum.

manding height unguarded. Their infantry moved forward in close columns and occupied their key points. Within twenty-four hours the whole 36th Division was firmly established and the last German defence line south of Rome penetrated.

The success of the 36th U.S. Division did not bear immediate fruit. The enemy hung on desperately both in the Alban Hills and at Valmontone, although the retreat of most of their army had now been deflected northwards towards Avezzano and Arsoli, where they were hunted by the Xth and XIIIth British Corps and the aircraft of the tactical air force.

Unhappily, the mountainous country stopped us using our great strength in armour, which otherwise could have been employed to much advantage.

On June 2 the IInd U.S. Corps captured Valmontone and drove westwards. That night German resistance broke, and next day the VIth U.S. Corps in the Alban Hills, with the British 1st and 5th Divisions on its left, pressed on towards Rome. The IInd American Corps led them by a short head. They found the bridges mostly intact, and at 7.15 p.m. on June 4 the head of their 88th Division entered the Piazza Venezia, in the heart of the capital.

THE LANDING IN NORMANDY

Zero hour struck between June 6 and June 7, 1944: the landing in Normandy. After fierce fighting of epic proportions, the Allies established a bridgehead near Caen on the night of June 7. The attack on Germany was launched.

Once ashore, the first need of the Allies was to consolidate the immediate defence of their beaches and form a continuous front by expanding from them. The enemy fought stubbornly and were not easily overcome. In the American sector the marshes near Carentan and at the mouth of the river Vire hampered our movements, and everywhere the country was suited to infantry defence. The *bocage* which covers much of Normandy consists of a multitude of small fields divided by banks, with ditches and very high hedges. Artillery support for an attack is thus hindered by lack of good observation and it was extremely difficult to use tanks. It was infantry fighting all the way, with every little field a potential strong-point. Nevertheless good progress was made, except for the failure to capture Caen.

This small but famous town was to be the scene of bitter struggles over many days. To us it was important, because, apart from the fact that there was good ground to the east for constructing air-strips, it was the hinge on which our whole plan turned. Montgomery's intention was to make a great left wheel by the American forces, with Caen as their left-hand pivot. It was equally important for the Germans. If their lines were pierced there the whole of their Seventh Army would be forced southeastward towards the Loire, opening a gap between it and the Fifteenth Army in the north. The way to Paris would then be open. Thus in the following weeks Caen became the scene of ceaseless attacks and the most stubborn defence, drawing towards it a great part of the German divisions, and especially their armour. This was a help as well as a hindrance.

The Germans, though the reserve divisions of their Fifteenth Army were still held intact north of the Seine, had of course been reinforced from elsewhere, and by June 12 twelve divisions were in action, four of them Panzers. This was less than we had expected. The tremendous air offensive had hampered all the enemy's communications. Every bridge across the Seine below Paris and the principal bridges across the river Loire were by now destroyed. Most of the reinforcing troops had to use the roads and railways running through the gap between Paris and Orléans, and were subjected to continuous and damaging attacks by day and night from our air forces. A German report of July 8 said, "From Paris to the west and southwest all rail communications are broken." Not only were the enemy unable to reinforce quickly, but their divisions arrived piecemeal, short of equipment,

Top: an Italian-American serviceman poses with the small French phrase-book that was distributed to all military personnel landed in Normandy.

Close-up of a German paratrooper from the Green Devils regiment lying in ambush near Caen.

Southampton (U.K.),
June 5, 1944: an endless
succession of landing
craft moored at the
dock waiting for D-day.
All units are covered
with camouflage nets.

and fatigued by long night marches, and they were thrown into the line as they came. The German command had no chance to form a striking force behind the battle for a powerful, well-concerted counter-offensive.

By June 11 the Allies had formed a continuous front inland, and our fighters were operating from half a dozen forward air-strips. The next task was to secure a lodgment area big enough to hold sufficient forces for the decisive break-out. The Americans thrust westward across the Cherbourg peninsula towards Barneville, on the western coast, which they reached on June 17. Simultaneously they advanced northward, and after sharp fighting stood before the outer defences of Cherbourg on the 22d. The enemy resisted stoutly till the 26th in order to carry out demolitions. These were so thorough that heavy loads could not be brought in through the port till the end of August.

On June 17, at Margival, near Soissons, Hitler held a conference with Rundstedt and Rommel. His two generals pressed on him strongly the folly of bleeding the German Army to death in Normandy. They urged that before it was destroyed the Seventh Army should make an orderly withdrawal to the Seine, where, together with the Fifteenth Army, it could fight a defensive but mobile battle with at least some hope of success. But Hitler would not agree. Here, as in Russia and Italy, he demanded that no ground should be given up and all should fight where they stood. The generals were of course right. Hitler's method of fighting to the death on all fronts at once lacked the important element of selection.

Close-up of a field artillery gun opening fire during the encounter near Carentan.

Some troops were flown to Normandy by glider. In this photograph, some of the aircraft have been destroyed during landing, some have landed safely, and others are still circling in the sky, protected by fighters.

A British frigate has just launched a depth charge aimed at a submarine in the English Channel. The hunt for submarines was incessant throughout the landing operations.

In the battle area along the coast our consolidation was making headway. Bombarding ships of all types, including battleships, continued to support the armies on shore, particularly in the eastern sector, where the enemy concentrated the bulk of his armour and where his batteries were most troublesome. U-boats and light surface vessels tried to attack, though with little success, but sea mines, which were mostly laid by aircraft, took a serious toll of Allied shipping and delayed our build-up. Attacks from enemy bases to the eastward, particularly from Havre, were warded off, and in the west an Allied naval bombarding squadron co-operated later with the American Army in the capture of Cherbourg. Across the beaches progress was good. In the first six days 326,000 men, 54,000 vehicles, and 104,000 tons of stores were landed. In spite of serious losses among landing-craft an immense supply organisation was rapidly taking shape. An average of more than two hundred vessels and

The battleship *Rodney*, off the coast of Normandy, opens fire against the German defences of the Atlantic Rampart.

Troops from the Third Canada Division land at Bernières-sur-Mer.

Aboard a U.S. landing craft, troops lie in ambush behind the hatch just moments before dashing ashore.

Aerial view of landing craft approaching the beach in Normandy, where other units have already established a bridgehead.

craft of all types was arriving daily with supplies. The gigantic problem of handling such a volume of shipping was aggravated by bad weather. Nevertheless remarkable progress was made. The Merchant Navy played an outstanding part. Their seamen cheerfully accepted all the risks of war and weather, and their staunchness and fidelity played an impressive part in the vast enterprise.

By June 19 the two "Mulberry" harbours, one at Arromanches, the other ten miles farther west, in the American sector, were making good progress. "Pluto," the submarine pipeline, was also well advanced. But then a four-day gale began which almost entirely prevented the landing of men and material, and did a great damage to the newly sunk breakwaters. Many floating bombardons which were not designed for such conditions broke from their moorings and crashed into other breakwaters and the anchored shipping. The harbour in the American sector was

ruined, and its serviceable parts were used to repair Arromanches. This gale, the like of which had not been known in June for forty years, was a severe misfortune. We were already behind our programme of unloading. The break-out was equally delayed, and on June 23 we stood only on the line we had prescribed for the 11th.

In the last week of June the British established a bridgehead across the river Odon south of Caen. Efforts to extend it southward and eastward across the river Orne were repelled. The southern sector of the British front was twice attacked by several Panzer divisions. In violent conflicts the Germans were severely defeated, with heavy losses from our air and powerful artillery. It was now our turn to strike, and on July 8 a strong attack on Caen was launched from the north and northwest. The first of the tactical bombardments by Allied heavy bombers, which henceforward were a marked feature, prepared the

On the shore known by the code name "Omaha Beach", some soldiers perform artificial respiration on a fellow soldier who almost drowned after the sinking of a landing craft.

Infantry units of the British navy, equipped with small motorcycles and bicycles, disembark from the landing craft in the sector known by the code name "Sword".

way. Royal Air Force heavy bombers dropped more than 2000 tons on the German defences, and at dawn British infantry, hampered unavoidably by the bomb-craters and the rubble of fallen buildings, made good progress. By July 10 all of Caen on our side of the river was gained and I could say to Montgomery, "Many congratulations on your capture of Caen."

The hour of the great American break-out under General Omar Bradley came at last. On July 25 their VIIth Corps struck southward from St. Lô, and the next day the VIIIth Corps, on their right, joined the battle. The bombardment by the United States Air Force had been devastating, and the infantry assault prospered. Then the armour leaped through and swept on to the key point of Coutances. The German escape route down that coast of Normandy was cut, and the whole German defence west of the Vire was in jeopardy and chaos. The roads were jammed with retreating troops and the Allied bombers and fighter-bombers took a destructive toll of men and vehicles. The advance drove forward. Avranches was taken on July 31, and soon afterwards the sea corner, opening the way to the Brittany peninsula, was turned. The Canadians, under General Crerar, made a simultaneous attack from Caen down the Falaise road. This was effectively opposed by four Panzer divisions. Montgomery, who still commanded the whole battle line, thereupon transferred the

A group of American paratroopers during mopping-up operations in a town center.

weight of the British attack to the other front, and gave orders to the British Second Army, under General Dempsey, for a new thrust from Caumont to Vire. Preceded again by heavy air bombing, this began on July 30, and Vire was reached a few days later.

The Third United States Army, under General Patton, had now been formed and was in action. He detached two armoured and three infantry divisions for the westward and southerly drive to clear the Brittany peninsula. The cut-off enemy at once retreated towards their fortified ports. The French Resistance Movement, which here numbered 30,000 men, played a notable part, and the peninsula was quickly overrun. By the end of the first week in August the Germans, amounting to 45,000 garrison troops and remnants of four divisions, had been pressed

into their defensive perimeters at St. Malo, Brest, Lorient, and St. Nazaire. Here they could be penned and left to wither, thus saving the unnecessary losses which immediate assaults would have required. The damage done to Cherbourg had been enormous, and it was certain that when the Brittany ports were captured they would take a long time to repair. The fertility of the "Mulberry" at Arromanches, the sheltered anchorages, and the unforeseen development of smaller harbours on the Normandy coast had lessened the urgency of capturing the Brittany ports, which had been so prominent in our early plans. Moreover, with things going so well we could count on gaining soon the far better French ports from Havre to the north. Brest, however, which held a large garrison, under an active commander, was dangerous, and

had to be eliminated. It surrendered on September 19 to violent attacks by three U.S. divisions.

While Brittany was thus being cleared or cooped the rest of Patton's Third Army drove eastward in the "long hook" which was to carry them to the gap between the Loire and Paris and down the Seine towards Rouen. The town of Laval was entered on August 6, and Le Mans on August 9. Few Germans were found in all this wide region, and the main difficulty was supplying the advancing Americans over long and ever-lengthening distances. Except for a limited air-lift, everything had still to come from the beaches of the original landing and pass down the western side of Normandy through Avranches to reach the front. Avranches therefore became the bottle-neck, and offered a tempting

opportunity for a German attack striking westward from the neighbourhood of Falaise. The idea caught Hitler's fancy, and he gave orders for the maximum possible force to attack Mortain, burst its way through to Avranches, and thus cut Patton's communications. The German commanders were unanimous in condemning the project. Realising that the battle for Normandy was already lost, they wished to use four divisions which had just arrived from the Fifteenth Army in the north to carry out an orderly retreat to the Seine. They thought that to throw any fresh troops westward was merely to "stick out their necks," with the certain prospect of having them severed. Hitler insisted on having his way, and on August 7 five Panzer and two infantry divisions delivered a vehement attack on Mortain from the east.

While a column of armoured vehicles stops in a small village in the Avranches region, a young woman offers a drink to the servicemen. In the foreground is a severely damaged SS automobile.

June 9, 1944: a group of German troops surrender during the Allied advance in the Carentan peninsula.

The blow fell on a single U.S. division, but it held firm and three others came to its aid. After five days of severe fighting and concentrated bombing from the air the audacious onslaught was thrown back in confusion, and, as the enemy generals had predicted, the whole salient from Falaise to Mortain, full of German troops, was at the mercy of converging attacks from three sides. To the south of it one corps of the Third United States Army had been diverted northward through Alençon to Argentan, which they reached on August 13. The First United States Army, under General Hodges, thrust southward from Vire, and the Second British Army towards Condé. The Canadian Army, supported again by heavy bombers, continued to press down the road from Caen to Falaise, and this time with greater success, for they reached their goal on August 17. The Allied air forces swept on to the crowded Germans within the long and narrow pocket, and with the artillery inflicted fearful slaughter. The Germans held stubbornly on to the jaws of the gap at Falaise and Argentan, and, giving priority to their armour, tried to extricate all that they could. But on August 17 command and control broke down and the scene became a shambles. The jaws closed on August 20, and although by then a considerable part of the enemy had been able to scramble eastward, no fewer than eight German divisions were annihilated. What had been the Falaise pocket was their

grave. Von Kluge reported to Hitler: "The enemy air superiority is terrific and smothers almost all our movements. Every movement of the enemy however is prepared and protected by his air forces. Losses in men and material are extraordinary. The morale of the troops has suffered very heavily under constant, murderous enemy fire."

The Third United States Army, besides clearing the Brittany peninsula and contributing with their "short hook" to the culminating victory at Falaise, thrust three corps eastward and northeastward from Le Mans. On August 17 they reached Orléans, Chartres, and Dreux. Thence they drove northwestward down the left bank of the river to meet the British advancing on Rouen. Our Second Army had experienced some delay. They had to reorganise after the Falaise battle and the enemy found means to improvise rearguard positions. However, the pursuit was pressed hotly, and all the Germans south of the Seine were soon seeking desperately to retreat across it, under destructive air attacks. None of the bridges destroyed by previous air bombardments had been repaired, but again there was a fairly adequate ferry system. Very few vehicles could be saved. South of Rouen immense quantities of transport were abandoned. Such troops as escaped over the ferries were in no condition to resist on the farther bank of the river.

Eisenhower was determined to avoid a battle for Paris. Stalingrad and Warsaw had proved the horrors of frontal assaults and patriotic risings, and he therefore resolved to encircle the capital and force the garrison to surrender or flee. By August 20 the time for action had come. Patton had crossed the Seine near Mantes, and his right flank had reached Fontainebleau. The French Underground had revolted. The police were on strike. The Prefecture was in Patriot hands. An officer of the Resistance reached Patton's headquarters with vital reports, and on the morning of Wednesday, August 23, these were delivered to Eisenhower at Le Mans.

Attached to Patton was the French 2d Armoured Division, under General Leclerc, which had landed in Normandy on August 1, and played an honourable part in the advance. De Gaulle arrived the same day, and was assured by the Allied Supreme Commander that when the time came—and as had been long agreed—Leclerc's troops would be the first in Paris. That evening the news of street fighting in the capital decided Eisenhower to act, and Leclerc was told to march. At 7.15 p.m. General Bradley delivered these instructions to the French commander, whose division was then quartered in the region of Argentan. The operation orders, dated August 23, began with the words, "Mission s'emparer de Paris…"

Leclerc wrote to de Gaulle: "I have had the impression…of living over again the situation of 1940 in reverse—complete disorder on the enemy side, their columns completely surprised." He decided to act boldly and evade rather than reduce the German concentra-

An American soldier poses next to the road sign outside Sainte Mère-Eglise, site of the landing of the first paratroops on the night of June 15.

149

U.S. servicemen speak with a wounded German soldier lying on barrack equipment left behind by German military units in a street of Cherbourg.

June 17, 1944: a Frenchman prays over the corpse of an American casualty.

tions. On August 24 the first detachments moved on the city from Rambouillet, where they had arrived from Normandy the day before. The main thrust, led by Colonel Billotte, son of the commander of the First French Army Group, who was killed in May 1940, moved up from Orléans. That night a vanguard of tanks reached the Porte d'Italie, and at 9.22 precisely entered the square in front of the Hôtel de Ville. The main body of the division got ready to enter the capital on the following day. Early next morning Billotte's armoured columns held both banks of the Seine opposite the Cité. By the afternoon the headquarters of the German commander, General von Choltitz, in the Hôtel Meurice, had been surrounded, and Choltitz surrendered to a French lieutenant, who brought him to Billotte. Leclerc had meanwhile arrived and established himself at the Gare Montparnasse, moving down in the afternoon to the Prefecture of Police. About four o'clock von Choltitz was taken before him. This was the end of the road from Dunkirk to Lake Chad and home again. In a low voice Leclerc spoke his thoughts aloud: "Maintenant, ça y est," and then in German he introduced himself to the vanquished. After a brief and brusque discussion the capitulation of the garrison was signed, and one by one their remaining strong-points were occu-

pied by the Resistance and the regular troops.

The city was given over to a rapturous demonstration. German prisoners were spat at, collaborators dragged through the streets, and the liberating troops fêted. On this scene of long-delayed triumph there arrived General de Gaulle. At 5 p.m. he reached the Rue St. Dominique, and set up his headquarters in the Ministry of War. Two hours later, at the Hôtel de Ville, he appeared for the first time as the leader of Free France before the jubilant population in company with the main figures of the Resistance and Generals Leclerc and Juin. There was a spontaneous burst of wild enthusiasm. Next afternoon, on August 26, de Gaulle made his formal entry on foot down the Champs Elysées to the Place de la Concorde, and then in a file of cars to Notre Dame. There was one fusillade from the rooftops by hidden collaborators. The crowd scattered, but after a short moment of panic the solemn dedication of the liberation of Paris proceeded to its end.

By August 30 our troops were crossing the Seine at many points. Enemy losses had been tremendous: 400,000 men, half of them prisoners, 1300 tanks, 20,000 vehicles, 1500 field guns. The German Seventh Army, and all divisions that had been sent to reinforce it, were torn to shreds. The Allied break-out from the beach-head had been delayed by bad weather and Hitler's mistaken resolve.

THE END OF THE CAMPAIGN IN ITALY

In the fall of 1944, the Allies decided to delay the offensive in Italy until the following spring. In April, once the western front had been cleared of German forces, they invaded the Po Valley.

The long, obstinate, and unexpected German resistance on all fronts had made us and the Americans very short of artillery ammunition, and our hard experiences of winter campaigning in Italy forced us to postpone a general offensive till the spring. But the Allied Forces, under General Eaker, and later under General Cannon, used their thirty-to-one superiority in merciless attacks on the supply lines which nourished the German armies. The most important one, from Verona to the Brenner Pass, where Hitler and Mussolini used to meet in their happier days, was blocked in many places for nearly the whole of March. Other passes were often closed for weeks at a time, and two divisions being transferred to the Russian front were delayed almost a month.

The enemy had enough ammunition and supplies, but lacked fuel. Units were generally up to strength, and their spirit was high in spite of Hitler's reverses on the Rhine and the Oder. In Northern Italy they had twenty-seven divisions, four of them Italian, against our equivalent of twenty-three drawn from the British Empire, the United States, Poland, Brazil, and Italy. The German High Command might have had little to fear had it not been for the dominance of our Air Forces, the fact that we had the initiative and could strike where we pleased, and their own ill-chosen defensive position, with the broad Po at their backs. They would have done better to yield Northern Italy and withdraw to the strong defences of the Adige, where they could have held us with much smaller forces, and sent troops to help their over-matched armies elsewhere, or have made a firm southern face for the National Redoubt in the Tyrol mountains, which Hitler may have had in mind as his "last ditch".

But defeat south of the Po spelt disaster. This must have been obvious to Kesselring.

Top: a girl from Ferrara and an infantryman kiss.

In a base of the Fifteenth Air Division, the pilots of a Mustang P-51 squadron are briefed by their commander before taking off on a mission in the Brenner region.

1944: a Mitchell B-25 bomber in action over a railroad and roadway bridge not far from Pietrasanta (near Lucca).

An Allied air raid over Emilia-Romagna. According to Churchill, Allied air superiority enabled the Allies to hit whatever they wished.

June 1, 1944: the ruins of the center of Recco (near Genoa) after a fierce air raid.

Hitler was of course the stumbling-block, and when Vietinghoff, who succeeded Kesselring, proposed a tactical withdrawal he was thus rebuffed: "The Fuehrer expects, now as before, the utmost steadiness in the fulfilment of your present mission to defend every inch of the North Italian areas entrusted to your command."

This eased our problem. If we could break through the Adriatic flank and reach the Po quickly all the German armies would be cut off and forced to surrender, and it was to this that Alexander and Clark bent their efforts when the stage was set for the final battle. The capture of Bologna, which had figured so much in our autumn plans, was no longer a principal object. The plan was for the Eighth Army, under General McCreery, to force a way down the road from Bastia to Argenta, a narrow, strongly defended passage, flooded on both sides, but leading to more open ground beyond. When this was well under way General Truscott's Fifth Army was to strike from the mountainous central front, pass west of Bologna, join hands with the Eighth Army

on the Po, and together pursue to the Adige. The Allied naval forces would make the enemy believe that amphibious landings were imminent on both east and west coasts.

In the evening of April 9, after a day of mass air attacks and artillery bombardment, the Eighth Army attacked across the river Senio, led by the Vth and the Polish Corps. On the 11th they reached the next river, the Santerno. The foremost brigade of the 56th Division and Commandos made a surprise landing at Menate, three miles behind the enemy, having been carried across the floods in a new type of amphibious troop-carrying tank called the Buffalo, which had come by sea from an advanced base in the Adriatic. By the 14th there was good news all along the Eighth Army front. The Poles took Imola. The New Zealand Division crossed the Sillaro. The 78th Division, striking north, took the bridge at Bastia and joined the attacks of the 56th on the Argenta road. The Germans knew well that this was their critical hinge and fought desperately.

That same day the Fifth Army began the

155

April 24, 1944: British infantrymen cross a canal of the Po River at Volano, during the occupation of Ferrara.

centre attack west of the Pistoia-Bologna road. After a week of hard fighting, backed by the full weight of the Allied Air Forces, they broke out from the mountains, crossed the main road west of Bologna, and struck north. On the 20th Vietinghoff, despite Hitler's commands, ordered a withdrawal. He tactfully reported that he had "decided to abandon the policy of static defence and adopt a mobile strategy". It was too late. Argenta had already fallen and the 6th British Armoured Division was sweeping towards Ferrara. Bologna was closely threatened from the east by the Poles and from the south by the 34th U.S. Division. It was captured on April 21, and here the Poles destroyed the renowned 1st

German Parachute Division. The Fifth Army pressed towards the Po, with the tactical air force making havoc along the roads ahead. Its 10th U.S. Mountain Division crossed the river on the 23rd, and the right flank of the Army, the 6th South African Division, joined the left of the Eighth. Trapped behind them were many thousand Germans, cut off from retreat, pouring into prisoners' cages or being marched to the rear. The offensive was a fine example of concerted land and air effort, wherein the full strength of the strategical and tactical air forces played its part. Fighter-bombers destroyed enemy guns, tanks, and troops; light and medium bombers attacked the lines of supply, and our heavy bombers struck by day and night at the rear installations.

We crossed the Po on a broad front at the heels of the enemy. All the permanent bridges had been destroyed by our Air Forces, and the ferries and temporary crossings were attacked with such effect that the enemy were thrown into confusion. The remnants who struggled across, leaving all their heavy equipment behind, were unable to reorganise on the far bank. The Allied armies pursued them to the Adige. Italian Partisans had long harassed the enemy in the mountains and their back areas. On April 25 the signal was given for a general rising, and they made widespread attacks. In many cities and towns, notably Milan and Venice, they seized control. Surrenders in North-West Italy became wholesale. The garrison of Genoa, four thousand strong, gave themselves up to a British liaison officer and the Partisans. On the 27th the Eighth Army crossed the Adige, heading for Padua, Treviso,

April 1945: a tank of the New Zealand forces is about to enter Massa Lombarda (near Ravenna).

April 20, 1945: two German casualties on the outskirts of Verona. U.S. troops are marching past a typical sample of Fascist architecture.

April 1945: in a town in the rear, not far from the front, small twin sisters watch a soldier setting up a warning sign.

and Venice, while the Fifth, already in Verona, made for Vicenza and Trento, its left extending to Brescia and Alessandria.

The naval campaign, though on a much smaller scale, had gone equally well. In January the ports of Split and Zadar had been occupied by the Partisans, and coastal forces from these bases harassed the Dalmatian shore and helped Tito's steady advance. In April alone at least ten actions were fought at sea, with crippling damage to the enemy and no loss of British ships.

The Navy had operated on both flanks during the final operations. On the west coast British, American, and French forces were continually in action, bombarding and harassing the enemy, driving off persistent

attacks by light craft and midget submarines, and clearing mines in the liberated ports. These activities led to the last genuine destroyer action in the Mediterranean. The former Yugoslav destroyer *Premuda*, captured by the Italians at the beginning of the war, left Genoa on the night of March 17, with two Italian destroyers, all manned by Germans, and tried to intercept a British convoy sailing from Marseilles to Leghorn. The British destroyers *Look-out* and *Meteor*, on patrol off the north point of Corsica, got warning and attacked. Both the Italian ships were sunk, the British suffering no loss or damage. By the time our armies reached the Adige the fighting at sea had virtually ended.

THE ATOMIC BOMB

August 6, 1945: the first atomic bomb was dropped on Hiroshima. This decision gained Japan's surrender, but placed the world under the threat of a future global war.

On July 17 world-shaking news had arrived. In the afternoon Stimson called at my abode and laid before me a sheet of paper on which was written, "Babies satisfactorily born." By his manner I saw something extraordinary had happened. "It means," he said, "that the experiment in the Mexican desert has come off. The atomic bomb is a reality." Although we had followed this dire quest with every scrap of information imparted to us, we had not been told beforehand, or at any rate I did not know, the date of the decisive trial. No responsible scientist would predict what would happen when the first full-scale atomic explosion was tried. Were these bombs useless or were they annihilating? Now we knew. The "babies" had been "satisfactorily born". No one could yet measure the immediate military consequences of the discovery, and no one has yet measured anything else about it.

Next morning a plane arrived with a full description of this tremendous event in the human story. Stimson brought me the report. I tell the tale as I recall it. The bomb, or its equivalent, had been detonated a the top of a pylon 100 feet high. Everyone had been cleared away for ten miles round, and the scientists and their staffs crouched behind massive concrete shields and shelters at about that distance. The blast had been terrific. An enormous column of flame and smoke shot up to the fringe of the atmosphere of our poor earth. Devastation inside a one-mile circle was absolute. Here then was a speedy end to the Second World War, and perhaps to much else besides.

The President invited me to confer with

Top: the mushroom cloud of the first atomic bombing.

The crew of the B-29 flying fortress *Enola Gay*, which dropped the atomic bomb on Hiroshima, pose just a few minutes before take-off. Commander Paul W. Tibbets is standing fourth from the left.

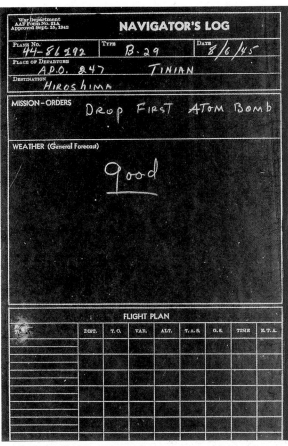

NAVIGATOR'S LOG

War Department
AAF Form No. 21A
Approved Sept. 15, 1942

PLANE NO.	TYPE	DATE
44-86292	B-29	8/6/45

PLACE OF DEPARTURE
A.P.O. 247   TINIAN

DESTINATION
HIROSHIMA

MISSION-ORDERS
Drop First Atom Bomb

WEATHER (General Forecast)
Good

FLIGHT PLAN

	DIST.	T.C.	VAR.	ALT.	T.A.S.	G.S.	TIME	E.T.A.

him forthwith. He had with him General Marshall and Admiral Leahy. Up to this moment we had shaped our ideas towards an assault upon the homeland of Japan by terrific air bombing and by the invasion of very large armies. We had contemplated the desperate resistance of the Japanese fighting to the death with Samurai devotion, not only in pitched battles, but in every cave and dugout. I had in my mind the spectacle of Okinawa island, where many thousands of Japanese, rather than surrender, had drawn up in line and destroyed themselves by hand-grenades after their leaders had solemnly performed the rite of *hara-kiri*. To quell the Japanese resistance man by man and conquer the country yard by yard might well require the loss of a million American lives and half that number of British—or more if we could get them there: for we were resolved to share the agony. Now all this nightmare picture had vanished. In its place was the vision—fair and bright indeed it seemed—of the end of the whole war in one or two violent shocks. I thought immediately myself of how the Japanese people, whose courage I had always admired, might find in the apparition of this almost supernatural weapon an excuse which would save their honour and release them from their obligation of being killed to the last fighting man.

Moreover, we should not need the Russians. The end of the Japanese war no longer depended upon the pouring in of their armies for the final and perhaps protracted slaughter. We had no need to ask favours of them. A few days later I minuted to Mr. Eden: "It is quite clear that the United States do not at the present time desire Russian participation in the war against Japan." The array of European problems could therefore be faced on their merits and according to the broad principles of the United Nations. We seemed suddenly to have become possessed of a merciful abridgment of the slaughter in the East and of a far happier prospect in Europe.

The *Enola Gay* in an air base on the Mariana Islands, after its mission to Hiroshima.

The *Enola Gay* navigator's log for August 6, 1945.

I have no doubt that these thoughts were present in the minds of my American friends. At any rate, there never was a moment's discussion as to whether the atomic bomb should be used or not. To avert a vast, indefinite butchery, to bring the war to an end, to give peace to the world, to lay healing hands upon its tortured peoples by a manifestation of overwhelming power at the cost of a few explosions, seemed, after all our toils and perils, a miracle of deliverance.

British consent in principle to the use of the weapon had been given on July 4, before the test had taken place. The final decision now lay in the main with President Truman, who had the weapon; but I never doubted what it would be, nor have I ever doubted since that he was right. The historic fact remains, and must be judged in the after-time, that the decision whether or not to use the atomic bomb to compel the surrender of Japan was never an issue. There was unanimous, automatic, unquestioned agreement around our table; nor did I ever hear the slightest suggestion that we should do otherwise.

It appeared that the American Air Force had prepared an immense assault by ordinary air-bombing on Japanese cities and harbours. These could certainly have been destroyed in a few weeks or a few months, and no one could say with what very heavy loss of life to the civilian population. But now, by using this new agency, we might not merely destroy cities, but save the lives alike of friend and foe.

The atomic bomb that was dropped on Hiroshima, before being loaded on the *Enola Gay*.

Japan's emperor Hirohito. Japan agreed to surrender only after assurances that Hirohito would be allowed to stay on the throne.

Panoramic view of Hiroshima's central district razed to the grround by the explosion, which killed over 100,000 and injured as many more.

The first Americans to arrive in Hiroshima after the bombing. On August 9, a second atom bomb was dropped on Nagasaki, but killed "only" 39,000.

One of the wounded in the bombing of Hiroshima. Many died a long time later, from the effects of the radiation.

An elderly Hiroshima couple stricken by radiation, in their home. Flies were everywhere.

In one of the Red Cross centers set up in Hiroshima, a nurse arranges the features of a boy who has just died from his wounds.

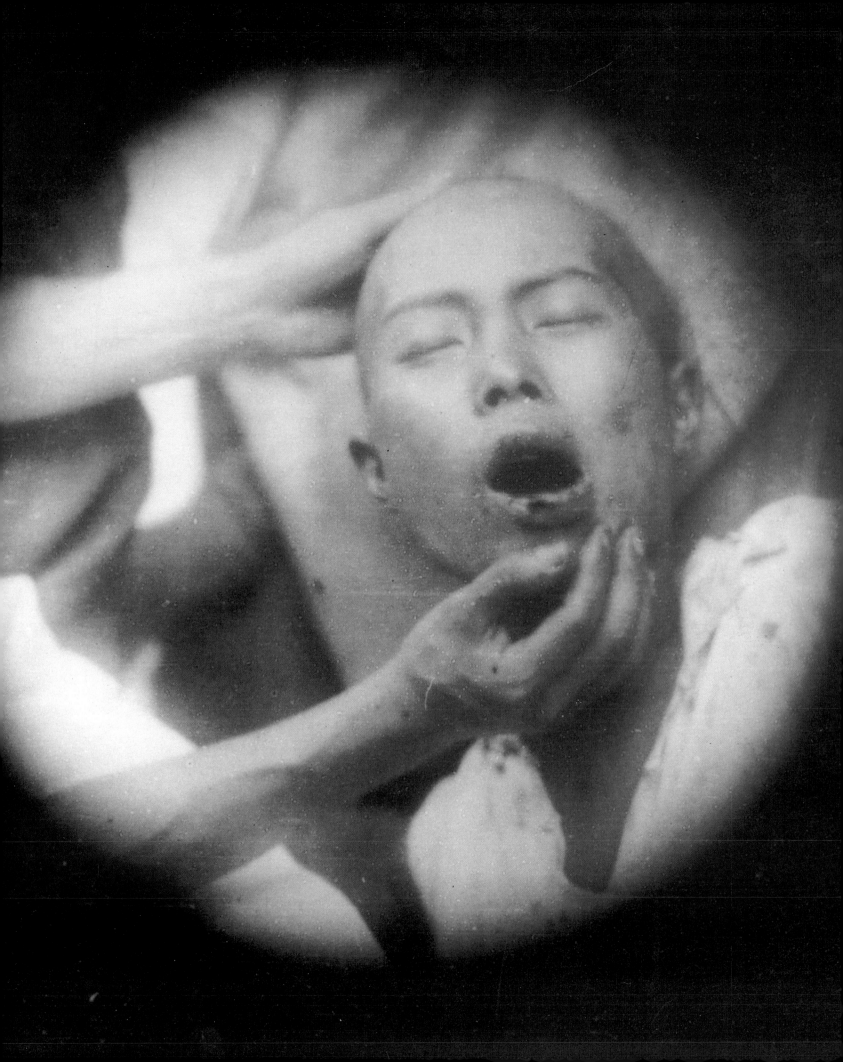

The Leaders

CHURCHILL

"I felt as if I were walking with destiny, and that all my past life had been but a preparation for this hour and for this trial."

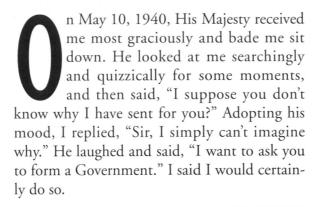

O n May 10, 1940, His Majesty received me most graciously and bade me sit down. He looked at me searchingly and quizzically for some moments, and then said, "I suppose you don't know why I have sent for you?" Adopting his mood, I replied, "Sir, I simply can't imagine why." He laughed and said, "I want to ask you to form a Government." I said I would certainly do so.

Winston Churchill *was born on November 30, 1874, at Blenheim Palace, to an old aristocratic family. His father had had important political roles. Churchill twice failed the admission exam at Sandhurst academy, but eventually graduated from it, as a cavalry officer, in 1894. He alternated between a military career and activity as war correspondent in Cuba (1895), Malakland (1897), and South Africa (1899-1900). After a first, failed attempt, he was elected to the House of Commons as a Conservative (1900), but in 1904 he joined the Liberals. He was Under-Secretary of State for the Colonies (1905-1908), President of the Board of Trade (1908-1910), Home Secretary (1910-1911), and First Lord of the Admiralty from 1911; the unfortunate incident in the Dardanelles led him to resign (November 1915) and join the fight in France. Later, he was Minister of Munitions (1917-1919), Secretary of State for War and Air (1919-1921), and Colonial Secretary (1921-1922). He retired from political life for two years and started writing a history of World War I (1923-1931). In 1924, he re-entered Parliament as a member of the Conservative Party, and became Chancellor of the Exchequer (1924-1929); after the defeat of the Conservative Party, he was chancellor of Aberdeen University (1929) and of Bristol University and published some autobiographical and historical works. As a Member of Parliament, he was among the first to express serious concerns about the rise of Hitler, while as a radical anti-Communist, he had never concealed his sympathies for Italian Fascism. He harshly criticised Chamberlain for his weakness towards Nazism, but he agreed to join the War Cabinet instituted on November 5, 1939, as First Lord of the Admiralty. After Chamberlain's resignation, he was appointed Prime Minister and assumed the leadership of the Defence Office, positions that he held throughout the war, which he directed from both the military and the political standpoint. In July 1945, just a few days before Japan's surrender, Churchill was defeated in the general election. In the following years, he fought against the Communist danger, for an Atlantic alliance, and for the European union. He regained power in October 1951 and retired in April 1955, handing over his office to his protégé, Anthony Eden. After The Second World War, for which he received the Nobel Prize in 1953, he published A History of the English-Speaking People (1956-1958). He died in London on January 24, 1965.*

Thus, then, on the night of the 10th of May, at the outset of this mighty battle, I acquired the chief power in the State, which henceforth I wielded in ever-growing measure for five years and three months of world war, at the end of which time, all our enemies having surrendered unconditionally or being about to do so, I was immediately dismissed by the British electorate from all further conduct of their affairs.

During these last crowded days of the political crisis my pulse had not quickened at any moment. I took it all as it came. But I cannot conceal from the reader of this truthful account that as I went to bed at about 3 a.m. I was conscious of a profound sense of relief. At last I had the authority to give directions over the whole scene. I felt as if I were walking with destiny, and that all my past life had been but a preparation for this hour and for this trial. Ten years in the political wilderness had freed me from ordinary party antagonisms. My warnings over the last six years had been so numerous, so detailed, and were now so terribly vindicated, that no one could gainsay me. I could not be reproached either for making the war or with want of preparation for it. I thought I knew a good deal about it all, and I was sure I should not fail. Therefore, although impatient for the morning, I slept soundly and had no need for cheering dreams. Facts are better than dreams.

When I woke about 8 a.m. I read all the telegrams, and from my bed dictated a continuous flow of minutes and directives to the departments and to the Chiefs of Staff Committee. These were typed in relays as they were done, and handed at once to General Ismay, Deputy-Secretary (Military) to the War Cabinet, and my representative on the Chiefs of Staff Committee, who came to see me early

as one, and the War Cabinet clothed us with ever more discretion, and sustained us with unwearied and unflinching constancy. There was no division, as in the previous war, between politicians and soldiers, between the "Frocks" and the "Brass Hats"—odious terms which darkened counsel. We came very close together indeed, and friendships were formed which I believe were deeply valued.

The efficiency of a war Administration depends mainly upon whether decisions emanating from the highest approved authority are in fact strictly, faithfully, and punctually obeyed. This we achieved in Britain in this time of crisis owing to the intense fidelity, comprehension, and whole-hearted resolve of the War Cabinet upon the essential purpose to which we had devoted ourselves. According to the directions given, ships, troops, and aeroplanes moved, and the wheels of factories spun. By all these processes, and by the confidence, indulgence, and loyalty by which I was upborne, I was soon able to give an integral direction to almost every aspect of the war. This was really necessary, be-

Churchill poses in a pinstriped suit, with a machine gun and cigar, during an inspection of coastal defences in northeastern Britain. This photograph was used repeatedly, with defamatory intention, by enemy propagandists.

On September 1, 1939, Germany attacked Poland. Churchill leaves No. 10 Downing Street after a consultation with Prime Minister Neville Chamberlain. Four days later, he entered the new War Cabinet as First Lord of the Admiralty.

each morning. Thus he usually had a good deal in writing to bring before the Chiefs of Staff Committee when they met at ten-thirty. They gave all consideration to my views at the same time as they discussed the general situation. Thus between three and five o'clock in the afternoon, unless there were some difficulties between us requiring further consultation, there was ready a whole series of orders and telegrams sent by me or by the Chiefs of Staff and agreed between us, usually giving all the decisions immediately required.

In total war it is quite impossible to draw any precise line between military and non-military problems.

I cannot say that we never differed among ourselves even at home, but a kind of understanding grew up between me and the British Chiefs of Staff that we should convince and persuade rather than try to overrule each other. This was of course helped by the fact that we spoke the same technical language, and possessed a large common body of military doctrine and war experience. In this ever-changing scene we moved

Churchill in the garden at No. 10 Downing Street with some of his closest military aides. From the left, sitting: Marshal Charles Portal, Marshal Alan Brooke, Admiral Andrew Cunningham; From the left, standing: General L. C. Hollis and General Hasting Ismay.

Accompanied by some officers, Churchill inspects the southern coastal defenses of Great Britain (July 1940).

August 28, 1940:
Churchill, with
binoculars, scans the
horizon beyond the
English Channel from
an antiaircraft
observation post in
Dover. On his left, the
mayor of Dover.

Accompanied by
admiral R. Burnett,
Churchill inspects a
fleet unit, that has
returned from escorting
a convoy with supplies
for the Soviet Union
(October 1942).

cause times were so very bad. The method was accepted because everyone realised how near were death and ruin. Not only individual death, which is the universal experience, stood near, but, incomparably more commanding, the life of Britain, her message, and her glory.

On Monday, May 13, I asked the House of Commons, which had been specially summoned, for a vote of confidence in the new Administration. After reporting the progress which had been made in filling the various offices, I said: "I have nothing to offer but blood, toil, tears, and sweat." In all our long history no Prime Minister had ever been able to present to Parliament and the nation a programme at once so short and so popular. I ended:

You ask, What is our policy? I will say: It is to wage war, by sea, land, and air, with all our might and with all the strength that God can give us: to wage war against a monstrous tyranny, never surpassed in the dark, lamentable catalogue of human crime. That is our policy. You ask, What is our aim? I can answer in one word: Victory—victory at all costs, victory in spite of all terror; victory, however long and hard the road may be; for without victory there is no survival. Let that be realised: no survival for the British Em-

pire; no survival for all that the British Empire has stood for, no survival for the urge and impulse of the ages, that mankind will move forward towards its goal. But I take up my task with buoyancy and hope. I feel sure that our cause will not be suffered to fail among men. At this time I feel entitled to claim the aid of all, and I say, "Come, then, let us go forward together with our united strength."

On the other hand, I was well aware of the strength of my position. I could count on the goodwill of the people for the share I had had in their survival in 1940. I did not underrate the broad, deep tide of national fidelity that bore me forward. The War Cabinet and the Chiefs of Staff showed me the highest loyalty. I was sure of myself. I made it clear, as occasion required, to those about me that I would not consent to the slightest curtailment of my personal authority and responsibility. The Press was full of suggestions that I should remain Prime Minister and make the speeches but cede the actual control of the war to someone else. I resolved to yield nothing to any quarter, to take the prime and direct personal responsibility upon myself, and to demand a Vote of Confidence from the House of Commons. I also remembered that wise French saying, "On ne règne sur les âmes que par le calme."

It was necessary above all to warn the House and the country of the misfortunes which impended upon us. There is no worse mistake in pubic leadership than to hold out false hopes soon to be swept away. The British people can face peril or misfortune with fortitude and buoyancy, but they bitterly resent being deceived or finding that those responsible for their affairs are themselves dwelling in a fool's paradise. I felt it vital, not only to my own position but to the whole conduct of the war, to discount future calamities by describing the immediate outlook in the darkest terms. It was also possible to do so at this juncture without prejudicing the military situation or disturbing that underlying confidence in ultimate victory which all were now entitled to feel.

My own position had not seemed to be affected in all this period of political tension and change at home and disaster abroad. I was too

much occupied with hourly business to have much time for brooding upon it. My personal authority even seemed to be enhanced by the uncertainties affecting several of my colleagues or would-be colleagues. I did not suffer from any desire to be relieved of my responsibilities. All I wanted was compliance with my wishes after reasonable discussion. Misfortunes only brought me and the Chiefs of Staff closer together, and this unity was felt through all the circles of the Government. There was no whisper of intrigue or dissidence, either in the War Cabinet or in the much larger number of Ministers of Cabinet rank. From outside however there was continuous pressure to change my method of conducting the war, with a view to obtaining better results than were now coming in. "We are all with the Prime Minister, but he has too much to do. He should be relieved of some of the burdens that fall upon him." This was the persistent view, and many theories were pressed.

I was entirely resolved to keep my full power of war-direction. This could only be exercised by combining the offices of Prime Minister and Minister of Defence. More difficulty and toil

May 8, 1945: from his office at No. 10 Downing Street, Churchill broadcasts the announcement of victory to the people of Great Britain.

Churchill with King George VI, in May 1944, during an official reception at Buckingham Palace for the prime ministers of the British Empire.

London, May 8, 1945: the crowd surrounds Churchill in Parliament square.

A moment of emotion for Churchill during a Conservative Party meeting in May 1948.

Opposite page: Churchill, with his dog Rufus, rests at his country house in Chartwell, Kent (1949).

are often incurred in overcoming opposition and adjusting divergent and conflicting views than by having the right to give decisions oneself. It is most important that at the summit there should be one mind playing over the whole field, faithfully aided and corrected, but not divided in its integrity. I should not of course have remained Prime Minister for an hour if I had been deprived of the office of Minister of Defence. The fact that this was widely known repelled all challenges, even under the most unfavourable conditions, and many well-meant suggestions of committees and other forms of impersonal machinery consequently fell to the ground.

HITLER

Hitler's photographs were chosen with care, by himself as well as by Nazi propagandists, to present the image of a steady and resolute man, like this one, or in many cases to emphasise his humane and cordial aspects.

In October 1918 a German corporal had been temporarily blinded by mustard gas in a British attack near Comines. While he lay in hospital in Pomerania defeat and revolution swept over Germany. The son of an obscure Austrian customs official, he had nursed youthful dreams of becoming a great artist. Having failed to gain entry to the Academy of Art in Vienna, he had lived in poverty in that capital and later in Munich. Sometimes as a house-painter, often as a casual labourer, he suffered physical privations and bred a harsh though concealed resentment that the world had denied him success. These misfortunes did not lead him into Communist ranks. By an honourable inversion he cherished all the more an abnormal sense of racial loyalty and a fervent and mystic admiration for Germany and the German people. He sprang eagerly to arms at the outbreak of the war, and served for four years with a Bavarian regiment on the Western Front.

As he lay sightless and helpless in hospital during the winter of 1918 his own personal failure seemed merged in the disaster of the whole German people. The shock of defeat, the collapse of law and order, the triumph of the French, caused this convalescent regimental orderly an agony which consumed his being, and generated those portentous and measureless forces of the spirit which may spell the rescue or the doom of mankind. The downfall of Germany seemed to him inexplicable by ordinary processes. Somewhere there had been a gigantic and monstrous betrayal. Lonely and pent within himself, the little soldier pondered and speculated upon the possible causes of the catastrophe, guided only by his narrow personal experiences. He had mingled in Vienna with

Adolf Hitler *was born on April 20, 1889, in Braunau, Austria, to a peasant family. He dreamt of becoming an architect, but only managed to be a mediocre painter. A volunteer in World War I, he moved to Germany after the Austrian-German defeat and joined the Workers' Party, which in 1920, became the National Socialist German Workers' Party (NSDAP). After a failed Putsch (1923) and a period in jail, he reorganised the party and created two paramilitary units (SA and SS). Between 1928 and 1930, the party grew enormously, thanks to the political and economic crisis and to Hitler's anti-Communist hypernationalism. He was nominated as Chancellor (January 30, 1933), and in the March elections he received 43.9% of the vote. On August 19, 1934, he became Head of State, and shortly after he imposed a dictatorship. With an expansionist program based on the tenet of the superiority of the German race, he invaded Rhineland (1936), Austria and the Sudeten (1938), and Czechoslovakia (1939), beginning World War II (September 1, 1939). Having lost the war, he committed suicide on April 30, 1945, in Berlin.*

extreme German Nationalist groups, and here he had heard stories of sinister, undermining activities of another race, foes and exploiters of the Nordic world––the Jews. His patriotic anger fused with his envy of the rich and successful into one overpowering hate.

When at length, as an unnoted patient, he was released from hospital, still wearing the uniform in which he had an almost schoolboyish pride, what scenes met his newly unscaled eyes! Fearful are the convulsions of defeat. Around him in the atmosphere of despair and frenzy glared the lineaments of Red Revolution. Armoured cars dashed through the streets of Munich scattering leaflets or bullets upon the fugitive wayfarers. His own comrades, with defiant red arm-bands on their uniform, were shouting slogans of fury against all that he cared for on earth. As in a dream everything suddenly became clear. Germany had been stabbed in the back and clawed down by the Jews, by the profiteers and intriguers behind the Front, by the accursed Bolsheviks in their international conspiracy of Jewish intellectuals. Shining before him he saw his duty, to save Germany from these plagues, to avenge her wrongs, and lead the master race to its long-decreed destiny.

The officers of his regiment, deeply alarmed by the seditious and revolutionary temper of

Munich, August 2, 1914: a public demonstration in favor of war. The day before, Germany had declared war on Russia; the following day, the declaration was extended to France. The young man circled in the photograph is Hitler, who enlisted on August 3.

their men, were very glad to find one, at any rate, who seemed to have the root of the matter in him. Corporal Hitler desired to remain mobilised, and found employment as a "political education officer" or agent. In this guise he gathered information about mutinous and subversive designs. Presently he was told by the Security officer for whom he worked to attend meetings of the local political parties of all complexions. One evening in September 1919 the Corporal went to a rally of the German Workers' Party in a Munich brewery, and here he heard for the first time people talking in the style of his secret convictions against the Jews, the speculators, the "November Criminals" who had brought Germany into the abyss. On September 16 he joined this party, and shortly afterwards, in harmony with his military work, undertook its propaganda. In February 1920 the first mass meeting of the German Workers' Party was held in Munich, and here Adolf Hitler himself dominated the proceedings and in twenty-five points outlined the party programme. He had now become a politician. His

campaign of national salvation had been opened. In April he was demobilised, and the expansion of the party absorbed his whole life. By the middle of the following year he had ousted the original leaders, and by his passion and genius forced upon the hypnotised company the acceptance of his personal control. Already he was "the Fuehrer". An unsuccessful newspaper, the *Voelkischer Beobachter,* was bought as the party organ.

The Communists were not long in recognising their foe. They tried to break up Hitler's meetings, and in the closing days of 1921 he organised his first units of storm-troopers. Up to this point all had moved in local circles in Bavaria. But in the tribulation of German life during these first post-war years many began here and there throughout the Reich to listen to the new gospel. The fierce anger of all Germany at the French occupation of the Ruhr in 1923 brought what was now called the National Socialist Party a broad wave of adherents. The collapse of the mark destroyed the basis of the German middle class, of whom many in

Hitler (first on the left, sitting) with some fellow soldiers during World War I. He fought valiantly in an infantry regiment for four years on the western front; he was promoted to corporal (November 1914), was injured (October 1916 and October 1918), and received two decorations for military valour (December 1914 and August 1918).

their despair became recruits of the new party and found relief from their misery in hatred, vengeance, and patriotic fervour.

At the beginning Hitler had made it clear that the path to power lay through aggression and violence against a Weimar Republic born from the shame of defeat. By November 1923 "the Fuehrer" had a determined group around him, among whom Goering, Hess, Rosenberg, and Roehm were prominent. These men of action decided that the moment had come to attempt the seizure of authority in the State of Bavaria. General von Ludendorff lent the military prestige of his name to the venture, and marched forward in the *Putsch*. It used to be said before the war: "In Germany there will be no revolution, because in Germany all revolutions are strictly forbidden." This precept was revived on this occasion by the local authorities in Munich. The police troops fired, carefully avoiding the General, who marched straight forward into their ranks and was received with respect. About twenty of the demonstrators were killed. Hitler threw himself upon the

At the end of the war, Hitler (indicated here by a cross on his chest) was still in a hospital in Pomerania: he had suffered serious injuries to his eyes from the effects of poisonous gas.

Hitler, still convalescing at Beelitz hospital, is shown here with the same dog as on the previous page: He was very fond of dogs.

Hitler in a traditional Bavarian outfit. Austrian by birth, he became a naturalised German only on February 24, 1932, shortly before acceding to power.

cal philosophy inscribed to the dead of the recent *Putsch*. When eventually he came to power there was no book which deserved more careful study from the rulers, political and military, of the Allied Powers. All was there—the programme of German resurrection, the technique of party propaganda; the plan for combating Marxism; the concept of a National-Socialist State; the rightful position of Germany at the summit of the world. Here was the new Koran of faith and war: turgid, verbose, shapeless, but pregnant with its message.

The main thesis of *Mein Kampf* is simple. Man is a fighting animal; therefore the nation, being a community of fighters, is a fighting unit. Any living organism which ceases to fight for its existence is doomed to extinction. A country or race which ceases to fight is equally doomed. The fighting capacity of a race depends on its purity. Hence the need for ridding it of foreign defilements. The Jewish race, owing to its universality, is of necessity pacifist and internationalist. Pacifism is the deadliest sin, for it means the surrender of the race in the fight for existence. The first duty of every country is therefore to nationalise the masses. Intelligence in the case of the individual is not of first importance; will and determination are the prime qualities. The individual who is born to command is more valuable than countless thousands of subordinate natures. Only brute force can ensure the survival of the race; hence the necessity for military forms. The race must fight; a race that rests must rust and perish. Had the German race been united in good time it would have been already master of the globe. The new Reich must gather within its fold all the scattered German elements in Europe. A race which has suffered defeat can be rescued by restoring its self-confidence. Above all things the army must be taught to believe in its own invincibility. To restore the German nation the people must be convinced that the recovery of freedom by force of arms is possible. The aristocratic principle is fundamentally sound. Intellectualism is undesirable. The ultimate aim of education is to produce a German who can be converted with the minimum of training into a soldier. The greatest upheavals

ground, and presently escaped with other leaders from the scene. In April 1924 he was sentenced to four years' imprisonment.

Although the German authorities had maintained order, and the German court had inflicted punishment, the feeling was widespread throughout the land that they were striking at their own flesh and blood, and were playing the foreigners' game at the expense of Germany's most faithful sons. Hitler's sentence was reduced from four years to thirteen months. These months in the Landsberg fortress were however sufficient to enable him to complete in outline *Mein Kampf*, a treatise on his politi-

Once again in a Bavarian outfit and, on the right, in the Nazi brown shirt. Hitler instituted the SA paramilitary organisation in August 1921; While the SS was formed in 1925.

Hitler celebrates the anniversary of the aborted putsch of November 9, 1923.

September 1923: a few weeks before the putsch, Hitler organised a National Socialist demonstration in Nuremberg. On the right is General Erich Ludendorff, who took part in the putsch.

in history would have been unthinkable had it not been for the driving force of fanatical and hysterical passions. Nothing could have been effected by the bourgeois virtues of peace and order. The world is now moving towards such an upheaval, and the new German State must see to it that the race is ready for the last and greatest decisions on this earth.

Foreign policy may be unscrupulous. It is not the task of diplomacy to allow a nation to founder heroically, but rather to see that it can prosper and survive. England and Italy are the only two possible allies for Germany. No country will enter into an alliance with a cowardly pacifist State run by democrats and Marxists. So long as Germany does not fend for herself, nobody will fend for her. Her lost provinces cannot be regained by solemn appeals to Heaven or by pious hopes in the League of Nations,

but only by force of arms. Germany must not repeat the mistake of fighting all her enemies at once. She must single out the most dangerous and attack him with all her forces. The world will only cease to be anti-German when Germany recovers equality of rights and resumes her place in the sun. There must be no sentimentality about Germany's foreign policy. To attack France for purely sentimental reasons would be foolish. What Germany needs is increase of territory in Europe. Germany's pre-war colonial policy was a mistake and should be abandoned. Germany must look for expansion to Russia, and especially to the Baltic States. No alliance with Russia can be tolerated. To wage war together with Russia against the West would be criminal, for the aim of the Soviets is the triumph of international Judaism.

Such were the "granite pillars" of his policy.

Usually in modern times when States have been defeated in war they have preserved their structure, their identity, and the secrecy of their archives. On this occasion, the war being fought to an utter finish, we have come into full possession of the inside story of the enemy. From this we can check up with some exactness our own information and performances. We have seen how in July 1936 Hitler had instructed the German General Staff to draw up mili-

tary plans for the occupation of Austria when the hour should strike. This operation was labelled "Case Otto". Now, a year later, on June 24, 1937, he crystallised these plans by a special directive. On November 5 he unfolded his future designs to the chiefs of his armed forces. Germany must have more "living space". This could best be found in Eastern Europe—Poland, White Russia, and the Ukraine. To obtain this would involve a major war, and incidentally the

April 1924: the principal defendants of the putsch.

The Fuehrer in Landsberg prison, where he spent less than a year. In 1933, his cell was opened to the public as a shrine.

extermination of the people then living in those parts. Germany would have to reckon with her two "hateful enemies", England and France, to whom "a German Colossus in the centre of Europe would be intolerable". In order to profit by the lead she had gained in munitions production and by the patriotic fervour aroused and represented by the Nazi Party, she must therefore make war at the first promising opportunity, and deal with her two obvious opponents before they were ready to fight.

Neurath, Fritsch, and even Blomberg, all of them influenced by the views of the German Foreign Office, General Staff, and Officer Corps, were alarmed by this policy. They thought that the risks to be run were too high. They recognised that by the audacity of the Fuehrer they were definitely ahead of the Allies in every form of rearmament. The Army was maturing month by month; the internal decay of France and the lack of will-power in Britain were favourable factors which might well run their full course. What was a year or two when all was moving so well? They must have time to complete the war machine, and a conciliatory speech now and again from the Fuehrer would keep these futile and degenerate democracies chattering. But Hitler was not sure of this. His genius taught him that victory would not be achieved by processes of certainty. Risks had to be run. The leap had to be made. He was flushed with his successes, first in rearmament, second in conscription, third in the Rhineland, fourth by the accession of Mussolini's Italy. To wait till everything was ready was probably to wait till all was too late. It is very easy for historians and other people, who do not have to live and act from day to day, to say that he would have had the whole fortunes of the world in his hands if he had gone on growing in strength for another two or three years before striking. However, this does not follow. There are no certainties in human life or in the life of States. Hitler was resolved to hurry, and have the war while he was in his prime.

On February 4, 1938, Hitler dismissed Fritsch, and himself assumed supreme command of the armed forces. So far as it is possible for one man, however gifted and powerful, however terrible the penalties he can inflict, to make his will effective over spheres so vast, the Fuehrer assumed direct control, not only of the policy of the State, but of the military machine. He had at this time something like the power of Napoleon after Austerlitz and Jena, without of course the glory of winning great battles by his personal direction on horseback, but with triumphs in the political and diplomatic field which all his circle and followers knew were due alone to him and to his judgment and daring.

Hitler was sure that the French political system was rotten to the core, and that it had infected the French Army. He knew the power of the Communists in France, and that it would be used to weaken or paralyse action once Ribbentrop and Molotov had come to terms and Moscow had denounced the French and British Governments for entering upon a capitalist and imperialist war. He was convinced that Britain was pacifist and degenerate. In his view, though Mr. Chamberlain and M. Daladier had been brought to the point of declaring war by a bellicose minority in England, they would both wage as little of it as they could, and once Poland had been crushed would accept the accomplished fact, as they had done a year before in the case of Czechoslovakia. On the repeated occasions which have been set forth Hitler's instinct had been proved right and the arguments and fears of his generals wrong. He did not understand the profound change which takes place in Great Britain and throughout the British Empire once the signal for war has been given; nor how those who have been the most strenuous for peace turn overnight into untiring toilers for victory. He could not comprehend the mental or spiritual force of our Island people, who, however much opposed to war or military preparation, had through the centuries come to regard victory as their birthright. In any case, the British Army could be no factor at the outset, and he was certain that the French nation had not thrown its

heart into the war. This was indeed true. He had his way, and his orders were obeyed.

Hitler had failed to quell or conquer Britain. It was plain that the Island would persevere to the end. Without the command of the sea or the air it had been deemed impossible to move German armies across the Channel. Winter with its storms had closed upon the scene. The German attempt to cow the British nation or shatter their war-making capacity and will-power by bombing had been foiled, and the Blitz was costly. There must be many months' delay before "Sea Lion" could be revived, and with every week that passed the growth, ripen-

A glorifying photograph from 1934, for the party congress.

1933: newly appointed chancellor, Hitler confers with former chancellor Franz von Papen (in the middle) and Defence Minister Werner Blomberg.

ing, and equipment of the British home armies required a larger "Sea Lion", with aggravated difficulties of transportation. Even three-quarters of a million men with all their furnishings would not be enough in April or May 1941. What chance was there of finding by then the shipping, the barges, the special landing-craft necessary for so vast an oversea stroke? How could they be assembled under ever-increasing British air-power? Meanwhile this air-power, fed by busy factories in Britain and the United States, and by immense training schemes for

pilots in the Dominions centred in Canada, would perhaps in a year or so make the British Air Force superior in numbers, as it was already in quality, to that of Germany. Can we wonder then that Hitler, once convinced that Goering's hopes and boasts had been broken, should turn his eyes to the East? Like Napoleon in 1804, he recoiled from the assault of the Island until at least the Eastern danger was no more. He must, he now felt, at all costs settle with Russia before staking everything on the invasion of Britain. Obeying the same forces and following the same thoughts as Napoleon when he marched the Grand Army from Boulogne to Ulm, Austerlitz, and Friedland, Hitler abandoned for the moment his desire and need to destroy Great Britain. That must now become the final act of the drama.

There is no doubt that he had made up his own mind by the end of September 1940. From that time forth the air attacks on Britain, though of-

ten on a larger scale through the general multiplication of aircraft, took second place in the Fuehrer's thoughts and German plans. They might be maintained as effective cover for other designs, but Hitler no longer counted on them for decisive victory. Eastward ho! Personally, on purely military grounds, I should not have been averse from a German attempt at the invasion of Britain in the spring or summer of 1941. I believed that the enemy would suffer the most terrific defeat and slaughter that any country had ever sustained in a specific military enterprise. But for that very reason I was not so simple as to expect it to happen. In war what you don't dislike is not usually what the enemy does. Still, in the conduct of a long struggle, when time seemed for a year or two on our side, and mighty allies might be gained, I thanked God that the supreme ordeal was to be spared our people. As will be seen from my papers written at the time, I never seriously contemplated a German descent upon England in 1941. By the end of 1941 the

boot was on the other leg; we were no longer alone; three-quarters of the world were with us. But tremendous events, measureless before they happened, were to mark that memorable year.

While to uninformed continentals and the outer world our fate seemed forlorn, or at best in the balance, the relations between Nazi Germany and Soviet Russia assumed the first position in world affairs. The fundamental antagonisms between the two despotic Powers resumed their sway once it was certain that Britain could not be stunned and overpowered like France and the Low Countries. To do him justice, Stalin tried his very best to work loyally and faithfully with Hitler, while at the same time gathering all the strength he could in the enormous mass of Soviet Russia. He and Molotov sent their dutiful congratulations on every German victory. They poured a heavy flow of food and essential raw materials into the Reich. Their Fifth Column Communists did what they could to disturb our factories. Their radio

Hitler greets a celebrity who has paid him a visit and is about to leave by car.

Vienna, March 15, 1938: on the night of March 11-12, Austria was annexed to Germany. As Hitler arrives in the former capital, he is greeted by Arthur Seyss-Inquart, the former Minister of Domestic Affairs and future Governor of the country, which became a mere province of the Reich, called Eastern Mark.

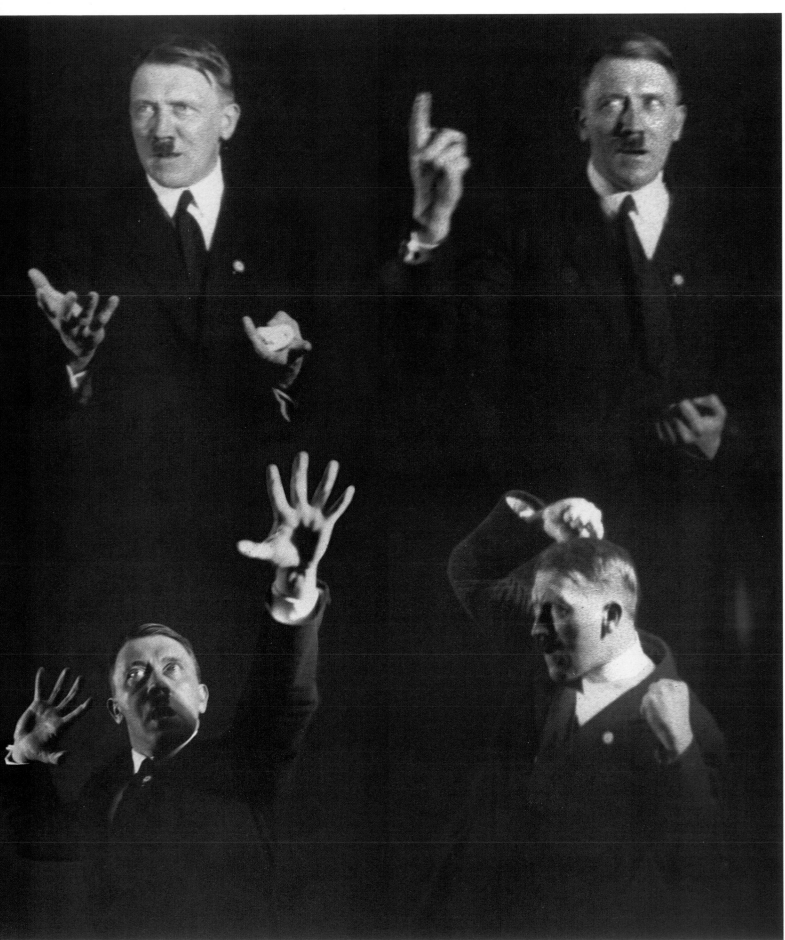

Hitler greeted by the Reichstag in 1939.

Berlin, March 24, 1936: Hitler delivers a speech to a Nazi assembly at the Deutschlandhalle.

powerful German army as a central reserve. In this way only could he use the high qualities of the German command and fighting troops, and at the same time take full advantage of the central position which he occupied, with its interior lines and remarkable communications. As General von Thoma said while a prisoner of war in our charge, "Our only chance is to create a situation where we can use the Army." Hitler had in fact made a spider's web and forgotten the spider. He tried to hold everything he had won. Enormous forces were squandered in the Balkans and in Italy which could play no part in the main decisions. A central reserve of thirty or forty divisions of the highest quality and mobility would have enabled him to strike at any one of his opponents advancing upon

A cheerful Führer during a telephone conversation.

In a photograph taken by Eva Braun, Hitler with a young guest in his residence at Berchtesgaden.

Eva Braun and Hitler relax. They married just hours before committing suicide together.

Hitler with his beloved German shepherd.

him and fight a major battle with good prospects of success. He could, for instance, have met the British and Americans at the fortieth or fiftieth day after their landing in Normandy a year later with fresh and greatly superior forces. There was no need to consume his strength in Italy and the Balkans, and the fact that he was induced to do so must be taken as the waste of his last opportunity.

Hitler had returned from the Feltre meeting convinced that Italy could only be kept in the war by purges in the Fascist Party and increasing pressure by the Germans on the Fascist leaders. Mussolini's sixtieth birthday fell on July 29, and Goering was chosen to pay him an official visit on this occasion. But during the course of July 25 alarming reports from Rome began to come in to Hitler's headquarters. By the evening it was clear that Mussolini had resigned or had been removed, and that Badoglio had been nominated by the King as his successor. It was finally decided that any major operation against the new Italian Government would require withdrawals of more divisions than could be spared from the Eastern Front in the event of the expected Russian offensive. Plans were made to rescue Mussolini, to occupy Rome, and to support Italian Fascism wherever possible. If Badoglio signed an armistice with the Allies, further plans were drawn up for seizing the Italian Fleet and occupying key positions throughout Italy, and for overawing Italian garrisons in the Balkans and in the Ægean.

"We must act," Hitler told his advisers on July 26. "Otherwise the Anglo-Saxons will steal a march on us by occupying the airports. The Fascist Party is at present only stunned, and will recover behind our lines. The Fascist Party is the only one that has the will to fight on our side. We must therefore restore it. All reasons advocating further delays are wrong; thereby we run the danger of losing Italy to the Anglo-Saxons. These are matters which a soldier cannot comprehend. Only a man with political insight can see his way clear."

In the foreground, the crater at the Berlin chancellery, where the presumed corpses of Hitler and Eva Braun were found.

Photographers crowd around the remains of Hitler.

Hitler's body—probably a fake wanted by Stalin.

was to take charge in the North both of the military and civil authorities, with the particular task of bringing back to German soil nearly two million refugees from the East. In the South General Kesselring was to command the remaining German armies. These arrangements were to take effect if Berlin fell.

Two days later, on April 22, Hitler made his final and supreme decision to stay in Berlin to the end. The capital was soon completely encircled by the Russians and the Fuehrer had lost all power to control events. It remained for him to organise his own death amid the ruins of the city. He announced to the Nazi leaders who remained with him that he would die in Berlin. Goering and Himmler had both left after the conference of the 20th, with thoughts of peace negotiations in their minds. Goering, who had gone south, assumed that Hitler had in fact abdicated by his resolve to stay in Berlin, and asked for confirmation that he should act formally as the successor to the Fuehrer. The reply was his instant dismissal from all his offices.

The last scenes at Hitler's headquarters have been described elsewhere in much detail. Of the personalities of his régime only Goebbels and Bormann remained with him to the end. The Russian troops were now fighting in the streets of Berlin. In the early hours of April 29 Hitler made his will. The day opened with the normal routine of work in the air-raid shelter under the Chancellery. News arrived of Mussolini's end. The timing was grimly appropriate. On the 30th Hitler lunched quietly with his suite, and at the end of the meal shook hands with those present and retired to his private room. At half-past three a shot was heard, and members of his personal staff entered the room to find him lying on the sofa with a revolver by his side. He had shot himself through the mouth. Eva Braun, whom he married secretly during these last days, lay dead beside him. She had taken poison. The bodies were burnt in the courtyard, and Hitler's funeral pyre, with the din of the Russian guns growing ever louder, made a lurid end to the Third Reich.

By the middle of April it had been clear that Hitler's Germany would soon be utterly destroyed. The invading armies drove onwards in their might and the space between them narrowed daily. Hitler had pondered where to make his last stand. As late as April 20 he still thought of leaving Berlin for the "Southern Redoubt" in the Bavarian Alps. That day he held a meeting of the principal Nazi leaders. As the German double front, East and West, was in imminent danger of being cut in twain by the spear-point thrust of the Allies, he agreed to set up two separate commands. Admiral Doenitz

MUSSOLINI

Mussolini, newly elected Premier. In his buttonhole is the badge of the National Fascist Party.

A photograph from the same series: Il Duce holds a schoolmaster's traditional blue-and-red pencil, which he used to underline official documents.

The friendship between the British and Italian peoples sprang from the days of Garibaldi and Cavour. Every stage in the liberation of Northern Italy from Austria and every step towards Italian unity and independence had commanded the sympathies of Victorian Liberalism. This had bred a warm and enduring response. The declaration in the original Treaty of Triple Alliance between Italy, Germany, and the Austro-Hungarian Empire stipulated that in no circumstances should Italy be drawn into war with Great Britain. British influence had powerfully contributed to the Italian accession to the Allied cause in the First World War. The rise of Mussolini and the establishment of Fascism as a counter to Bolshevism had in its early phases divided British opinion on party lines, but had not affected the broad foundations of goodwill between the peoples. We have seen that until Mussolini's designs against Abyssinia had raised grave issues he had ranged himself with Great Britain in opposition to Hitlerism and German ambitions. I have told in the previous volume the sad tale of how the Baldwin-Chamberlain policy about Abyssinia brought us the worst of

Benito Mussolini *was born on July 29, 1883, in Dovia di Predappio near Forlì, Italy. His father was a smith and his mother an elementary-school teacher. In 1900, he joined the Socialist Party, and became the leader of its revolutionary wing in 1912. At the outbreak of World War I, he left the party and fought as a volunteer. Later he founded the Fascist movement (March 23, 1919) on a nationalist platform. Socially Leftist, albeit increasingly right-wing, he obtained the endorsement of veterans, industrialists, and landowners with a virulent anti-Socialist action, until the king appointed him Prime Minister (October 30, 1922). He established a dictatorship on January 3, 1925, and initiated an expansionist policy with the Ethiopian war (1935-1936). After signing the Steel Pact with Hitler (May 22, 1939), he entered the war (June 10, 1940), but the king eventually removed him from office because of military defeats (July 25, 1943). Hitler appointed him head of the Italian Social Republic (September 1943), causing a civil war that ended with the shooting of Mussolini by the Partisans (Giulino di Mezzegna, near Como) on April 28, 1945.*

both worlds, how we estranged the Italian dictator without breaking his power, and how the League of Nations was injured without Abyssinia being saved. We have also seen the earnest but futile efforts made by Mr. Chamberlain, Sir Samuel Hoare, and Lord Halifax to win back during the period of appeasement Mussolini's lost favour. And finally there was the growth of Mussolini's conviction that Britain's sun had set, and that Italy's future could, with German help, be founded on the ruins of the British Empire. This had been followed by the creation of the Berlin-Rome Axis, in accordance with which Italy might well have been expected to enter the war against Britain and France on its very first day.

It was certainly only common prudence for Mussolini to see how the war would go before committing himself and his country irrevocably. The process of waiting was by no means unprofitable. Italy was courted by both sides, and gained much consideration for her interests, many profitable contracts, and time to improve her armaments. Thus the twilight months had passed. It is an interesting speculation what the Italian fortunes would have been if this policy had been maintained. The United States with its large Italian vote might well have made it clear to Hitler that an attempt to rally Italy to his side by force of arms would raise the gravest issues. Peace, prosperity, and growing power would have been the prize of a persistent neutrality. Once Hitler was embroiled with Russia this happy state might have been almost indefinitely prolonged, with ever-growing benefits, and Mussolini might have stood forth in the peace or in the closing year of the war as the wisest statesman the sunny peninsula and its industrious and prolific people had known. This was a more agreeable situation than that which in fact awaited him.

At the time when I was Chancellor of the Exchequer under Mr. Baldwin in the years after 1924 I did what I could to preserve the traditional friendship between Italy and Britain. I made a debt settlement with Count Volpi which contrasted very favourably with the arrangements made with France. I received the warmest expressions of gratitude from the Duce, and with difficulty escaped the highest decoration. Moreover, in the conflict between Fascism and Bolshevism there was no doubt where my sympathies and convictions lay. On the two occasions in 1927 when I met Mussolini our personal relations had been intimate and easy. I would never have encouraged Britain to make a breach with him about Abyssinia or roused the League of Nations against him unless we were prepared to go to war in the last extreme. He, like Hitler, understood and in a way respected my campaign for British rearmament, though he was very glad British public opinion did not support my view.

In the crisis we had now reached of the disastrous Battle of France it was clearly my duty as Prime Minister to do my utmost to keep Italy out of the conflict, and though I did not indulge in vain hopes I at once used what resources and influence I might possess. Six days after becoming head of the Government I wrote at the Cabinet's desire the appeal to Mussolini which, together with his answer, was published two years later in very different circumstances.

Prime Minister to Signor Mussolini 16.V.40
Now that I have taken up my office as Prime Minister and Minister of Defence I look back to our meetings in Rome and feel a desire to speak words of goodwill to you as Chief of the Italian nation across what seems to be a swiftly-widening

Mussolini in a series of propaganda images meant to illustrate his multiform vitality: with a lion cub, on the snow, swimming, and threshing wheat. This last photograph was taken in Aprilia on July 4, 1938.

gulf. Is it too late to stop a river of blood from flowing between the British and Italian peoples? We can no doubt inflict grievous injuries upon one another and maul each other cruelly, and darken the Mediterranean with our strife. If you so decree, it must be so; but I declare that I have never been the enemy of Italian greatness, nor ever at heart the foe of the Italian lawgiver. It is idle to predict the course of the great battles now raging in Europe, but I am sure that whatever may happen on the Continent England will go on to the end, even quite alone, as

we have done before, and I believe with some assurance that we shall be aided in increasing measure by the United States, and, indeed, by all the Americas.

I beg you to believe that it is in no spirit of weakness or of fear that I make this solemn appeal, which will remain on record. Down the ages above all other calls comes the cry that the joint heirs of Latin and Christian civilisation must not be ranged against one another in mortal strife. Hearken to it, I beseech you in all honour and respect, before the dread signal is given. It will never be given by us.

The response was hard. It had at least the merit of candour.

Signor Mussolini to Prime Minister 18.v.40

I reply to the message which you have sent me in order to tell you that you are certainly aware of grave reasons of an historical and contingent character which have ranged our two countries in opposite camps. Without going back very far in time I remind you of the initiative taken in 1935 by your Government to organise at Geneva sanctions against Italy, engaged in securing for herself a small space in the African sun without causing the slightest injury to your interests and territories or those of others. I remind you also of the real and actual state of servitude in which Italy finds herself in her own sea. If it was to honour your signature that your Government declared war on Germany, you will understand that the same sense of honour and of respect for engagements assumed in the Italian-German Treaty guides Italian policy to-day and to-morrow in the face of any event whatsoever.

This photograph was meant to emphasise the importance that the Fascist régime placed on cinematography, especially on the propaganda films produced by the Istituto LUCE.

201

From this moment we could have no doubt of Mussolini's intention to enter the war at his most favourable opportunity. His resolve had in fact been made as soon as the defeat of the French armies was obvious. On May 13 he had told Ciano that he would declare war on France and Britain within a month. His official decision to declare war on any date suitable after June 5 was imparted to the Italian Chiefs of Staff on May 29. At Hitler's request the date was postponed to June 10.

I thought it the moment to address the Italian people by the broadcast, and on the night of December 23 I reminded them of the long friendship between Britain and Italy. Now we were at war. ". . .Our armies are tearing and will tear your African Empire to shreds and tatters. . . . How has all this come about, and what is it all for?"

Italians, I will tell you the truth. It is all because of one

April 25, 1938: Mussolini lays the foundation stone of the city of Pomezia.

Rome, April 18, 1939: Mussolini inspects the construction of the new EUR district in Rome.

Mussolini during an official visit to Padua, in 1940.

Mussolini and King Victor Emmanuel III during the maneuvers of August 1938. Southern Italy, 1938.

Mussolini and the people: with children, with a working woman, and with a group of Young Italians.

man. One man and one man alone has ranged the Italian people in deadly struggle against the British Empire, and has deprived Italy of the sympathy and intimacy of the United States of America. That he is a great man I do not deny, but that after eighteen years of unbridled power he has led your country to the horrid verge of ruin can be denied by none. It is one man who, against the Crown and Royal Family of Italy, against the Pope and all the authority of the Vatican and of the Roman Catholic Church, against the wishes of the Italian people, who had no lust for this war, has arrayed the trustees and inheritors of ancient Rome upon the side of the ferocious pagan barbarians.

I read out the message I had sent to Mussolini on becoming Prime Minister and his reply of May 18, 1940, and I continued:

Where is it that the Duce has led his trusting people after eighteen years of dictatorial power? What hard choice is open to them now? It is to stand up to the battery of the whole British Empire on sea, in the air, and in Africa, and the vigorous counter-attack of the Greek nation; or, on the other hand, to call in Attila over the Brenner Pass

with his hordes of ravenous soldiery and his gangs of Gestapo policemen to occupy, hold down, and protect the Italian people, for whom he and his Nazi followers cherish the most bitter and outspoken contempt that is on record between races.

There is where one man and one man only has led you; and there I leave this unfolding story until the day comes—as come it will—when the Italian nation will once more take a hand in shaping its own fortunes.

It is curious that on this same day Mussolini, speaking of the morale of the Italian Army, remarked to Ciano, "I must nevertheless recognise that the Italians of 1914 were better than these. It is not flattering for the *régime*, but that's how it is." And the next day, looking out of the window: "This snow and cold are very good. In this way our good-for-nothing Italians, this mediocre race, will be improved." Such were the bitter and ungrateful reflections which the failure of the Italian Army in Libya and Albania had wrung from the heart of this dark figure after six months of aggressive war on what he had thought was the decadent British Empire.

Mussolini now had to bear the brunt of the military disasters into which he had, after so many years of rule, led his country. He had exercised almost absolute control and could not cast the burden on the Monar-

chy, Parliamentary institutions, the Fascist Party, or the General Staff. All fell on him. Now that the feeling that the war was lost spread throughout well-informed circles in Italy the blame fell upon the man who had so imperiously thrust the nation on to the wrong and the losing side. These convictions formed and spread widely during the early months of 1943. The lonely dictator sat at the summit of power, while military defeat and Italian slaughter in Russia, Tunis, and Sicily were the evident prelude to direct invasion.

In vain he made changes among the politicians and generals. In February General Ambrosio had succeeded Cavallero as Chief of the Italian General Staff. Ambrosio, together with the Duke of Acquarone, the Minister of Court, were personal advisers of the King and had the confidence of the Royal Circle. For months they had been hoping to overthrow the Duce and put an end to the Fascist régime. But Mussolini still dwelt in the European scene as if he were a principal factor. He was affronted when his new military chief proposed the immediate withdrawal of the Italian divisions from the Balkans. He regarded these forces as the counterpoise to German

Hitler greets Mussolini at the train station in Munich on June 18, 1940.

May 1938: during an official visit to Rome, Hitler listens to Giulio Quirino Giglioli, curator of the Augustan Roman exhibition.

Mussolini, Galeazzo Ciano, and Joachim von Ribbentrop in Florence on October 28, 1940, the anniversary of the March on Rome. That same day Italy attacked Greece.

predominance in Europe. He did not realise that defeats abroad and internal demoralisation had robbed him of his status as Hitler's ally. He cherished the illusion of power and consequence when the reality had gone. Thus he resisted Ambrosio's formidable request. So durable however was the impression of his authority and the fear of his personal action in extremity that there was prolonged hesitation throughout all the forces of Italian society about how to oust him. Who would "bell the cat"? Thus the spring had passed with invasion by a mighty foe, possessing superior power by land, sea, and air, drawing ever nearer.

At 5 p.m on the 24th the Grand Council met. Care appears to have been taken by the Chief of Police that they should not be disturbed by violence. Mussolini's musketeers, his personal bodyguard, were relieved of their duty to guard the Palazzo Venezia, which was also filled with armed police. The Duce unfolded his case, and the Council, who were all dressed in their black Fascist uniform, took up the discussion. Mussolini ended: "War is always a party war—a war of the party which desires it; it is always one man's war—the war of the man who declared it. If to-day this is called Mussolini's war, the war in 1859 could have been called

Cavour's war. This is the moment to tighten the reins and assume the necessary responsibility. I shall have no difficulty in replacing men, in turning the screw, in bringing forces to bear not yet engaged, in the name of our country, whose territorial integrity is to-day being violated."

Grandi then moved a resolution calling upon the Crown to assume more power and upon the King to emerge from obscurity and assume

Ciampino airport (Rome), at the end of 1939: accompanied by Ettore Muti, Secretary of the National Fascist Party, Mussolini reviews some air force crews.

Mussolini inspects an artillery unit in 1939.

Gradisca, September 20, 1938: Mussolini inspects a Bersaglieri regiment. On his right is Party Secretary Starace.

his responsibilities. He delivered what Mussolini describes as "a violent philippic", "the speech of a man who was at last giving vent to a long-cherished rancour." The contacts between members of the Grand Council and the Court became evident. Mussolini's son-in-law, Ciano, supported Grandi. Everyone present was now conscious that a political convulsion impended. The debate continued till midnight, when Scorza, secretary of the Fascist Party, proposed adjourning till next day. But Grandi leaped to his feet, shouting, "No, I am against the proposal. We have started this business and we must finish it this very night!" It was after two o'clock in the morning when the voting took place. "The position of each member of the Grand Council," writes Mussolini, "could be discerned even before the voting. There was a group of traitors who had already negotiated with the Crown, a group of accomplices, and a group of uninformed who probably did not re-

alise the seriousness of the vote, but they voted just the same." Nineteen replied "Yes" to Grandi's motion and seven "No". Two abstained. Mussolini rose. "You have provoked a crisis of the régime. So much the worse. The session is closed." The party secretary was about to give the salute to the Duce when Mussolini checked him with a gesture, saying, "No, you are excused." They all went away in silence. None slept at home.

Meanwhile the arrest of Mussolini was being quietly arranged. The Duke of Acquarone, the Court Minister, sent instructions to Ambrosio, whose deputies and trusted agents in the police and the Carabinieri acted forthwith. The key telephone exchanges, the police headquarters, and the offices of the Ministry of the Interior were quietly and unobtrusively taken over. A small force of military police was posted out of sight near the Royal villa.

Mussolini spent the morning of Sunday, July

March 18, 1941: atop Mount Nasta, on the Greek front, Mussolini observes the posts in that sector.

25, in his office, and visited some quarters in Rome which had suffered by bombing. He asked to see the King, and was granted an audience at five o'clock. "I thought the King would withdraw his delegation of authority of June 10, 1940, concerning the command of the armed forces, a command which I had for some time past been thinking of relinquishing. I entered the villa therefore with a mind completely free from any forebodings, in a state which, looking back on it, might really be called utterly unsuspecting." On reaching the Royal abode he noticed that there were everywhere reinforcements of Carabinieri. The King, in Marshal's uniform, stood in the doorway. The two men entered the drawing-room. The King said, "My dear Duce, it's no longer any good. Italy has gone to bits. Army morale is at rock-bottom. The soldiers don't want to fight any more. . . . The Grand Council's vote is terrific——nineteen votes for Grandi's motion, and among them four holders of the Order of the Annunciation! . . . At this moment you are the most hated man in Italy. You can no longer count on more than one friend. You have one friend left, and I am he. That is why I tell you that you need have no fears for your personal safety, for which I will ensure protection. I have been thinking that the man for the job now is Marshal Badoglio. . . ."

Mussolini replied, "You are taking an extremely grave decision. A crisis at this moment would mean making the people think that peace was in sight, once the man who declared war had been dismissed. The blow to the Army's morale would be serious. The crisis would be considered as a triumph for the Churchill-Stalin set-up, especially for Stalin. I realise the people's hatred. I had no difficulty in recognising it last night in the midst of the Grand Council. One can't govern for such a long time and impose so many sacrifices without provoking resentments. In any case, I wish good luck to the man who takes the situation in hand." The King accompanied Mussolini to the door. "His face," says Mussolini, "was livid and he looked smaller than ever, almost dwarfish. He shook my hand and went in again. I descended the few steps and went towards my car. Suddenly a Carabinieri captain stopped me and said, 'His Majesty has charged me with the protection of your person.' I was continuing towards my car when the captain said to me, pointing to a motor-ambulance standing near by, 'No. We must get in there.' I got into the ambulance, together with my secretary. A lieutenant, three Carabinieri, and two police agents in plain clothes got in as well as the captain, and placed themselves by the door armed with machine-guns. When the door was closed the ambulance drove off at top speed. I still

A characteristic expression for Mussolini during a speech.

Mussolini in the courtyard of Villa Feltrinelli, his Salò residence, with his personal German physician, Paul Zachariae.

September 12, 1943: Mussolini and the German officer Otto Skorzeny, one of those who liberated him from the prison on the Gran Sasso.

thought that all this was being done, as the King had said, in order to protect my person."

Later that afternoon Badoglio was charged by the King to form a new Cabinet of Service chiefs and civil servants, and in the evening the Marshal broadcast the news to the world. Two days later the Duce was taken on Marshal Badoglio's order to be interned on the island of Ponza.

Thus ended Mussolini's twenty-one years' dictatorship in Italy, during which he had raised the Italian people from the Bolshevism into which they might have sunk in 1919 to a position in Europe such as Italy had never held before. A new impulse had been given to the national life. The Italian Empire in North Africa was built. Many important public works in Italy were completed. In 1935 the Duce had by his will-power overcome the League of Nations—"Fifty nations led by one"—and was able to complete his conquest of Abyssinia. His régime was far too costly for the Italian people to bear, but there is no doubt that it appealed during its period of success to very great numbers of Italians. He was, as I had addressed him at the time of the fall of France, "the Italian lawgiver." The alternative to his rule might well have been a Communist Italy, which would have brought perils and misfortunes of a different character both upon the Italian people and Europe. His fatal mistake was the declaration of war on France and Great Britain following Hitler's victories in June 1940. Had he not done this he could well have maintained Italy in a balancing position, courted and rewarded by both sides and deriving an unusual wealth and prosperity from the struggles of other countries. Even when the issue of the war became certain Mussolini would have been welcomed by the Allies. He had much to give to shorten its course. He could have timed his moment to declare war on Hitler with art and care. Instead he took the wrong turning. He never understood the strength of Britain, nor the long-enduring qualities of Island resistance and sea-power. Thus he marched to ruin. His great roads will remain a monument to his personal power and long rein.

But there was to be no turning back. Mussolini's half-hearted "Hundred Days" began. At the end of September he set up his headquarters on the shores of Lake Garda. This pitiful shadow Government is known as the "Republic of Salo". Here the squalid tragedy was played out. The dictator and lawgiver of Italy for more than twenty years dwelt with his mistress in the hands of his German masters, ruled by their will, and cut off from the outside world by carefully chosen German guards and doctors.

For Mussolini also the end had come. Like Hitler he seems to have kept his illusions until almost the last moment. Late in March he had paid a final visit to his German partner, and returned to his headquarters on Lake Garda buoyed up with the thought of the secret weapons which could still lead to victory. But the rapid Allied advance from the Apennines made these hopes vain. There was hectic talk of a last stand in the mountainous areas on the Italo-Swiss frontier. But there was no will to fight left in the Italian Socialist Republic.

On April 25 Mussolini decided to disband the remnants of his armed forces and to ask the Cardinal Archbishop of Milan to arrange a meeting with the underground Military Committee of the Italian National Liberation Movement. That afternoon talks took place in the Archbishop's palace, but with a last furious gesture of independence Mussolini walked out. In the evening, followed by a convoy of thirty vehicles, containing most of the surviving leaders of Italian Fascism, he drove to the prefecture at Como. He had no coherent plan, and as discussion became useless it was each man for himself. Accompanied by a handful of supporters, he attached himself to a small German convoy heading towards the Swiss frontier. The commander of the column was not anxious for trouble with Italian Partisans. The Duce was persuaded to put on a German great-coat and helmet. But the little party was stopped by Partisan patrols; Mussolini was recognised and taken into custody. Other members, including his mistress, Signorina Petacci, were also arrested. On Communist instructions the Duce and his mistress were taken out in a car next day and shot. Their bodies, together with others, were sent to Milan and strung up head downwards on meat-hooks in a petrol station on the Piazzale Loreto, where a group of Italian Partisans had lately been shot in public.

Such was the fate of the Italian dictator.

A photograph of the final scene was sent to me, and I was profoundly shocked.

Images from the Italian Social Republic: Mussolini with San Marco marines training in Germany.

Mussolini encourages a very young soldier from the mobile Bersaglieri brigade, Nera, as they get ready to leave for a fight against the Partisans.

In Milan, Il Duce greets the residents; at his side is Alessandro Pavolini.

Mussolini with a casualty in Gardone.

April 25, 1945: Mussolini leaves Milan. In the last photograph taken of him alive, he is leaving the prefecture.

The bodies of Mussolini and Claretta Petacci.

Prime Minister to Field-Marshal Alexander (Italy) 10 May 45

I have seen the photograph.

The man who murdered Mussolini made a confession, published in the *Daily Express*, gloating over the treacherous and cowardly method of his action. In particular he said he shot Mussolini's mistress. Was she on the list of war criminals? Had he any authority from anybody to shoot this woman? It seems to me the cleansing hand of British military power should make inquiries on these points.

But at least the world was spared an Italian Nuremberg.

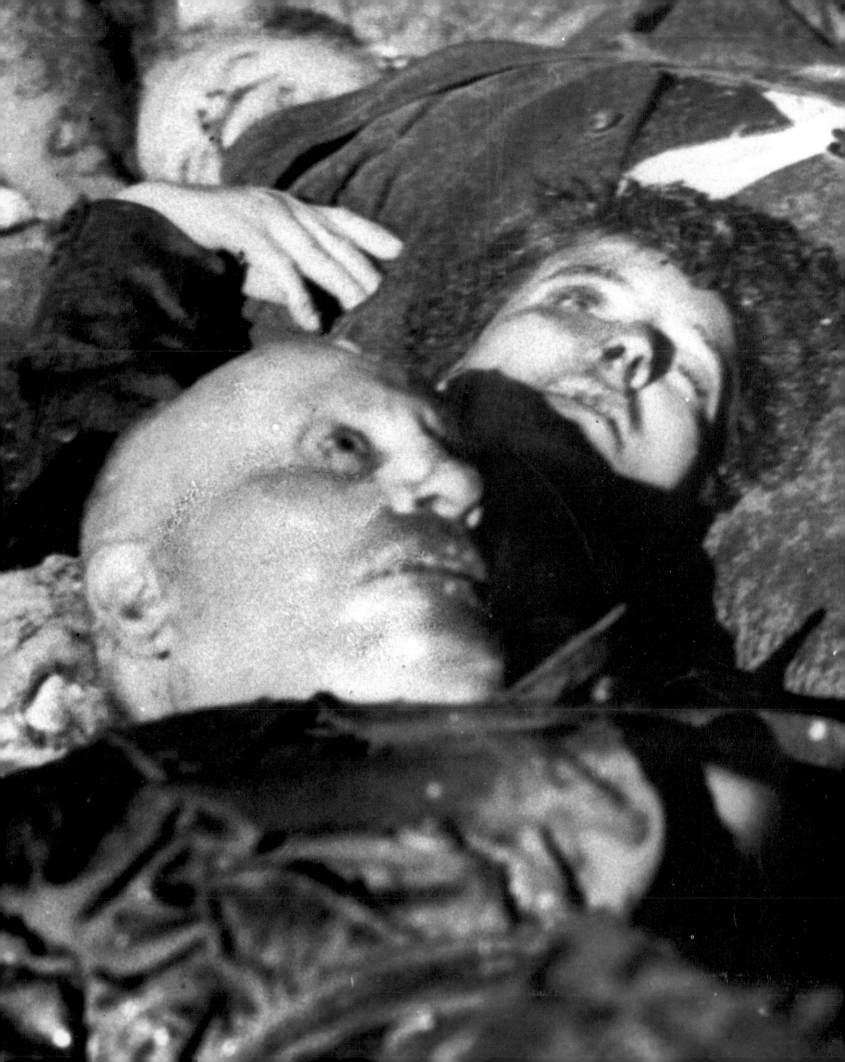

CHAMBERLAIN

"I had described him in Shakespeare's words as the 'packhorse in our great affairs', and Chamberlain had accepted this description as a compliment."

On May 28, 1937, after King George VI had been crowned, Mr. Baldwin retired. His long public services were suitably rewarded by an Earldom and the Garter. He laid down the wide authority he had gathered and carefully maintained, but had used as little as possible. He departed in a glow of public gratitude and esteem. There was no doubt who his successor should be. Mr. Neville Chamberlain had, as Chancellor of the Exchequer, not only done the main work of the Government for five years past, but was the ablest and most forceful Minister, with high abilities and an historic name. I had described him a year earlier at Birmingham in Shakespeare's words as the "packhorse in our great affairs", and he had accepted this description as a compliment. I had no expectation that he would wish to work with me, nor would he have been wise to do so at such a time. His ideas were far different from mine on the treatment of the dominant issues of the day. But I welcomed the accession to power of a live, competent, executive figure. While still Chancellor of the Exchequer he had involved himself in a fiscal proposal for a small-scale national defence contribution which had been ill-received by the Conservative Party and was of course criticised by the Opposition. I was able, in the first days of his Premiership, to make a speech upon this subject which helped him to withdraw, without any loss of dignity, from a position which had become untenable. Our relations continued to be cool, easy, and polite both in public and in private.

Mr. Chamberlain made few changes in the Government. He had had disagreements with Mr. Duff Cooper about War Office administration, and much surprised him by offering him advancement to the great key office of the Admiralty. The Prime Minister evidently did not know the eyes through which his new First Lord, whose early career had been in the Foreign Office, viewed the European scene. In my turn I was astonished that Sir Samuel Hoare, who had just secured a large expansion of the naval programme, should wish to leave the Admiralty for

Arthur Neville Chamberlain *was born on March 18, 1869, in Birmingham, to a family with a significant political background (his father and brother both held government offices). Lord Mayor of Birmingham (1911), a Member of Parliament for the Conservative Party from 1918, and Chancellor of the Exchequer (1923-1924 and 1931-1937), Chamberlain was able to balance British finances, and in 1937 he became Prime Minister. He was excessively weak toward Germany, especially during the crisis of Czechoslovakia, when he signed the Munich Pact (September 29, 1938) for the German annexation of Sudetenland. When Hitler invaded Czechoslovakia, despite the pact, Chamberlain re-instated conscription, signed agreements with Poland, Greece, and Rumania, and entered into negotiations with the USSR. However, he hesitated before declaring war on Germany, thus incurring the antagonism of the Labour Party, which made it impossibile to form the vast coalition Cabinet he had planned. The German invasion of Norway (April 1940) was fatal to his prestige, and on May 10 he resigned, yielding the leadership of the government to Churchill. Chamberlain died few months later, in London, on November 9, 1940.*

Chamberlain on May 28, 1937, when war still seemed far away.

With his wife, Mary Henriette, Chamberlain casts his vote for a new Member of Parliament to replace one who died (May 1939).

Accompanied by his wife at the very beginning of the war (September 7, 1939), Chamberlain demonstrates how to carry a gas mask on a stroll.

the Home Office. Hoare seems to have believed that prison reform in a broad humanitarian sense would become the prevailing topic in the immediate future; and since his family was connected with the famous Elizabeth Fry, he had a strong personal sentiment about it.

I may here set down a comparative appreciation of these two Prime Ministers, Baldwin and Chamberlain, whom I had known so long and under whom I had served or was to serve. Stanley Baldwin was the wiser, more comprehending personality, but without detailed executive capacity. He was largely detached from foreign and military affairs. He knew little of Europe, and disliked what he knew. He had a deep knowledge of British party politics, and represented in a broad way some of the strengths and many of the infirmities of our Island race. He had fought five General Elections as leader of the Conservative Party and had won three of them. He had a genius for waiting upon events and an imperturbability under adverse criticism. He was singularly adroit in letting events work for him, and capable of seizing the ripe moment when it came. He seemed to me to revive the impressions history gives us of Sir Robert Walpole, without of course the eighteenth-century corruption, and he was master of British politics for nearly as long.

Neville Chamberlain, on the other hand, was alert, businesslike, opinionated and self-confi-

dent in a very high degree. Unlike Baldwin, he conceived himself able to comprehend the whole field of Europe, and indeed the world. Instead of a vague but none the less deep-seated intuition, we had now a narrow, sharp-edged efficiency within the limits of the policy in which he believed. Both as Chancellor of the Exchequer and as Prime Minister he kept the tightest and most rigid control upon military expenditure. He was throughout this period the masterful opponent of all emergency measures. He had formed decided judgments about all the political figures of the day, both at home and abroad, and felt himself capable of dealing with them. His all-prevading hope was to go down to history as the great Peacemaker, and for this he was prepared to strive continually in the teeth of facts, and face great risks for himself and his country. Unhappily he ran into tides the force of which he could not measure, and met hurricanes from which he did not flinch, but with

which he could not cope. In these closing years before the war I should have found it easier to work with Baldwin, as I knew him, than with Chamberlain; but neither of them had any wish to work with me except in the last resort.

The morning of the 10th of May dawned, and with it came tremendous news. Boxes with telegrams poured in from the Admiralty, the War Office, and the Foreign Office. The Germans had struck their long-awaited blow. Holland and Belgium were both invaded. Their frontiers had been crossed at numerous points. The whole movement of the German Army upon the invasion of the Low Countries and of France had begun.

At about ten o'clock Sir Kingsley Wood came to see me, having just been with the Prime Minister. He told me that Mr. Chamberlain was inclined to feel that the great battle which had broken upon us made it necessary for him to remain at his post. Kingsley Wood had told him that, on

the contrary, the new crisis made it all the more necessary to have a National Government, which alone could confront it, and he added that Mr. Chamberlain had accepted this view. At eleven o'clock I was again summoned to Downing Street by the Prime Minister. There once more I found Lord Halifax. We took our seats at the table opposite Mr. Chamberlain. He told us that he was satisfied that it was beyond his power to form a National Government. The response he had received from the Labour leaders left him in no doubt of this. The question therefore was whom he should advise the King to send for after his own resignation had been accepted. His demeanour was cool, unruffled, and seemingly quite detached from the personal aspect of the affair. He looked at us both across the table.

I have had many important interviews in my public life, and this was certainly the most important. Usually I talk a great deal, but on this occasion I was silent. Mr. Chamberlain evidently

September 1939: Winston Churchill, First Lord of the Admiralty, and Neville Chamberlain.

March 31, 1939: Chamberlain in front of No. 10 Downing Street, after the meeting at which the Cabinet was agreed to offer Poland "unconditional warrant". In keeping its word, Britain entered the war the following September.

had in his mind the stormy scene in the House of Commons two nights before, when I had seemed to be in such heated controversy with the Labour Party. Although this had been in his support and defence, he nevertheless felt that it might be an obstacle to my obtaining their adherence at this juncture. I do not recall the actual words he used, but this was the implication. His biographer, Mr. Feiling, states definitely that he preferred Lord Halifax. As I remained silent a very long pause ensued. It certainly seemed longer than the two minutes which one observes in the commemorations of Armistice Day. Then at length Halifax spoke. He said that he felt that his position as a Peer, out of the House of Commons, would make it very difficult for him to discharge the duties of Prime Minister in a war like this. He would be held responsible for everything, but would not have the power to guide the assembly upon whose confidence the life of every Government depended. He spoke for some minutes in this sense, and by the time he had finished it was clear that the duty would fall upon me—had in fact fallen upon me. Then for the first time I spoke. I said I would have no communication with either of the Opposition parties until I had the King's Commission to form a Government. On this the momentous conversation came to an end, and we reverted to our ordinary easy and familiar manners of men who had worked for years together and whose lives in and out of office had been spent in all the friendliness of British politics.

ROOSEVELT

"Roosevelt was the greatest champion of freedom who has ever brought help and comfort from the New World to the Old."

Two images of Roosevelt during the 1932 presidential campaign, after the 1929 Crash. The sign in the bottom photograph proved correct, since Roosevelt succeeded in rapidly improving the economy.

It had been intended that we should steam up the Potomac and motor to the White House, but we were all impatient after nearly ten days at sea to end our journey. We therefore arranged to fly from Hampton Roads, and landed after dark on December 22 at the Washington airport. There was the President waiting in his car. I clasped his strong hand with comfort and pleasure. We soon reached the White House, which was to be in every sense our home for the next three weeks. Here we were welcomed by Mrs. Roosevelt, who thought of everything that could make our stay agreeable.

I must confess that my mind was so occupied with the whirl of events and the personal tasks I had to perform that my memory till refreshed had preserved but a vague impression of these days. The outstanding feature was of course my contacts with the President. We saw each other for several hours every day, and lunched always together, with Harry Hopkins as a third. We talked of nothing but business, and reached a great measure of agreement on many points, both large and small. Dinner was a more social occasion, but equally intimate and friendly.

The President punctiliously made the preliminary cocktails himself, and I wheeled him in his chair from the drawing-room to the lift as a mark of respect, and thinking also of Sir Walter Raleigh spreading his cloak before Queen Elizabeth. I formed a very strong affection, which grew with our years of comradeship, for this formidable politician who had imposed his will for nearly ten years upon the American scene, and whose heart seemed to respond to many of the impulses that stirred my own. As we both, by need or habit, were forced to do much of our work in bed, he visited me in my room whenever he felt inclined, and encouraged me to do the same to him. Hopkins was just across the passage from my bedroom, and next door to him my travelling map room was soon installed. The President was much interested in this institution, which Captain Pim had perfected. He liked to come and study attentively the large maps of all the theatres of war which soon covered the walls, and on which the movement of fleets and armies was so accurately and swiftly recorded. It was not long before he established a map room of his own of the highest efficiency.

On my return to the White House all was ready for the signature of the United Nations Pact. Many telegrams had passed between Washington, London, and Moscow, but now all was settled. The President had exerted his most fervent efforts to persuade Litvinov, the Soviet Ambassador, newly restored to favour by the turn of events, to accept the phrase "religious freedom". He was invited to luncheon with us in the President's room on purpose. After his hard experiences in his own country he had to be careful. Later on the President had a long talk with him alone about his soul and the dangers of hell-fire. The accounts which Mr. Roosevelt gave us on several occasions of what he said to the Russian were impressive. Indeed,

---

Franklin Delano Roosevelt *was born in Hyde Park, New York, on January 10, 1882, to a family that had already produced a President (his cousin Theodore Roosevelt). A graduate of Harvard in 1904, he entered politics when he was elected Senator for the state of New York in 1910. A Democratic candidate for the vice-presidency in the 1920 elections, he was defeated; the following year, he contracted poliomyelitis, and he increasingly lost the use of his legs. In 1929, he was elected Governor of New York, and in 1932 he won the presidential election against former Republican President Hoover by a large majority. He succeeded in lifting the U.S. out of the Great Depression with the New Deal; a program of government intervention in the economy, and by developing a social and labor-union democracy. Re-elected in 1936 and in 1940, he supported democratic countries in their fight against Germany from the beginning, but brought the U.S. into the war only after Japan's attack on Pearl Harbor (December 7, 1941). He was re-elected for the fourth time in 1944, but died shortly before the end of the war, in Warm Springs, Arkansas, on April 12, 1945.*

**August 1939: Roosevelt
answers questions from
the press at the White
House.**

August 1939: Roosevelt answers questions from the press at the White House.

**November 1939: the
President asks Congress
to revise the neutrality
law and to give him full
powers.**

on one occasion I promised Mr. Roosevelt to recommend him for the position of Archbishop of Canterbury if he should lose the next Presidential election. I did not however make any official recommendation to the Cabinet or the Crown upon this point, and as he won the election in 1944 it did not arise. Litvinov reported the issue about "religious freedom" in evident fear and trembling to Stalin, who accepted it as a matter of course. The War Cabinet also got their point in about "social security", with which, as the author of the first Unemployment Insurance Act, I cordially concurred. After a spate of telegrams had flowed about the world for a week agreement was reached throughout the Grand Alliance.

The title of "United Nations" was substituted by the President for that of "Associated Powers". I thought this a great improvement. I showed my friend the lines from Byron's Childe Harold:

Here, where the sword United Nations drew,
Our countrymen were warring on that day!
And this is much—and all—which will not pass
away.

The President was wheeled in to me on the morning of January 1. I got out of my bath, and agreed to the draft. The Declaration could not by itself win battles, but it set forth who we were and what we were fighting for. Later that day Roosevelt, I, Litvinov, and Soong, representing China, signed this majestic document in the President's study. It was left to the State Department to collect the signatures of the remaining twenty-two nations.

While at Palm Beach I was of course in constant touch by telephone with the President and the British Staffs in Washington, and also when necessary I could speak to London. An amusing, though at the moment disconcerting, incident occurred. Mr. Wendell Willkie had asked to see me. At this time there was tension between him and the President. Roosevelt had not seemed at all keen about my meeting prominent members of the Opposition, and I had consequently so far not done so. Having regard however to Wendell Willkie's visit to England a year before, in January 1941, and to the cordial relations I had established with him, I felt that I ought not to leave American shores without seeing him. This was also our Ambassador's advice. I therefore put a call through to

Roosevelt broadcasting a speech in 1939, during his third term. He was the only U.S. President to be elected four times (1932, 1936, 1940, and 1944).

him on the evening of the 5th. After some delay I was told, "Your call is through." I said in effect, "I am so glad to speak to you. I hope we may meet. I am travelling back by train tomorrow night. Can you not join the train at some point and travel with me for a few hours? Where will you be on Saturday next?" A voice came back: "Why, just where I am now, at my desk." To this I replied, "I do not understand." "Whom do you think you are speaking to?" I replied, "To Mr. Wendell Willkie, am I not?" "No," was the answer, "you are speaking to the President." I did not hear this very well, and asked, "Who?" "You are speaking to me," came the answer, "Franklin Roosevelt." I said, "I did not mean to trouble you at this moment. I was trying to speak to Wendell Willkie, but your telephone exchange seems to have made a mistake." "I hope you are getting on all right down there and enjoying yourself," said the Presi-

dent. Some pleasant conversation followed about personal movements and plans, at the end of which I asked, "I presume you do not mind my having wished to speak to Wendell Willkie?" To this Roosevelt said, "No." And this was the end of our talk.

The President prepared to depart. But I said to him, "you cannot come all this way to North Africa without seeing Marrakesh. Let us spend two days there. I must be with you when you see the sunset on the snows of the Atlas Mountains." I worked on Harry Hopkins also in this sense. It happened there was a most delightful villa, of which I knew nothing, at Marrakesh which the American Vice-Consul, Mr. Kenneth Pendar, had been lent by an American lady, Mrs. Taylor. This villa would accommodate the President and me, and there was plenty of outside room for our entourages. So it was decided that we should all go to Marrakesh. Roosevelt and I drove together the 150 miles across the desert–already it seemed to me to be beginning to get greener–and reached the famous oasis. My description of Marrakesh was "the Paris of the Sahara", where all the caravans had come from Central Africa for centuries to be heavily taxed *en route* by the tribes in the mountains and afterwards swindled in the Marrakesh markets, receiving the return, which they greatly valued, of the gay life of the city, including fortune-tellers, snake-charmers, masses of food and drink, and on the whole the largest and most elaborately organised brothels in the African continent. All these institutions were of long and ancient repute.

It was agreed between us that I should provide the luncheon, and Tommy was accordingly charged with the task. The President and I drove together all the way, five hours, and talked a great deal of shop, but also touched on lighter matters. Many thousand American troops were posted along the road to protect us from any danger, and aeroplanes circled ceaselessly overhead. In the evening we arrived at the villa, where we were very hospitably and suitably entertained by Mr. Pendar. I took the President up the tower of the villa. He was carried in a chair, and sat enjoying a wonderful sunset on the snows of the Atlas. We had a very jolly dinner, about fifteen or sixteen, and we all sang songs. I sang, and the President joined in the choruses, and at one moment was about to try a solo. However, someone interrupted and I never heard this.

My illustrious colleague was to depart just after dawn on the 25th for his long flight by Lagos and Dakar and so across to Brazil and then up to Washington. We had parted the night before, but he came round in the morning on the way to the aeroplane to say another good-bye. I was in bed, but would not hear of letting him go to the airfield alone, so I jumped up and put on my zip, and nothing else except slippers, and in this informal garb I drove with him to the airfield, and went on the plane and saw him comfortably settled down, greatly admiring his courage under all his physical disabilities and feeling very anxious about the hazards he had to undertake. These aeroplane journeys had to be taken as a matter of course during the war. None the less I always regarded them as dangerous excursions. However, all was well.

President Roosevelt died suddenly on Thursday, April 12, at Warm Springs, Georgia. He was sixty-three. In the afternoon, while he was having his portrait painted, he suddenly collapsed, and died a few hours later without regaining consciousness.

Indeed, it may be said that Roosevelt died at the supreme climax of the war, and at the mo-

January 1932: New York Governor Roosevelt with his wife, Eleanor; in November, he was elected President for the first time.

June 1942: Roosevelt contracted poliomyelitis as an adult; he was often confined to a wheelchair, but only rarely was he photographed with crutches.

August 1942: President Roosevelt decorates General James H. Doolittle for his actions in the war against Japan; in the background, with the general's wife, are Henry H. Harnold and George Marshall.

December 1942: Roosevelt decorates General Mark W. Clark on a visit to Sicily.

June 1941: the President examines an ad inviting people to buy Treasury bonds for the defence.

ment when his authority was most needed to guide the policy of the United States. When I received these tidings early in the morning of Friday, the 13th, I felt as if I had been struck a physical blow. My relations with this shining personality had played so large a part in the long, terrible years we had worked together. Now they had come to an end, and I was overpowered by a sense of deep and irreparable loss. I went down to the House of Commons, which met at eleven o'clock, and in a few sentences proposed that we should pay our respects to the memory of our great friend by immediately adjourning. This unprecedented step on the occasion of the death of the head of a foreign State was in accordance with the unanimous wish of the Members, who filed slowly out of the chamber after a sitting which had lasted only eight minutes.

All the nations paid their tributes in one form or another to Roosevelt's memory. Black-bordered flags were hung in Moscow, and the Supreme Soviet, when it met, stood in silence. The Japanese Premier expressed "profound sympathy" to the Americans in the loss of their leader, to whom he assigned the responsibility for "the Americans' advantageous position today". The German radio said, in contrast, "Roosevelt will go down in history as the man at whose instigation the present war spread into a Second World War, and as the President who finally succeeded in bringing his greatest opponent, the Bolshevik Soviet Union, to power."

In my message to Mrs. Roosevelt I said:

Accept my most profound sympathy in your grievous loss, which is also the loss of the British nation and of the cause of freedom in every land. I feel so deeply for you all. As for myself, I have lost a dear and cherished friendship which was forged in the fire of war. I trust you may find consolation in the magnitude of his work and the glory of his name.

And to Harry Hopkins, who had been my precious link on so many occasions:

I understand how deep your feelings of grief must be. I feel with you that we have lost one of our greatest friends and one of the most valiant champions of the causes for which we fight. I feel a very painful personal loss, quite apart from the ties of

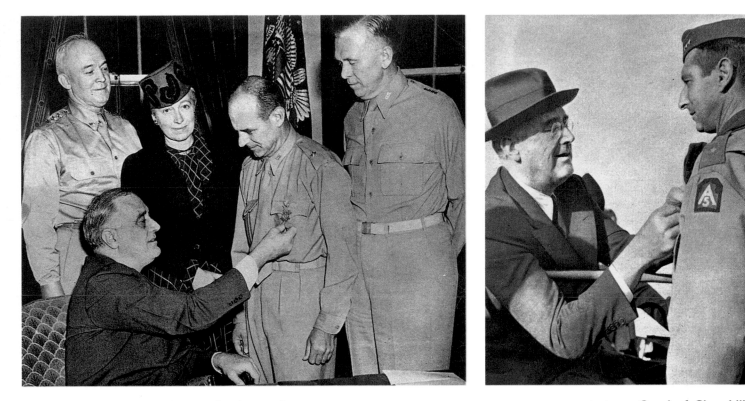

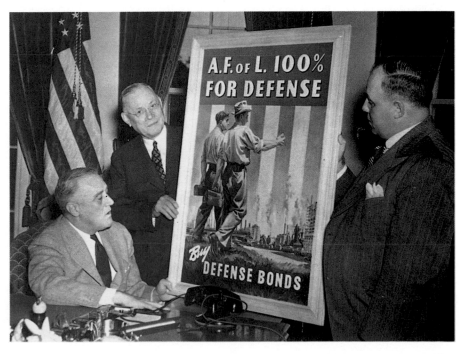

public action which bound us so closely together. I had a true affection for Franklin.

When Parliament met on Tuesday, April 17, I moved an address to the King conveying to His Majesty the deep sorrow of the House and their profound sympathy with Mrs. Roosevelt and with the Government and people of the United States. It is customary for the leaders of all parties to speak in support of such a motion, but there developed a spontaneous feeling that it should be left to me alone to speak for the Commons. I cannot find to-day words which I prefer to those I uttered in the emotion of this melancholy event.

"My friendship," I said, "with the great man to whose work and fame we pay our tribute to-day began and ripened during this war. I had met him, but only for a few minutes, after the close of the last war, and as soon as I went to the Admiralty in September 1939 he telegraphed inviting me to correspond with him direct on naval or other matters if at any time I felt inclined. Having obtained the permission of the Prime Minister, I did so. Knowing President Roosevelt's keen interest in sea warfare, I furnished him with a stream of information about our naval affairs, and about the various actions, including especially the action of the Plate River, which lighted the first gloomy winter of the war.

"When I became Prime Minister, and the war broke out in all its hideous fury, when our own life and survival hung in the balance, I was already in a position to telegraph to the President on terms of an association which had become most intimate, and to me most agreeable. This continued through all the ups and downs of the world struggle until Thursday last, when I received my last messages from him. These messages showed no falling-off in his accustomed clear vision and vigour upon perplexing

Overleaf: Churchill and Roosevelt in September 1944 in Quebec, during one of their numerous meetings.

only after official solutions have not been reached at other stages. To this correspondence there must be added our nine meetings—at Argentia, three in Washington, at Casablanca, at Teheran, two at Quebec, and last of all at Yalta—comprising in all about 120 days of close personal contact, during a great part of which I stayed with him at the White House or at his home at Hyde Park or in his retreat in the Blue Mountains, which he called Shangri-La.

"I conceived an admiration for him as a statesman, a man of affairs, and a war leader. I felt the utmost confidence in his upright, inspiring character and outlook, and a personal regard—affection, I must say—for him beyond my power to express to-day. His love of his own country, his respect for its constitution, his power of gauging the tides and currents of its mobile public opinion, were always evident, but added to these were the beatings of that generous heart which was always stirred to

and complicated matters. I may mention that this correspondence, which of course was greatly increased after the United States' entry into the war, comprises, to and fro between us, over 1,700 messages. Many of these were lengthy messages, and the majority dealt with those more difficult points which come to be discussed upon the level of heads of Governments

anger and to action by spectacles of aggression and oppression by the strong against the weak. It is indeed a loss, a bitter loss to humanity, that those heart-beats are stilled for ever.

"President Roosevelt's physical affliction lay heavily upon him. It was a marvel that he bore up against it through all the many years of tumult and storm. Not one man in ten millions, stricken and crippled as he was, would have attempted to plunge into a life of physical and mental exertion and of hard, ceaseless political controversy. Not one in ten millions would have tried, not one in a generation would have succeeded, not only in entering this sphere, not only in acting vehemently in it, but in becoming indisputable master of the scene. In this extraordinary effort of the spirit over the flesh, of will-power over physical infirmity, he was inspired and sustained by that noble woman his devoted wife, whose high ideals marched with his own, and to whom the deep and respectful sympathy of the House of Commons flows out to-day in all fullness.

"There is no doubt that the President foresaw the great dangers closing in upon the pre-war world with far more prescience than most well-informed people on either side of the Atlantic, and that he urged forward with all his power such precautionary military prepara-

November 10, 1944: President Roosevelt, just elected for the fourth time, with Vice President-elect Harry Truman and outgoing Vice President Henry A. Wallace.

Admiral Chester Nimitz explains the situation in the Pacific to General Douglas MacArthur, President Roosevelt, and Admiral William D. Leahy (1944).

On this page: two images of Roosevelt with General Dwight D. Eisenhower, who succeeded Truman in the White House.

233

Haile Selassie, King of Ethiopia met with Roosevelt in Egypt in February 1945.

Still in Egypt in February 1945, Roosevelt met with King Farouk aboard a U.S. ship.

Ibn-Saud, King of Saudi Arabia, between Roosevelt and Marine Colonel Eddy Quincey, who represented the U.S. in Arabia.

tions as peace-time opinion in the United States could be brought to accept. There never was a moment's doubt, as the quarrel opened, upon which side his sympathies lay. The fall of France, and what seemed to most people outside this Island the impending destruction of Great Britain, were to him an agony, although he never lost faith in us. They were an agony to him not only on account of Europe, but because of the serious perils to which the United States herself would have been exposed had we been overwhelmed or the survivors cast down under the German yoke. The bearing of the British nation at that time of stress, when we were all alone, filled him and vast numbers of his countrymen with the warmest sentiments towards our people. He and they felt the Blitz of the stern winter of 1940-41, when Hitler set himself to 'rub out' the cities of our country, as much as any of us did, and perhaps more indeed, for imagination is often more torturing than reality. There is no doubt that the bearing of the British, and above all of the Londoners, kindled fires in American bosoms far harder to quench than the conflagrations from which we were suffering. There was also at that time, in spite of General Wavell's victories—all the more indeed because of the reinforcements which were sent from this country to him—the appre-

hension widespread in the United States that we should be invaded by Germany after the fullest preparation in the spring of 1941. It was in January that the President sent to England the late Mr. Wendell Willkie, who, although a political rival and an opposing candidate, felt as he did on many important points. Mr. Willkie brought a letter from Mr. Roosevelt, which the President had written in his own hand, and this letter contained the famous lines of Longfellow:

Sail on, O ship of State!
Sail on, O Union, strong and great!
Humanity with all its fears,
With all the hopes of future years,
Is hanging breathless on thy fate.

"At about that same time he devised the extraordinary measure of assistance called Lend-Lease, which will stand forth as the most unselfish and unsordid financial act of any country in all history. The effect of this was greatly to increase British fighting power, and for all the purposes of the war effort to make us, as it were, a much more numerous community. In that autumn I met the President for the first time during the war at Argentia, in Newfoundland, and together we drew up the declaration which has since been called the Atlantic Charter, and which will, I trust, long remain a guide for both our peoples and for other peoples of the world.

"All this time, in deep and dark and deadly secrecy, the Japanese were preparing their act of treachery and greed. When next we met in Washington, Japan, Germany, and Italy had declared war upon the United States, and both our countries were in arms, shoulder to shoulder. Since then we have advanced over the land and over the sea through many difficulties and disappointments, but always with a broadening measure of success. I need not dwell upon the series of great operations which have taken place in the Western Hemisphere, to say nothing of that other immense war proceeding on the other side of the world. Nor need I speak of the plans which we made with our great Ally, Russia, at Teheran, for these have now been carried out for all the world to see.

"But at Yalta I noticed that the President was ailing. His captivating smile, his gay and charming manner, had not deserted him, but his face

This historic photograph has become the symbol of the Yalta Conference (February 1-11, 1945), at which Churchill, Roosevelt, and Stalin delineated the world balance of the post-war era.

A luncheon at Livadia Palace during the Yalta Conference. On the left, US Under-Secretary of State Edward Stettinius attempts a toast, almost unnoticed by the other guests; across the table, Soviet Foreign Minister Molotov, and Churchill, Roosevelt, Stalin, and Soviet ideologue Mikhail Suslov.

had a transparency, an air of purification, and often there was a far-away look in his eyes. When I took my leave of him in Alexandria harbour I must confess that I had an indefinable sense of fear that his health and his strength were on the ebb. But nothing altered his inflexible sense of duty. To the end he faced his innumerable tasks unflinching. . . . When death came suddenly upon him he had 'finished his mail'. That portion of his day's work was done. As the saying goes, he died in harness, and we may well say in battle harness, like his soldiers, sailors, and airmen, who side by side with ours are carrying on their task to the end all over the world. What an enviable death was his! He had brought his country through the worst of its perils and the heaviest of its toils. Victory had cast its sure and steady beam upon him.

"In the days of peace he had broadened and stabilised the foundations of American life and union. In war he had raised the strength, might, and glory of the great Republic to a height never attained by any nation in history. With her left hand she was leading the advance of the conquering Allied Armies into the heart of Germany, and with her right, on the other side of the globe, she was irresistibly and swiftly breaking up the power of Japan. And all the time ships, munitions, supplies, and food of every kind were aiding on a gigantic scale her Allies, great and small. . . .

"But all this was no more than worldly power and grandeur, had it not been that the causes of human freedom and social justice, to which so much of his life had been given, added a lustre. . . which will long be discernible among men. He has left behind him a band of resolute and able men handling the numerous interrelated parts of the vast American war machine. He has left a successor who comes forward with firm step and sure conviction to carry on the task to its appointed end. For us it remains only to say that in Franklin Roosevelt there died the greatest American friend we have ever known, and the greatest champion of freedom who has ever brought help and comfort from the New World to the Old."

STALIN

"The Russian dictator possessed a swift and complete mastery of a problem hitherto novel to him."

Stalin during a moment of relaxation in 1930, and with some close aides, in 1934: from the left (standing), Voro£ilov, Kaganovi™, Kujby£ev; (sitting) Orgionikidze, Molotov, and Kirov.

Nothing that any of us could do pierced the purblind prejudice and fixed ideas which Stalin had raised between himself and the terrible truth. Although on German estimates 186 Russian divisions were massed behind the Soviet boundaries, of which 119 faced the German front, the Russian armies to a large extent were taken by surprise. The Germans found no signs of offensive preparations in the forward zone, and the Russian covering troops were swiftly overpowered. Something like the disaster which had befallen the Polish Air Force on September 1, 1939, was now to be repeated on a far larger scale on the Russian airfields, and many hundreds of Russian planes were caught at daybreak and destroyed before they could get into the air. Thus the ravings of hatred against Britain and the United States which the Soviet propaganda machine cast upon the midnight air were overwhelmed at dawn by the German cannonade. The wicked are not always clever, nor are dictators always right.

On August 12, 1942 I reached Moscow. There was placed at my disposal, as aide-de-camp, an enormous, splendid-looking officer (I believe of a princely family under the Czarist régime), who also acted as our host and was a model of courtesy and attention. A number of veteran servants in white jackets and beaming smiles waited on every wish or movement of the guests. A long table in the dining-room and various sideboards were laden with every delicacy and stimulant that supreme power can command. I was conducted through a spacious reception room to a bedroom and bathroom of almost equal size. Blazing, almost dazzling, electric lights displayed the spotless cleanliness. The hot and cold water gushed. I longed for a hot bath after the length and the heat of the journey. All was instantly prepared. I noticed that the basins were not fed by separate hot and cold water taps and that they had no plugs. Hot and cold turned on at once through a single spout, mingled to exactly the temperature one desired. Moreover, one did not wash one's hands in the basins, but under the flowing current of the taps. In a modest way I have adopted this system at home. If there is no scarcity of water it is far the best.

After all necessary immersions and ablutions we were regaled in the dining-room with every form of choice food and liquor, including of course caviare and vodka, but with many other dishes and wines from France and Germany far beyond our mood or consuming powers. Besides, we had but little time before starting for Moscow. I had told Molotov that I should be

Iosif Vissarionovich Dzhugashvili, a.k.a **Stalin** *("man of steel"), was born in Gori, Georgia, on December 21, 1879. In 1898 he joined the Social-democrat Party, and he was incarcerated and deported to Siberia several times (1913-1917). Back in Petrograd in March 1917, he participated in the October Revolution, and became a member of the first Soviet government as Commissar of Nationalities (1917-1922). On April 3, 1922, he was elected Secretary of the Communist Party. After Lenin's death (January 2, 1924), he defeated his rival Trotsky in the fight for succession, and set up a personal dictatorship that led to the great purges of 1934-1938. Against an internationalist policy, he opted for "socialism in only one country", to be realized through five-year plans as well as mandatory collectivisation and industrialisation. On August 23, 1939, he signed the Soviet-German Non-Aggression Pact, but when Germany attacked the USSR (June 22, 1941), he became one of the leaders of the anti-German coalition. At the end of the conflict, he initiated the Cold War by promoting Communism in the republics of Eastern Europe. He died in Moscow on March 5, 1953.*

ready to see Stalin that night, and he proposed seven o'clock.

I reached the Kremlin, and met for the first time the great Revolutionary Chief and profound Russian statesman and warrior with whom for the next three years I was to be in intimate, rigorous, but always exciting, and at times even genial, association. Our conference lasted nearly four hours. As our second aeroplane had not arrived with Brooke, Wavell, and Cadogan, there were present only Stalin, Molotov, Voroshilov, myself, Harriman, and our Ambassador, with interpreters. I have based this account upon the record which we kept, subject to my own memory, and to the telegrams I sent home at the time.

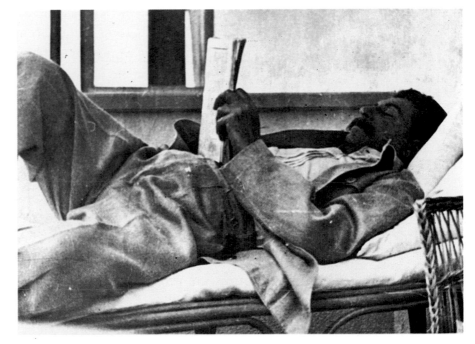

Stalin in 1936, with Molotov (head of the Council of People's Commissars) and Voro£ilov (Defense People's Commissar).

Stalin with Mixim Gorky, in 1930. Two years later, Gorky was nominated as president of the Writers' Union, but in 1936 he died mysteriously, possibly a victim of Stalinist purges.

The first two hours were bleak and sombre. I began at once with the question of the Second Front, saying that I wished to speak frankly and would like to invite complete frankness from Stalin. I would not have come to Moscow unless he had felt sure that he would be able to discuss realities. When M. Molotov had come to London I had told him that we were trying to make plans for a diversion in France. I had also made it clear to M. Molotov that I could make no promises about 1942, and had given M. Molotov a memorandum to this effect. Since then an exhaustive Anglo-American examination of the problem had been carried out. The British and American Governments did not feel themselves able to undertake a major operation in September, which was the latest month in which the weather was to be counted upon. But, as M. Stalin knew, they were preparing for a very great operation in 1943. For this purpose a million American troops were now scheduled to reach the United Kingdom at their point of assembly in the spring of 1943, making an expeditionary force of 27 divisions, to which the British Government were prepared to add 21 divisions. Nearly

half of this force would be armoured. So far only two and a half American divisions had reached the United Kingdom, but the big transportation would take place in October, November, and December.

I told Stalin that I was well aware that this plan offered no help to Russia in 1942, but thought it possible that when the 1943 plan was ready it might well be that the Germans would have a stronger army in the West than they now had. At this point Stalin's face crumpled up into a frown, but he did not interrupt. I then said I had good reasons against an attack on the French coast in 1942. We had only enough landing-craft for an assault landing on a fortified coast—enough to throw ashore six divisions and maintain them. If it were successful, more divisions might be sent, but the limiting factor was landing-craft, which were now being built in very large numbers in the United Kingdom, and especially in the United States. For one division which could be carried this year it would be possible next year to carry eight or ten times as many.

Stalin, who had begun to look very glum, seemed unconvinced by my argument, and asked if it was impossible to attack any part of the French coast. I showed him a map which indicated the difficulties of making an air umbrella anywhere except actually across the Straits. He did not seem to understand, and asked some questions about the range of fighter planes. Could they not, for instance, come and go all the time? I explained that they could indeed come and go, but at this range they would have no time to fight, and I added that an air umbrella to be of any use had to be kept open. He then said that there was not a single German division in France of any value, a statement which I contested. There were in France twenty-five German divisions, nine of which were of the first line. He shook his head. I said that I had brought the Chief of the Imperial General Staff and General Sir Archibald Wavell with me in order that such points might be examined in detail with the Russian General

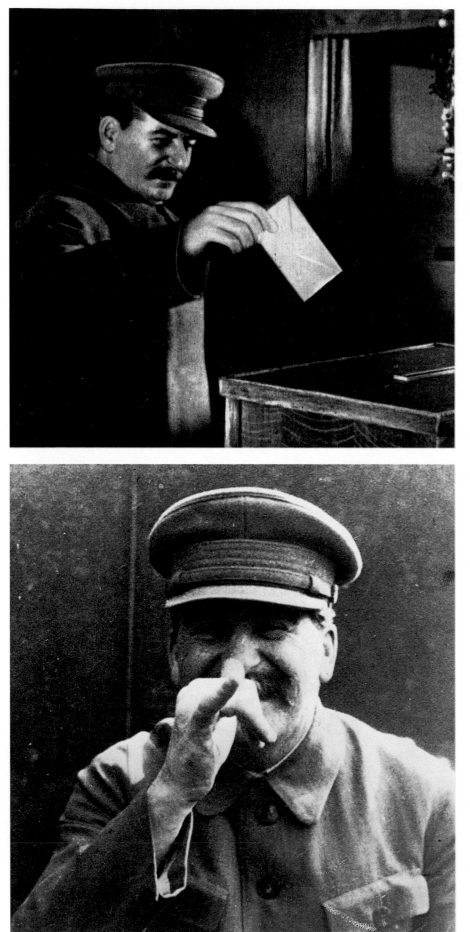

Staff. There was a point beyond which statesmen could not carry discussions of this kind.

Stalin, whose glumness had by now much increased, said that, as he understood it, we were unable to create a second front with any large force and unwilling even to land six divisions. I said that this was so. We could land six divisions, but the landing of them would be more harmful than helpful, for it would greatly injure the big operation planned for next year. War was war but not folly, and it would be folly to invite a disaster which would help nobody. I said I feared the news I brought was not good news. If by throwing in 150,000 to 200,000 men we could render him aid by drawing away from the Russian front appreciable Germans forces, we would not shrink from this course on the grounds of loss. But if it drew no men away and spoiled the prospects for 1943 it would be a great error.

Stalin, who had become restless, said that his view about war was different. A man who was not prepared to take risks could not win a war. Why were we so afraid of the Germans? He could not understand. His experience showed that troops must be blooded in battle. If you did not blood your troops you had no idea what their value was. I inquired whether he had ever asked himself why Hitler did not come to England in 1940, when he was at the height of his power and we had only 20,000 trained troops, 200 guns, and 50 tanks. He did not come. The fact was that Hitler was afraid of the operation. It is not so easy to cross the Channel. Stalin replied that this was no analogy. The landing of Hitler in England would have been resisted by the people, whereas in the case of a British landing in France the people would be on the side of the British. I pointed out that it was all the more important therefore not to expose the people of France by a withdrawal to the vengeance of Hitler and to waste them when they would be needed in the big operation in 1943.

There was an oppressive silence. Stalin at length said that if we could not make a landing in France this year he was not entitled to demand it or to insist upon it, but he was bound to say that he did not agree with my arguments.

I then unfolded a map of Southern Europe, the Mediterranean, and North Africa. What was a "Second Front"? Was it only a landing on a fortified coast opposite England? Or could it take the form of some other great enterprise which might be useful to the common cause? I thought it better to bring him southward by steps. If, for instance, we could hold the enemy in the Pas de Calais by our concentrations in Britain, and at the same time attack elsewhere—for instance, in the Loire, the Gironde, or alternatively the Scheldt—this was full of promise. There indeed was a general picture of next year's big operation. Stalin feared that it was not practicable. I said that it would indeed be difficult to land a million men, but that we should have to persevere and try.

We then passed on to the bombing of Germany, which gave general satisfaction. M. Stalin emphasised the importance of striking at the morale of the German population. He said he attached the greatest importance to bombing, and that he knew our raids were having a tremendous effect in Germany.

After this interlude, which relieved the tension, Stalin observed that from our long talk it seemed that all we were going to do was no "Sledgehammer", no "Round-up", and pay our way by bombing Germany. I decided to get the worst over first and to create a suitable background for the project I had come to unfold. I did not therefore try at once to relieve the gloom. Indeed, I asked specially that there should be the plainest speaking between friends and comrades in peril. However, courtesy and dignity prevailed.

The moment had now come to bring "Torch" into action. I said that I wanted to revert to the question of a Second Front in 1942, which was what I had come

Stalin casting a vote in 1937, and in two peculiar poses, which somehow symbolised his half ironic, half threatening attitude towards Churchill.

Two scenes from the signing of the German-Soviet Non-Aggression Pact at the Kremlin, on August 23, 1939. In the top photograph, Foreign Minister Molotov (sitting), Chief of General Staff Marshal Šapošnikov, an interpreter, German Foreign Minister Joachim von Ribbentrop, Stalin, and Mikhail Suslov.

for. I did not think France was the only place for such an operation. There were other places, and we and the Americans had decided upon another plan, which I was authorised by the American President to impart to Stalin secretly. I would now proceed to do so. I emphasised the vital need of secrecy. At this Stalin sat up

and grinned and said that he hoped that nothing about it would appear in the British Press.

I then explained precisely Operation "Torch". As I told the whole story Stalin became intensely interested. His first question was what would happen in Spain and Vichy France. A little later on he remarked that the operation was militarily right, but he had political doubts about the effect on France. He asked particularly about the timing, and I said not later than October 30, but the President and all of us were trying to pull it forward to October 7. This seemed a great relief to the three Russians.

I then described the military advantages of freeing the Mediterranean, whence still another front could be opened. In September we must win in Egypt, and in October in North Africa, all the time holding the enemy in Northern France. If we could end the year in possession of North Africa we could threaten the belly of Hitler's Europe, and this operation should be considered in conjunction with the 1943 operation. That was what we and the Americans had decided to do.

To illustrate my point I had meanwhile drawn a picture of a crocodile, and explained to Stalin with the help of this picture how it was our intention to attack the soft belly of the crocodile as we attacked his hard snout. And Stalin, whose interest was now at a high pitch, said, "May God prosper this undertaking."

I emphasised that we wanted to take the strain off the Russians. If we attempted that in Northern France we should meet with a rebuff. If we tried in North Africa we had a good chance of victory, and then we could help in Europe. If we could gain North Africa Hitler would have to bring his Air Force back, or otherwise we would destroy his allies, even, for instance, Italy, and make a landing. The operation would have an important influence on Turkey and on the whole of Southern Europe, and all I was afraid of was that we might be forestalled. If North Africa were won this year we could make a deadly attack upon Hitler next year. This marked the turning-point in our conversation.

Stalin then began to present various political difficulties. Would not an Anglo-American seizure of "Torch" regions be misunderstood in France? What were we doing about de Gaulle? I said that at this stage we did not wish him to intervene in the operation. The [Vichy] French were likely to fire on de Gaullists but unlikely to fire on Americans. Harriman backed this very strongly by referring to reports, on which the President relied, by American agents all over "Torch" territories, and also to Admiral Leahy's opinion.

At this point Stalin seemed suddenly to grasp the strategic advantages of "Torch". He recounted four main reasons for it: first, it would hit Rommel in the back; second, it would overawe Spain; third, it would produce fighting between Germans and Frenchmen in France; and, fourth, it would expose Italy to the whole brunt of the war.

I was deeply impressed with this remarkable statement. It showed the Russian Dictator's swift and complete mastery of a problem hitherto novel to him. Very few people alive could have comprehended in so few minutes the rea-

sons which we had all so long been wrestling with for months. He saw it all in a flash.

I mentioned a fifth reason, namely, the shortening of the sea route through the Mediterranean. Stalin was concerned to know whether we were able to pass through the Straits of Gibraltar. I said it would be all right. I also told him about the change in the command in Egypt, and of our determination to fight a decisive battle there in late August or September. Finally, it was clear that they all liked "Torch", though Molotov asked whether it could not be in September.

I then added, "France is down and we want to cheer her up." France had understood Madagascar and Syria. The arrival of the Americans would send the French nation over to our side. It would intimidate Franco. The Germans

might well say at once to the French, "Give us your Fleet and Toulon." This would stir anew the antagonisms between Vichy and Hitler.

I then opened the prospect of our placing an Anglo-American Air Force on the southern flank of the Russian armies in order to defend the Caspian and the Caucasian mountains and generally to fight in this theatre. I did not however go into details, as of course we had to win our battle in Egypt first, and I had not the President's plans for the American contribution. If Stalin like the idea we would set to work in detail upon it. He replied that they would be most grateful for this aid, but that the details of location, etc., would require study. I was very keen on this project, because it would bring about more hard fighting between the Anglo-American air-power and the Germans, all of which aided the gaining of mastery in the air under more fertile conditions than looking for trouble over the Pas de Calais.

We then gathered round a large globe, and I explained to Stalin the immense advantages of clearing the enemy out of the Mediterranean. I told Stalin I should be available should he wish to see me again. He replied that the Russian custom was that the visitor should state his wishes and that he was ready to receive me at any time. He now knew the worst, and yet we parted in an atmosphere of goodwill.

The meeting had now lasted nearly four hours. It took half an hour, more to reach State Villa No. 7. Tired as I was, I dictated my telegram to the War Cabinet and the President after midnight, and then, with the feeling that

July 1941, central Russian front: Iakov Dzhugashvili, Stalin's eldest son and an artillery lieutenant in the Red Army, has been captured by the Germans.

at least the ice was broken and a human contact established, I slept soundly and long.

Late the next morning I awoke in my luxurious quarters. It was Thursday, August 13—to me always "Blenheim Day". I had arranged to visit M. Molotov in the Kremlin at noon in order to explain to him more clearly and fully the character of the various operations we had in mind. I pointed out how injurious to the common cause it would be if owing to recriminations about dropping "Sledgehammer" we were forced to argue publicly against such enterprises. I also explained in more detail the political setting of "Torch". He listened affably, but contributed nothing. I proposed to him that I should see Stalin at 10 p.m. that night, and later in the day got word that eleven o'clock

would be more convenient, and as the subjects to be dealt with would be the same as those of the night before, would I wish to bring Harriman? I said "Yes", and also Cadogan, Brooke, Wavell, and Tedder, who had meanwhile arrived safely from Teheran in a Russian plane. They might have had a very dangerous fire in their Liberator.

Before leaving this urbane, rigid diplomatist's room I turned to him and said, "Stalin will make a great mistake to treat us roughly when we have come so far." For the first time Molotov unbent. "Stalin," he said, "is a very wise man. You may be sure that, however he argues, he understands all. I will tell him what you say."

I returned in time for luncheon to State Villa Number Seven.

Out of doors the weather was beautiful. It was just like what we love most in England—when we get it. I thought we would explore the domain. State Villa Number Seven was a fine large, brand-new country house standing in its own extensive lawns and gardens in a fir wood of about twenty acres. There were agreeable walks, and it was pleasant in the beautiful August weather to lie on the grass or pine-needles. There were several fountains, and a large glass tank filled with many kinds of goldfish, who were all so tame that they would eat out of your hand. I made a point of feeding them every day. Around the whole was a stockade, perhaps fifteen feet high, guarded on both sides by police and soldiers in considerable numbers. About a hundred yards from the

Stalin's son was electrocuted in April 1943 on the galvanised wire fence of Sachsenhausen concentration camp, where he had been detained and from which he was attempting to escape.

Stalin, in 1942, with marshal Vorošilov, who was one of Stalin's favorites and did not receive any command at the front during the war; the dictator entrusted him with training reserves.

house was an air-raid shelter. At the first opportunity we were conducted over it. It was of the latest and most luxurious type. Lifts at either end took you down eighty or ninety feet into the ground. Here were eight or ten large rooms inside a concrete box of massive thickness. The rooms were divided from each other by heavy sliding doors. The lights were brilliant. The furniture was stylish "Utility", sumptuous and brightly coloured. I was more attracted by the goldfish.

We all repaired to the Kremlin at 11 p.m., and were received only by Stalin and Molotov, with their interpreter. Then began a most unpleasant discussion. Stalin handed me a document. When it was translated I said I would answer it in writing, and that he must understand we had made up our minds upon the course to be pursued and that reproaches were vain. Thereafter we argued for about two hours, during which he said a great many disagreeable things, especially about our being too much afraid of fighting the Germans, and if we tried it like the Russians we should find it not so bad; that we had broken our promise about "Sledgehammer"; that we had failed in delivering the supplies promised to Russia and only sent remnants after we had taken all we needed for ourselves. Apparently these complaints were addressed as much to the United States as to Britain.

I repulsed all his contentions squarely, but without taunts of any kind. I suppose he is not

Stalin, in 1942, with marshal Vorošilov, who was one of Stalin's favorites and did not receive any command at the front during the war; the dictator entrusted him with training reserves.

used to being contradicted repeatedly, but he did not become at all angry, or even animated. He reiterated his view that it should be possible for the British and Americans to land six or eight divisions on the Cherbourg peninsula, since they had domination of the air. He felt that if the British Army had been fighting the Germans as much as the Russian Army it would not be so frightened of them. The Russians, and indeed the R.A.F., had shown that it was possible to beat the Germans. The British infantry could do the same provided they acted at the same time as the Russians.

I interposed that I pardoned the remarks which Stalin had made on account of the bravery of the Russian Army. The proposal for a landing in Cherbourg overlooked the existence of the Channel. Finally Stalin said we could

Stalin and Churchill at the Kremlin during a meeting in August 1942.

Eden, Churchill, and Stalin at a reception at the Soviet embassy in Teheran, during the conference (November 28-December 1, 1943) that decided to undertake the Anglo-American landing on the northern coast of France.

Stalin and Vorošilov at a parade at Red Square in Moscow, soon after the end of the war. Behind them is Nikita Khrushchev, who succeeded Stalin and in 1956 denounced his crimes and purges, in which Khrushchev himself had taken part.

carry it no further. He must accept our decision. He then abruptly invited us to dinner at eight o'clock the next night.

Accepting the invitation, I said I would leave by plane at dawn the following morning—i.e., the 15th. Joe seemed somewhat concerned at this, and asked could I not stay longer. I said certainly, if there was any good to be done, and that I would wait one more day anyhow. I then exclaimed that there was no ring of comrade-

ship in his attitude. I had travelled far to establish good working relations. We had done our utmost to help Russia, and would continue to do so. We had been left entirely alone for a year against Germany and Italy. Now that the three great nations were allied, victory was certain, provided we did not fall apart, and so forth. I was somewhat animated in this passage, and before it could be translated he made the remark that he liked the tone of my utterance.

Thereafter the talk began again in a somewhat less tense atmosphere.

He plunged into a long discussion of two Russian trench mortars firing rockets, which he declared were devastating in their effects, and which he offered to demonstrate to our experts if they could wait. He said he would let us have all information about them, but should there not be something in return? Should there not be an agreement to exchange information about inventions? I said that we would give them everything without any bargaining, except only those devices which, if carried in aeroplanes over the enemy lines and shot down, would make our bombing of Germany more difficult. He accepted this. He also agreed that his military authorities should meet our generals, and this was arranged for three o'clock in the afternoon. I said they would require at least four hours to go fully into the various technical questions involved in "Sledge-hammer", "Round-up", and "Torch". He observed at one moment that "Torch" was "militarily correct", but that the political side required more delicacy—i.e., more careful handling. From time to time he returned to "Sledgehammer", grumbling about it. When he said our promise had not been kept I replied, "I repudiate that statement. Every promise has been kept," and I pointed to the *aide-mémoire* I gave Molotov. He made a sort of apology, saying that he was expressing his sincere and honest opinions, that there was no mistrust between us, but only a difference of view.

Finally I asked about the Caucasus. Was he going to defend the mountain chain, and with how many divisions? At this he sent for a relief model, and, with apparent frankness and evident knowledge, explained the strength of this barrier, for which he said twenty-five divisions were available. He pointed to the various passes and said they would be defended. I asked were they fortified, and he said, "Yes, certainly." The Russian front line, which the enemy had not yet reached, was north of the main range. He said they would have to hold out for two months, when the snow would make the mountains impassable. He declared himself quite confident of their ability to do this, and also recounted in detail the strength of the Black Sea Fleet, which was gathered at Batum.

All this part of the talk was easier, but when Harriman asked about the plans for bringing American aircraft across Siberia, to which the Russians had only recently consented after

Stalin and Roosevelt at the Yalta Conference, in February 1945.

251

long American pressing, he replied, curtly, "Wars are not won with plans." Harriman backed me up throughout, and we neither of us yielded an inch nor spoke a bitter word.

Stalin made his salute and held out his hand to me on leaving, and I took it.

In the course of one of my later talks with Stalin I said, "Lord Beaverbrook has told me that when he was on his mission to Moscow in October 1941 you asked him, 'What did Churchill mean by saying in Parliament that he had given me warnings of the impending German attack?' I was of course," said I, "referring to the telegram I sent you in April '41," and I produced the telegram which Sir Stafford Cripps had tardily delivered. When it was read and translated to him Stalin shrugged his shoulders. "I remember it. I did not need any warnings. I knew war would come, but I thought I might gain another six months or so." In the common cause I refrained from asking what would have happened to us all if we had gone down for ever while he was giving Hitler so much valuable material, time, and aid.

An official 1945 photograph of Stalin.

Moscow, May 1945: a group of children cheer Stalin during the victory celebrations.

The first official meeting after Roosevelt's death between Stalin, Churchill, and Truman, President since April 12, 1945.

DE GAULLE

"I understood and admired, while I resented, his arrogant demeanour."

Under an impassive, unperturbable demeanour he seemed to me to have a remarkable capacity for feeling pain. I preserved the impression, in contact with this very tall, phlegmatic man: "Here is the Constable of France."

In spite of the Armistice and Oran and the ending of our diplomatic relations with Vichy, I never ceased to feel a unity with France. People who have not been subjected to the personal stresses which fell upon prominent Frenchmen in the awful ruin of their country should be careful in their judgments of individuals. It is beyond the scope of this story to enter the maze of French politics. But I felt sure that the French nation would do its best for the common cause according to the facts presented to it. When they were told that their only salvation lay in following the advice of the illustrious Marshal Pétain, and that England, which had given them so little help, would soon be conquered or give in, very little choice was offered to the masses. But I was sure they wanted us to win, and that nothing would give them more joy than to see us continue the struggle with vigour. It was our first

General de Gaulle in London in the summer of 1940, after he assumed the command of the combatants of Free France.

Charles de Gaulle *was born in Lille, France, on November 22, 1890. The son of a teacher, he graduated from the military academy of Saint-Cyr in 1912. He was captured by the Germans during World War I (1916). Marshal Pétain appointed him a member of the War Cabinet (1925-1927). At the outbreak of World War II, he was a colonel; he was promoted to general, and nominated as Under-Secretary of National Defence (June 6, 1940). After the creation of the Pétain government and the request for armistice (June 16), de Gaulle, from London, made an appeal for resistance (June 18); Pétain had him sentenced to death. He organised a Free French Army and the Resistance movement. President of two provisional governments (1944 and 1945), he resigned in 1946. He founded the Rassemblement du peuple français (RPF), and re-entered the government in 1958. He prepared a constitution that gave ample powers to the President of the Republic, and in the same year he was elected to that very office, a mandate that was renewed in 1965. Defeated in a referendum for the reformation of the Senate, on April 28, 1969, he retired from political life. He died on November 9, 1970 at Colombey-les-Deux-Eglises.*

duty to give loyal support to General de Gaulle in his valiant constancy. On August 7 I signed a military agreement with him which dealt with practical needs. His stirring addresses were made known to France and the world by the British broadcast. The sentence of death which the Pétain Geovernment passed upon him glorified his name. We did everything in our power to aid him and magnify his movement.

At the same time it was necessary to keep in touch not only with France, but even with Vichy. I therefore always tried to make the best of them. I was very glad when at the end of the year the United States sent an Ambassador to Vichy of so much influence and character as Admiral Leahy, who was himself so close to the President. I repeatedly encouraged Mr. Mackenzie King to keep his representative, the skilful and accomplished M. Dupuy, at Vichy.

Here at least was a window upon a courtyard to which we had no other access. On July 25 I sent a minute to the Foreign Secretary in which I said: "I want to promote a kind of collusive conspiracy in the Vichy Government whereby certain members of that Government, perhaps with the consent of those who remain, will levant to North Africa in order to make a better bargain for France from the North African shore and from a position of indepen-

London, June 18, 1940: on British radio, de Gaulle reads his famous appeal to the French to resist the German foe.

dence. For this purpose I would use both food and other inducements, as well as the obvious arguments." It was in this spirit that I was to receive in October a certain M. Rougier, who represented himself as acting on the personal instructions of Marshal Pétain. This was not because I or my colleagues had any respect for Marshal Pétain, but only because no road that led to France should be incontinently barred. Our consistent policy was to make the Vichy Government and its members feel that, so far as we were concerned, it was never too late to mend. Whatever had happened in the past, France was our comrade in tribulation, and nothing but actual war between us should prevent her being our partner in victory.

This mood was hard upon de Gaulle, who had risked all and kept the flag flying, but whose handful of followers outside France could never claim to be an effective alternative

London, July 1940: de Gaulle inspects French soldiers who have responded to his appeal. The second from the left is his son, Philippe.

One of de Gaulle's curious expressions.

De Gaulle in Plymouth, as he leaves a French submarine in July 1940.

Previous pages: the meeting in Casablanca (January 24, 1943) between General Giraud, Roosevelt, de Gaulle, and Churchill. Giraud, military and civilian head of French North Africa, strongly disagreed with de Gaulle.

Marrakech, February 1943: de Gaulle and Churchill inspect French units in training.

French Government. Nevertheless, we did our utmost to increase his influence, authority, and power. He for his part naturally resented any kind of truck on our part with Vichy, and thought we ought to be exclusively loyal to him. He also felt it to be essential to his position before the French people that he should maintain a proud and haughty demeanour towards "perfidious Albion", although an exile, dependent upon on our protection and dwelling in our midst. He had to be rude to the British to prove to French eyes that he was not a British puppet. He certainly carried out this policy with perserverance. He even one day explained this technique to me, and I fully comprehended the extraordinary difficulties of his problem. I always admired his massive strength.

In these pages various severe statements, based on events of the moment, are set down

about General de Gaulle, and certainly I had continuous difficulties and many sharp antagonisms with him. There was however a dominant element in our relationship. I could not regard him as representing captive and prostrate France, nor indeed the France that had a right to decide freely the future for herself. I knew he was no friend of England. But I always recognised in him the spirit and conception which, across the pages of history, the word "France" would ever proclaim. I understood and admired, while I resented, his arrogant demeanour. Here he was—a refugee, an exile from his country under sentence of death, in a position entirely dependent upon the goodwill of the British Government, and also now of the Untied States. The Germans had conquered his country. He had no real foothold anywhere. Never mind; he defied all. Always, even when he was behaving worst, he

May 30, 1943: de Gaulle
disembarks in Algiers,
to meet Giraud, with
whom he will share the
presidency of the
National Liberation
Committee until the
following October.

seemed to express the personality of France—a great nation, with all its pride, authority, and ambition. It was said in mockery that he thought himself the living representative of Joan of Arc, whom one of his ancestors is supposed to have served as a faithful adherent. This did not seem to me as absurd as it looked. Clemenceau, with whom it was said he also compared himself, was a far wiser and more experienced statesman. But they both gave the same impression of being unconquerable Frenchmen.

In spite of the tension with General de Gaulle about Peyrouton, Boisson, and Flandin, all of whom had been arrested by the Free French authorities in December, I determined to make an effort to renew friendly relations with him before returning home. On New Year's Day I asked him to dine and sleep at the villa on January 3. "This," I said, "would give us an opportunity of long-needed talks.

My wife is with me here, and if Madame de Gaulle would care to accompany you it would give us both much pleasure." The General evidently thought the notice too short. I ought to have known that he would not sleep anywhere in North Africa but in a French official residence. He pleaded the pressure of his other engagements. So I let it alone. However, having learnt later that he would arrive in Marrakesh on January 12, I invited him to luncheon that day, and he accepted. Mr. Duff Cooper and Lady Diana, Lord Beaverbrook, Mr. Nairn the Consul and his wife, were also our guests. The General arrived in the best of humour, greeted Mrs. Churchill in English, and spoke it throughout the meal. To make things equal I spoke French.

After luncheon the ladies went off to visit the bazaars, and de Gaulle and I and the other men settled down in the garden for a long talk. I had a lot of awkward subjects to deal with,

Paris, July 14, 1945: during the celebration of the anniversary of the storming of the Bastille, de Gaulle greets General Eisenhower. Beside him is Admiral Harold R. Stark.

and I thought my speaking French would add a lighter touch to them. Mr. Nairn, who made a few notes afterwards, records, "I heard Mr. Churchill say to Mr. Duff Cooper in English in a very audible whisper, 'I'm doing rather well, aren't I? Now that the General speaks English so well he understands my French perfectly.' Then everyone, General de Gaulle setting the example, burst out laughing. The Prime Minister continued in French, but the super sensitive General was completely disarmed and ready to accept Mr. Churchill's comments in a friendly and helpful spirit."

The comments were numerous and serious. Why was he pursuing this vendetta against the French notabilities who had fallen into his power? Did he not realise how much difficulty he made for himself in the United States? How angry the President was with him? How much we all depended on American aid and goodwill?

Why should he complicate his own task by this and all sorts of other needless friction? Why should he always try to offend these powerful Governments, without whose help he could not live? Upon a smaller point, why had he driven General Georges, whom I had specially brought from France to make things easier, off the Committee? At this de Gaulle said he had offered General Georges the Chancellorship of the Legion of Honour. I asked what reply he had received. "I received no reply," he answered. I said I was not surprised. Had he the Chancellorship to bestow? But all ended pleasantly, and the General proposed that I should attend a review he would hold in my honour the next morning, which I agreed to do. And accordingly de Gaulle and I stood on a small platform while quite a large array of French and Moroccan troops marched past for an hour amid the cheers of the inhabitants of the Marrakesh oasis.

CHIANG KAI-SHEK

"I was impressed by his calm, reserved, and efficient personality."

Chiang Kai-shek as a young man.

The Renown reached Alexandria on the morning of November 21, and I flew at once to the desert landing-ground near the Pyramids. Here Mr. Casey had placed at my disposal the agreeable villa he was using. We lay in a broad expanse of Kasserine woods, thickly dotted with the luxurious abodes and gardens of the cosmopolitan Cairo magnates. Generalissimo Chiang Kai-shek and Madame had already been ensconced half a mile away. The President was to occupy the spacious villa of the American Ambassador Kirk, about three miles down the road to Cairo. I went to the desert airfield to welcome him when he arrived in the "Sacred Cow" from Oran the next morning, and we drove to his villa together.

The Staffs congregated rapidly. The headquarters of the Conference and the venue of all the British and American Chiefs of Staff was at the Mena House Hotel, opposite the Pyramids, and I was but half a mile away. The whole place bristled with troops and anti-aircraft guns, and the strictest cordons guarded all approaches. Everyone set to work at once at their various levels upon immense mass of business which had to be decided or adjusted.

What we had apprehended from Chiang Kai-shek's presence now in fact occurred. The talks of the British and American Staffs were sadly distracted by the Chinese story, which was lengthy, complicated, and minor. Moreover, as will be seen, the President, who took an exaggerated view of the Indian-Chinese sphere, was soon closeted in long conferences with the Generalissimo. All hope of persuad-

Chiang Kai-shek *was born in Zhejiang on October 31, 1897, to a family of merchants and farmers. He completed his military studies in Japan (1907-1911). In 1923, he was appointed head of a military academy, and in 1925, after Sun Yat-sen's death, he headed the Kuomintang (the nationalist National People's Party). He became Prime Minister of Northern China in 1927, the same year he distanced himself from the Communists, whom he would later try to exterminate in a series of campaigns (1930-1935). After setting up a totalitarian régime, he was forced to come to an agreement with the Communists during the war against Japan (1937-1945), when China took part in World War II on the side of democracies. At the end of the conflict, the civil war between Nationalists and Communists resumed; and was won by the latter under Mao Tse-tung's leadership (1949). Chiang Kai-shek was forced to flee with his followers to the island of Taiwan, where he founded a Nationalist state (1950), of which he became president for life. In 1972, he nominated his son Chiang King-kuo as Prime Minister. He died in Taipei in 1975.*

ing Chiang and his wife to go and see the Pyramids and enjoy themselves till we returned from Teheran fell to the ground, with the result that Chinese business occupied first instead of last place at Cairo. The President, in spite of my arguments, gave the Chinese the promise of a considerable amphibious operation across the Bay of Bengal within the next few months. This would have cramped "Overlord" for landing- and tank-landing craft, which had now become the bottle-neck, far

more than any of my Turkey and Ægean projects. It would also have hampered grievously the immense operations we were carrying out in Italy. On November 29 I wrote to the Chiefs of Staff: "The Prime Minister wishes to put on record the fact that he specifically refused the Generalissimo's request that we should undertake an amphibious operation simultaneously with the land operations in Burma." It was not until we returned from Teheran to Cairo that I at length prevailed up-

Maymyo (Burma), April 1942: Chiang Kai-shek and his wife, Soong Mei-ling, with U.S. General Joseph Stilwell at the end of the Allied military conference.

265

on the President to retract his promise. Even so, many complications arose. Of this more anon.

I of course took occasion to visit the Generalissimo at his villa, where he and his wife were suitably installed. This was the first time I had met Chiang Kai-shek. I was impressed by his calm, reserved, and efficient personality. At this moment he stood at the height of his power and fame. To American eyes he was one of the dominant forces in the world. He was the champion of "the New Asia". He was certainly a steadfast defender of China against Japanese invasion. He was a strong anti-Communist. The accepted belief in American circles was that he would be the head of the great Fourth Power in the world after the victory had been won. All these views and values have since been cast aside by many of those who held them. I, who did not in those days share excessive estimates of Chiang Kai-shek's power or of the future helpfulness of China, may record the fact that the Generalissimo is still serving the same causes which at this time had gained him such wide renown. He has however since been beaten by the Communists in his own country, which is a very bad thing to be.

I had a very pleasant conversation with Madame Chiang Kai-shek, and found her a most remarkable and charming personality. I told her how much I had regretted that we could not find an occasion for a meeting at the time when we had both been in America together, and we agreed that no undue formalities should stand in the way of our talks in the future. The President had us all photographed together at one of our meetings at his villa, and although both the Generalissimo and his wife are now regarded as wicked and corrupt reactionaries by many of their former admirers I am glad to keep this as a souvenir.

Chiang Kai-shek in 1942.

Chiang Kai-shek with Jawaharlal Nehru, the leader of India's anti-Japanese faction.

Chiang Kai-shek toasts to victory with Mao Tse-tung; shortly thereafter, they clashed in a civil war.

TITO

Tito, with an injured arm, during the war of resistance .

I reached Naples that afternoon, and was installed in the palatial though somewhat dilapidated Villa Rivalta, with a glorious view of Vesuvius and the bay. Here General Wilson explained to me that all arrangements had been made for a conference next morning with Tito and Subašić, the new Yugoslav Prime Minister of King Peter's Government in London. They had already arrived in Naples, and would dine with us the next night.

On the morning of August 12 Marshal Tito came up to the villa. He wore a magnificent gold and blue uniform which was very tight under the collar and singularly unsuited to the blazing heat. The uniform had been given him by the Russians, and, as I was afterwards informed, the gold lace came from the United States. I joined him on the terrace of the villa, accompanied by Brigadier Maclean and an interpreter.

I suggested that the Marshal might first like to see General Wilson's War Room, and we moved inside. The Marshal, who was attended by two ferocious-looking bodyguards, each carrying automatic pistols, wanted to bring them with him in case of treachery on our part. He was dissuaded from this with some difficulty, and proposed to bring them to guard him at dinner instead.

I led the way into a large room, where maps of the battle-fronts covered the walls. I began by displaying the Allied front in Normandy and indicating our broad strategic moves against the German armies in the West. I pointed out Hitler's obstinacy in refusing to yield an inch of territory, how numerous divisions were locked up in Norway and in the Baltic provinces, and said that his correct strategy would be to withdraw his troops from the Balkans and concentrate them on the main battle-fronts. Allied pressure in Italy and the Russian advance from the east might force him to go, but we must reckon on the possibility of his staying. As I talked I pointed on the map to the Istrian peninsula, and asked Tito where, if we were able to reach it from the east coast of Italy, his forces could be sent to co-operate with us. I explained that it would help if a small port could be opened on the Yugoslav coast so that we could send in war material by sea. In June and July we had sent nearly two thousand tons of stores to his forces by air, but could do much more if we had a port. Tito said that although German opposition had intensified lately, and Yugoslav losses increased, he was able to raise considerable forces in Croatia and Slovenia, and he would certainly favour an operation against the Istrian peninsula, in which Yugoslav forces would join.

We now moved into a small sitting-room, and I began to question him about his relations with the Royal Yugoslav Government. He said that violent fighting still continued between

---

Josip Broz, *a.k.a.* **Tito,** *was born in Kumrovec, Croatia, on May 25, 1892. The son of a peasant, he left school at age 12 to become a blue-collar worker. During World War I, he fought in the Austro-Hungarian Army and was captured by the Russians (1915). Freed in the course of the 1917 Revolution, he joined the Bolsheviks, and in 1923 he went back to Croatia, part of the newly formed Yugoslavia, as a Communist agent. In 1928, he was arrested and incarcerated for six years. As the secretary of the clandestine Yugoslavian Communist Party he went to Moscow (1938-1939), then secretly returned to Yugoslavia. He led the Resistance against the Germans during the 1941 invasion. After liberation (March 1945), he maintained power as premier, and founded a Socialist republic based on the recognition of individual nationalities. However, on June 28, 1948, he officially broke his ties with the USSR by refusing to obey Stalin's policy, and declared Yugoslavia non-aligned with either of the two opposed blocs. He fostered the administration of productive activities through an autonomous "national way" toward Socialism. He was president for life from 1971, and died in Ljubljana on May 4, 1980.*

the Partisans and Mihailovic, whose power rested on German and Bulgar help. Reconciliation was unlikely. I replied that we had no desire to intervene in internal Yugoslav affairs, but wanted his country to be strong, united, and independent. Dr. Subašić was very loyal to this idea. Moreover, we ought not to let the King down. Tito said that he understood our obligation towards King Peter, but was not able to do anything about it until after the war, when the Yugoslav people themselves would decide.

I then turned to the future, and suggested that the right solution for Yugoslavia would be a democratic system based on the peasantry, and perhaps some gradual measure of agrarian reform where the holdings were too small. Tito assured me that, as he had stated publicly, he had no desire to introduce the Communist system into Yugoslavia, if only because most European countries after the war would probably be living under a democratic régime. Developments in small countries depended on relations between the Great Powers. Yugoslavia should be able to profit by the growing improvement in these relations and develop along democratic lines. The Russians had a mission with the Partisans, but its members, far from expressing any idea of introducing the Soviet system into Yugoslavia, had spoken against it.

I asked Tito if he would reaffirm his statement about Communism in public, but he did not wish to do this as it might seem to have been forced upon him. It was agreed that he should however discuss the suggestion with Dr. Subasic, whom he was meeting for the first time that afternoon.

We then lunched together, and arranged that if the talks with Dr. Subašić made favourable progress we should meet again the following evening. In the meantime I undertook to draft a memorandum on Yugoslav affairs, and the Marshal promised to send me a letter on certain specific matters about supplies.

Early in the day Tito had met General Gammell, Chief of Staff to General Wilson, and been given an important memorandum on Allied projects in Istria and thereabouts. It read as follows:

Caserta, August 1944: Churchill between Tito and Ivan Subasic, the Yugoslavian Prime Minister in exile in London.

Tito wearing the uniform described by Churchill on page 268.

utmost admiration, are not satisfied that sufficient recognition has been given to the power and rights of the Serbian people, or to the help which has been given, and will be continued, by His Majesty's Government.

The Yugoslavs objected to my suggestion that the Partisan movement was divorced from the Serbian people. I did not press this point, particularly as Tito had said that he was prepared later on to make a public statement about not introducing Communism into Yugoslavia after the war. We then discussed a possible meeting between him and King Peter. I said that democracy had flowered in England under constitutional monarchy, and thought that Yugoslavia's international position would be stronger under a king than as a republic. Tito said his country had had an unfortunate experience with her King, and it would take time for King Peter to live down his connection with Mihailovic. He had no objection in principle to meeting the King, but thought that the moment had not yet come. We therefore agreed to leave it to him and Dr. Subašić to decide on the most opportune occasion.

TRUMAN

"A man of exceptional character and ability, simple and direct methods of speech, and a great deal of self-confidence and resolution."

Harry Truman, thirty-third President of the United States.

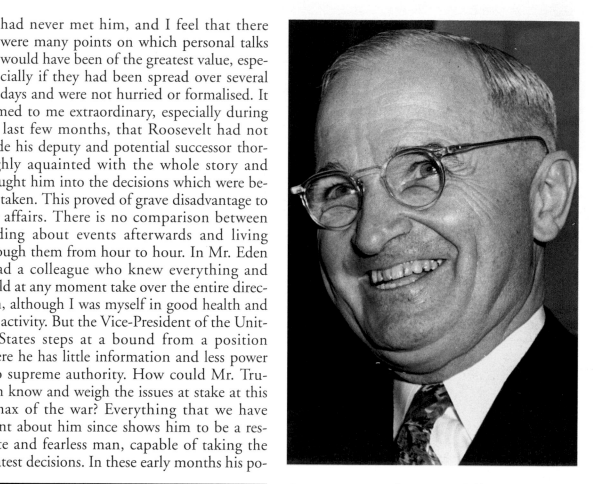

I had never met him, and I feel that there were many points on which personal talks would have been of the greatest value, especially if they had been spread over several days and were not hurried or formalised. It seemed to me extraordinary, especially during the last few months, that Roosevelt had not made his deputy and potential successor thoroughly aquainted with the whole story and brought him into the decisions which were being taken. This proved of grave disadvantage to our affairs. There is no comparison between reading about events afterwards and living through them from hour to hour. In Mr. Eden I had a colleague who knew everything and could at any moment take over the entire direction, although I was myself in good health and full activity. But the Vice-President of the United States steps at a bound from a position where he has little information and less power into supreme authority. How could Mr. Truman know and weigh the issues at stake at this climax of the war? Everything that we have learnt about him since shows him to be a resolute and fearless man, capable of taking the greatest decisions. In these early months his po-

sition was one of extreme difficulty, and did not enable him to bring his outstanding qualities fully into action.

President Truman arrived in Berlin the same day as I did. I was eager to meet a potentate with whom my cordial relations, in spite of differences, had been established by the correspondence included in this volume. I called on him the morning after our arrival, and was impressed with his gay, precise, sparkling manner and obvious power of decision.

On July 18 I lunched alone with the President, and we touched on many topics. I spoke of the melancholy position of Great Britain, who had spent more than half her foreign investments for the common cause when we were

Harry Truman *was born on May 25, 1892 in Lamar, Missouri, to a family of farmers. During World War I, he was an officer in France. In 1919, he opened a men's clothing store, which went bankrupt after two years. Unemployed, he joined the Democratic Party. Elected Senator of Missouri (1935-1945), during World War II he was chairman of a research commission for national defence, and in 1944 he was elected Vice-President with Roosevelt, whose office assumed after Roosevelt's sudden death (April 12, 1945). He authorized the use of atomic bombs on Hiroshima and Nagasaki. On March 12, 1947, he disclosed the principles of the so-called Truman doctrine, to contain the Communist expansion, and argued for the need for the Cold War, which included the Marshall Plan as an aid to Western nations threatened by Communism. His domestic policy followed in the steps of Roosevelt's New Deal, and in 1948 he was re-elected. As another element in the fight against Communism, he created NATO (1949), and decided that the U.S. should intervene in the Korean war (1950). He did not seek candidacy in the 1952 election. He died in Lamar on December 26, 1972.*

all alone, and now emerged from the war with a great external debt of three thousand million pounds. This had grown up through buying supplies from India, Egypt, and elsewhere, with no Lend-Lease arrangement, and would impose upon us an annual exportation without any compensatory import to nourish the wages fund. He followed this attentively and with sympathy, and declared that the United States owed Great Britain an immense debt for having held the fort at the beginning. "If you had gone down like France," he said, "we might be fighting the Germans on the American coast at the present time. This justifies us in regarding these matters as above the purely financial plane." I said I had told the election crowds that we were living to a large extent upon American imported food, for which we could not pay, but we had no intention of being kept by any country, however near to us in friendship. We should have to ask for help to become a going concern again, and until we got our wheels turning properly we could be of little use to world security or any of the high purposes of San Francisco. The President said he would do his very utmost, but of course I knew all the difficulties he might have in his own country.

I then spoke about Imperial Preference, and explained that it might cause a split in the Conservative Party if it were not wisely handled. I had heard that America was making great reductions in her tariff. The President said it had been reduced by 50 per cent., and he now had authority to reduce it by another 50 per cent., leaving it at one-quarter of its pre-war height. I replied that this was a great factor, and would have a powerful influence on our Dominions, especially Canada and Australia.

The President raised the subject of air and communications. He had great difficulties to face about airfields in British territory, especially in Africa, which the Americans had built at enormous cost. We ought to meet them on this and arrange a fair plan for common use. I assured him that if I continued to be responsible I would reopen the question with him personally. It would be a great pity if the Americans got worked up about bases and air traffic and set themselves to make a win of it all costs. We must come to the best arrangement in our common interests. President Roosevelt knew well that I wished to go much further on this matter of airfields and other bases, and would have liked to have a reciprocal arrangement between our two countries all over the world.

June 1945: two months into his presidency, Truman examines a document in the Oval Office. Behind him are the former Ambassador to Moscow, Admiral Joseph E. Davies, the Chief of Staff, Admiral William D. Leahy, and close aide Harry Hopkins.

Truman when he was still vice president, having lunch with Roosevelt at the White House.

275

Truman has just decorated Eisenhower, who will be his successor.

April 12, 1945: Truman is sworn in as President. His wife is at the center.

cy of the United Nations. I said that was all right so long as the facilities were shared between Britain and the United States. There was nothing in it if they were made common to everybody. A man might propose marriage to a young lady, but it was not much use if he were told that she would always be a sister to him. I wanted, under whatever form or cloak, a continuation of the existing war-time system of reciprocal facilities between Britain and the United States about bases and fuelling points.

The President seemed in full accord with this, if it could be presented in a suitable fashion and did not appear to take crudely the form of a military alliance *à deux*. These last were not his words, but give the impression I got of his mind. Encouraged by this, I went on with my long-cherished idea of keeping the organisation of the Combined Chiefs of Staff in being, at any rate until the world calmed down after the great storm and until there was a world structure of such proved strength and capacity that we could safely confide ourselves to it.

The President was replying to this in an encouraging way when we were interrupted by his officers reminding him that he must now start off to see Marshal Stalin. He was good enough to say that this had been the most enjoyable luncheon he had had for many years, and how earnestly he hoped the relations I had had with President Roosevelt would be continued between him and me. He invited personal friendship and comradeship, and used many expressions at intervals in our discussion which I could not easily hear unmoved. I felt that here was a man of exceptional character and ability, with an outlook exactly along the line of Anglo-American relations as they had developed, simple and direct methods of speech, and a great deal of self-confidence and resolution.

Britain was a smaller Power than the United States, but she had much to give. Why should not an American battleship calling at Gibraltar be able to get the torpedoes to fit her tubes and the shells to fit her guns? Why should we not share facilities for defence all over the world? We could add 50 per cent. to the mobility of the American fleet.

Mr. Truman replied that all these sentiments were very near his own heart. Any plan would have to be fitted in, in some way, with the poli-

RIBBENTROP

"He told me: 'Ah, England may be very clever, but this time she will not bring the world against Germany'."

One day in 1937 I had a meeting with Herr von Ribbentrop, German Ambassador to Britain. In one of my fortnightly articles I had noted that he had been misrepresented in some speech he had made. I had of course met him several times in society. He now asked me whether I would come to see him and have a talk. He received me in the large upstairs room at the German Embassy. We had a conversation lasting for more than two hours. Ribbentrop was most polite, and we ranged over the European scene, both in respect of armaments and policy. The gist of his statement to me was that Germany sought the friendship of England (on the Continent we are still often called "England"). He said he could have been Foreign Minister of Germany, but he had asked Hitler to let him come over to London in order to make the full case for an Anglo-German entente or even alliance. Germany would stand guard for the British Empire in all its greatness and extent. They might ask for the return of the German colonies, but this was evidently not cardinal. What was required was that Britain should give Germany a free hand in the East of Europe.

She must have her Lebensraum, or living-space, for her increasing population. Therefore Poland and the Danzig Corridor must be absorbed. White Russia and the Ukraine were indispensable to the future life of the German Reich of some seventy million souls. Nothing less would suffice. All that was asked of the British Commonwealth and Empire was not to interfere. There was a large map on the wall, and the Ambassador several times led me to it to illustrate his projects.

After hearing all this I said at once that I was sure the British Government would not agree to give Germany a free hand in Eastern Europe. It was true we were on bad terms with Soviet Russia and that we hated Communism as much as Hitler did, but he might be sure that even if France were safeguarded Great Britain would never disinterest herself in the fortunes of the Continent to an extent which would enable Germany to gain the domination of Central and Eastern Europe. We were actually standing before the map when I said this. Ribbentrop turned abruptly away. He then said, "In that case, war is inevitable. There is no way out. The Fuehrer is resolved. Nothing will stop him and nothing will stop us." We then returned to our chairs. I was only a private Member of Parliament, but of some prominence. I thought it right to say to the German Ambassador—in fact, I remember the words well, "When you talk of war, which no doubt would be general war, you must not underrate England. She is a curious country, and few foreigners can understand her mind. Do not judge by the attitude of the present Administration. Once a great cause is presented to the people all kinds of unexpected actions might be taken by this very Government and by the British nation." And I repeated, "Do not underrate England. She is very clever. If you plunge us all into another Great War she will bring the whole

Joachim von Ribbentrop *was born on April 30, 1893, in Wesel, Germany, to a family of officers. He spent a few years in Canada. He fought in World War I, and then started a career as an international travelling salesman. An employee of the champagne vintner Henkel, he married Henkel's daughter. He joined the National Socialist Party only in 1932. Thanks to his knowledge of the Anglo-Saxon world, Hitler appointed him ambassador to London from August 1936 until February 4, 1938, when he became minister of Foreign Affairs. His profound anti-British feelings were instrumental in convincing Hitler that Britain would not risk a war. He signed the Steel Pact with Italy (May 22, 1939) and scored a personal success with the German-Soviet Non-Aggression Pact (August 23, 1939). Later, though, he favoured the attack on the USSR, opening a second, immense front, and he did not try to prevent the involvement of the United States in the conflict. He eventually lost Hitler's esteem. Captured by the Allies, he was tried and hanged in Nuremberg on October 16, 1946.*

world against you, like last time." At this the Ambassador rose in heat and said, "Ah, England may be very clever, but this time she will not bring the world against Germany." We turned the conversation on to easier lines, and nothing more of note occurred. The incident however remains in my memory, and as I reported it at the time to the Foreign Office I feel it right to put it on record.

When he was on trial for his life by the conquerors Ribbentrop gave a distorted version of this conversation and claimed that I should be summoned as a witness. What I have set down about it is what I should have said had I been called.

Herr von Ribbentrop was at this time about to leave London to take up his duties as Foreign Secretary in Germany. Mr. Chamberlain gave a farewell luncheon in his honour at No. 10 Downing Street. My wife and I accepted the Prime Minister's invitation to attend. There were perhaps sixteen people present. My wife sat next to Sir Alexander Cadogan, near one end of the table. About half-way through the meal a Foreign Office mes-

senger brought him an envelope. He opened it and was absorbed in the contents. Then he got up, walked round to where the Prime Minister was sitting, and gave him the message. Although Cadogan's demeanour would not have indicated that anything had happened, I could not help noticing the Prime Minister's evident preoccupation. Presently Cadogan came back with the paper and resumed his seat. Later I was told its contents. It said that Hitler had invaded Austria and that the German mechanised forces were advancing fast upon Vienna. The meal proceeded without the slightest interruption, but quite soon Mrs. Chamberlain, who had received some signal from her husband, got up, saying, "Let us *all* have coffee in the drawing-room." We trooped in there, and it was evident to me and perhaps to some others that Mr. and Mrs. Chamberlain wished to bring the proceedings to an end. A kind of general restlessness pervaded the company, and everyone stood about ready to say good-bye to the guests of honour.

However, Herr von Ribbentrop and his wife did not seem at all conscious of this atmosphere. On the contrary,

Nuremberg, September 11, 1938: Ribbentrop, at the center, during an SS parade.

Ribbentrop shortly after the outbreak of World War II.

279

August 1940: in the park of his castle at Fusch, Ribbentrop follows the explanation of a Luftwaffe general on a map of Europe.

May 1, 1942: a moment of family life during the war.

April 1940: Hitler and Ribbentrop walk beside the railroad line by which they arrived at the western front for an inspection.

they tarried for nearly half an hour engaging their host and hostess in voluble conversation. At one moment I came in contact with Frau von Ribbentrop, and in a valedictory vein I said, "I hope England and Germany will preserve their friendship." "Be careful you don't spoil it," was her graceful rejoinder. I am sure they both knew perfectly well what had happened, but thought it was a good manœuvre to keep the Prime Minister away from his work and the telephone. At length Mr. Chamberlain said to the Ambassador, "I am sorry I have to go now to attend to urgent business," and without more ado he left the room. The Ribbentrops lingered on, so that most of us made our excuses and our way home. Eventually I suppose they left. This was the last time I saw Herr von Ribbentrop before he was hanged.

HESS

On Sunday, May 11, I was spending the week-end at Ditchley. During the evening news kept coming in of the heavy air raid on London of the night before. There was nothing I could do about it, so I watched the Marx Brothers in a comic film which my hosts had arranged. I went out twice to inquire about the damage, and heard it was bad. The merry film clacked on, and I was glad of the diversion. Presently a secretary told me that somebody wanted to speak to me on the telephone on behalf of the Duke of Hamilton. The Duke was a personal friend of mine, and was commanding a fighter-sector in the East of Scotland, but I could not think of any business he might have with me which could not wait till the morning. However, the caller pressed to speak with me, saying the matter was one of urgent Cabinet importance. I asked Mr. Bracken to hear what he had to say. After a few minutes Mr. Bracken told me that the Duke said he had an amazing piece of information to report. I therefore sent for him. On arrival he told me that a German pris-

oner whom he had interviewed alone said he was Rudolf Hess. "Hess in Scotland!" I thought this was fantastic. The report however was true.

Piloting his own plane and dressed as a flight-lieutenant of the Luftwaffe, he had flown from Augsburg and baled out. At first he gave his name as "Horn", and it was not till after his reception at a military hospital near Glasgow, where he had been brought for minor injuries caused by his drop, that it was learned who he was. He was soon removed by various stages to the Tower, and thence to other places of captivity in this country, and remained here till October 6, 1945, when in the cells of Nuremberg he rejoined such of his colleagues as had survived the war and were being tried for their lives by the conquerors.

I never attached any serious importance to this escapade. I knew it had no relation to the march of events. Throughout Britain, the United States, Russia and above all Germany, there was a profound sensation, and books have been written about it all. I shall merely set down here what I believe to be the true story.

Rudolf Hess was a good-looking, youngish man to whom Hitler took a fancy, and who became an intimate member of his personal staff. He worshipped the Fuehrer, and felt passionately about the world issue at stake. He dined at Hitler's table, often alone or with two or three. He knew and was capable of understanding Hitler's inner mind—his hatred of Soviet Russia, his lust to destroy Bolshevism, his admiration for Britain and earnest wish to be friends with the British Empire, his contempt for most other countries. No one knew Hitler better or saw him more often in his unguarded moments. With the coming of actual war there was a change. Hitler's meal-time company grew

Rudolf Hess *was born on April 26, 1894, in Alexandria, Egypt. His father was a German merchant who had moved to Egypt. He took part in World War I as an airman, and joined the National Socialist Party in June 1920. He had a central role in Hitler's putsch of 1923, and was incarcerated with him. He also helped in the writing of Mein Kampf. Hitler appointed him Personal Secretary (1925), Representative, and Deputy Fuehrer (1933), and second in succession after Göering (1939). On May 10, 1941, he climbed into his personal plane and left for Scotland, where he parachuted and was captured. Much has been said about what might have led him to this action (the main hypothesis is that he wanted to propose peace as a form of anti-Soviet pact), but ultimately his decision may have been prompted by his precarious mental health. He received a life sentence at Nuremberg (1946), and spent the rest of his life in Spandau Prison in Berlin. In spite of numerous controversies and initiatives (even international ones) to free him, especially after 1968, he remained there until his death in 1987.*

could get at the heart of Britain and make its King believe how Hitler felt towards her, the malign forces that now ruled in this ill-starred island and had brought so many needless miseries upon it would be swept away. How could Britain survive? France was gone. The U-boats would soon destroy all sea communications; the German air attack would overpower British industry and beat down British cities.

But to whom should he turn? There was the Duke of Hamilton who was known to the son of his political adviser, Haushofer. He knew also that the Duke of Hamilton was Lord Steward. A personage like that would probably be dining every night with the King and have his private ear. Here was a channel of direct access.

"It seemed," said a German Press notice a few days later, "that Party Member Hess lived in a state of hallucination, as a result of which he felt he would bring about an understanding be-

Hess in the Landsberg fortress, where he was incarcerated after the putsch of 1923; although he managed to escape to Austria, Hess gave himself up in order to share jail term with Hitler; during that period, he served as a secretary in the writing of Mein Kampf.

perforce. Generals, admirals, diplomats, high functionaries, were admitted from time to time to this select circle of arbitrary power. The Deputy Fuehrer found himself in eclipse. What were party demonstrations now? This was a time for deeds, not for antics.

We must discount to some extent the merits of his action by a certain strain of jealousy which affected his nature at finding that under war conditions he no longer played his old part of friendly confidant with the beloved Fuehrer. Here, he felt, are all these generals and others who must be admitted to the Fuehrer's intimacy, and crowd his table. They have their parts to play. But I, Rudolf, by a deed of superb devotion will surpass them all and bring to my Fuehrer a greater treasure and easement than all of them put together. I will go and make peace with Britain. My life is nothing. How glad I am to have a life to cast away for such a hope! Such moods, however naïve, were certainly neither wicked nor squalid.

Hess's idea of the European scene was that England had been wrested from her true interests and policy of friendship with Germany, and above all from alliance against Bolshevism, by the war-mongers, of whom Churchill was the superficial manifestation. If only he, Rudolf,

tween England and Germany.... The National Socialist Party regrets that this idealist fell a victim to his hallucination. This however will have no effect on the continuance of the war which has been forced on Germany." For Hitler the event was embarrassing. It was as if my trusted colleague the Foreign Secretary, who was only a little younger than Hess, had parachuted from a stolen Spitfire into the

Hess, Hitler, and a secretary in the Berchtesgaden residence; the Fuehrer is signing letters and sending out photographs dedicated to his admirers.

grounds of Berchtesgaden. The Nazis no doubt found some relief in arresting Hess's adjutants.

Hess's own explanations to the doctors were hardly more illuminating. On May 22 his doctor reported as follows: "He said he was horrified at the heavy air raids on London in 1940, and loathed the thought of killing young children and their mothers. This feeling was intensified when he contemplated his own wife and son, and led to the idea of flying to Britain and arranging peace with the large anti-war faction which he thought existed in this country. He stressed that personal advantage played no part in this scheme—it was an increasing idealistic urge."

"It was with such thoughts in his mind that he was impressed on hearing Karl Haushofer express similar sentiments, and mention the Duke of Hamilton as a person of common sense, who must be horrified at this senseless slaughter. Haushofer had also remarked that he had seen Hess on three occasions in a dream piloting an aeroplane he knew not where. Hess took these remarks, coming from such a man, as a message to fly to this country as an emissary of peace, to seek the Duke of Hamilton, who would conduct him to King George. The British Government would be thrown out of office and a party desiring peace installed in its place. He was insistent that he would have no

dealings with that 'clique'—the ruling Administration—who would do all in their power to thwart him, but he was very vague as to what statesmen would replace them, and seemed to be extremely ill-informed as to the names and standing of our politicians. . . . He described how he approached Willi Messerschmidt and obtained facilities for long-distance flying inside Germany in training for the event, and how when he was prepared he set out on his voyage. He maintained that there were no confederates, and that he showed considerable skill in arranging his journey, working out the route himself, and flying with an accuracy which enabled him to land only some ten miles from his destination, Dungavel."

The Cabinet invited Lord Simon to interview him, and on June 10 a meeting took place. "When the Fuehrer, " said Hess, "had come to the conclusion that common sense could not prevail in England, he acted just according to the rule of conduct of Admiral Lord Fisher: 'Moderation in war is folly. If you strike, strike hard and wherever you can. But I can confirm that it was indeed always difficult for the Fuehrer to give orders for these [air and U-boat] attacks. It pained him deeply. He was constantly in full sympathy with the English people who were victims of this method of

May 1941: the wreck of Hess's Messerschmidt BF-110, which crashed to the ground after he parachuted.

Hess with his son, Wolf Rudiger, shortly before his "mission" to Great Britain.

An undated photograph
of Hess in Spandau
prison (Berlin), where
he was incarcerated
from 1946 until his
death in 1987.

Hess, seated between
Goering and Ribbentrop,
at the 1948 Nuremberg
trials, where he received
a life sentence.

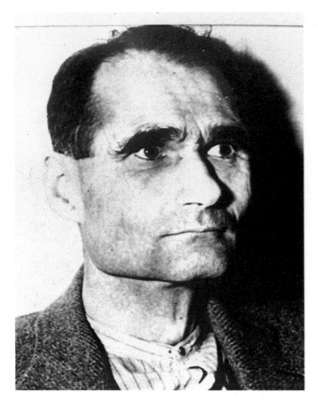

you know, there is a good deal of courage in this country, and we are not very fond of threats!"

Considering how closely Hess was knit to Hitler, it is surprising that he did not know of, or that if he knew he did not disclose, the impending attack on Russia, for which such vast preparations were being made. The Soviet Government were deeply intrigued by the Hess episode, and they wove many distorted theories around it. Three years later when I was in Moscow on my second visit I realised the fascination which this topic had for Stalin. He asked me at the dinner table what was the truth about the Hess mission. I said shortly what I have written here. I had the feeling that he believed there had been some deep negotiation or plot for Germany and Britain to act together in the invasion of Russia which had miscarried. Remembering what a wise man he is, I was surprised to find him silly on this point. When the interpreter made it plain that he did not believe what I said, I replied through my interpreter, "When I make a statement of facts within my knowledge I expect it to be accepted." Stalin received this somewhat abrupt response with a genial grin. "There are lots of things that happen even here in Russia which our Secret Service do not necessarily tell me about." I let it go at that.

waging war. . . . He said that even if victorious one should not impose any severe conditions on a country with which it was desired to come to an agreement." Then, the keynote for Hess: "I thought that if England once knew of this fact if might be possible that England on her part would be ready for agreement." If only England knew how kind Hitler really was, surely she would meet his wishes!

Much learned medical investigation has been devoted to Hess's mental state. Certainly he was a neurotic, a split soul seeking peace in the pursuit of power and position and in the worship of a leader. But he was more than a medical case. He believed passionately in his vision of Hitler's mind. If only England could share it too, how much suffering could be saved and how easy it would be to agree! A free hand for Germany in Europe and for Britain in her own Empire! Other minor conditions were the return of the German colonies, the evacuation of Iraq, and an armistice and peace with Italy. As it was, England's position was hopeless. If she did not agree to these conditions "sooner or later the day will come when she will be forced to accede to them". To this Lord Simon replied: "I do not think that that particular argument will be very good for the British Cabinet, because,

Reflecting upon the whole of this story, I am glad not to be responsible for the way in which Hess has been and is being treated. Whatever may be the moral guilt of a German who stood near to Hitler, Hess had, in my view, atoned for this by his completely devoted and frantic deed of lunatic benevolence. He came to us of his own free will, and, though without authority, had something of the quality of an envoy. He was a medical and not a criminal case, and should be so regarded.

January 9, 1944: the Verona trials against the "traitors" of July 25, 1943. From the left: Emilio De Bono, Luciano Gottardi, Ciano, Carlo Pareschi, Giovanni Marinelli, and Tullio Cianetti, the only one who was not sentenced to death.

Verona, January 11, 1944: a priest administers the Extreme Unction to Galeazzo Ciano, who had just been executed.

me that my children were in imminent danger. After they had pledged themselves to take me to Spain, they deported me and my family, against my will, to Bavaria. Now, I have been nearly three months in the prisons of Verona, abandoned to the barbarous treatment of the S.S. My end is near, and I have been told that in a few days my death will be decided, which to me will be no more nor less [than] a release from this daily martyrdom. And I prefer death to witnessing the shame and irreparable damage of an Italy which has been under Hun domination.

The crime which I am now about to expiate is that of having witnessed and been disgusted by the cold, cruel, and cynical preparation for this war by Hitler and the Germans. I was the only foreigner to see at close quarters this loathsome clique of bandits preparing to plunge the world into a bloody war. Now, in accordance with gangster rule, they are planning to suppress a dangerous witness. But they have miscalculated, for already a long time ago I put a diary of mine and various documents in a safe place, which will prove, more than I myself could, the crimes committed by those people with whom later that tragic and vile puppet Mussolini associated himself through his vanity and disregard of moral values.

I have made arrangements that as soon as possible after my death these documents, of the existence of which Sir Percy Loraine was aware at the time of his Mission in Rome, should be put at the disposal of the Allied Press.

Perhaps what I am offering you to-day is but little, but that and my life are all I can offer to the cause of liberty and justice, in the triumph of which I fanatically believe.

This testimony of mine should be brought to light so that the world may know, may hate and may remember, and that those who will have to judge the future should not be ignorant of the fact that the misfortune of Italy was not the fault of her people, but due to the shameful behaviour of one man.

Yours sincerely,
G. Ciano

It is always interesting to see the reactions of the other side. The reader is already acquainted with Count Ciano, and should not be too hard on weak people who follow easily into wrong courses the temptations of affluence and office. Those who have successfully resisted all such temptations should form the tribunal. When Ciano faced the firing squad he paid his debts to the full. Villains are made of a different texture. We must not however imagine that it is better to be a rare villain than a Ciano or one of the multitudinous potential Cianos.

EDEN

Eden as an army captain during World War I, in 1918.

Rome, February 25, 1934: Foreign Secretary Eden at the exhibition of the Fascist Revolution.

Leaving the exhibition in the company of Dino Alfieri (on his left), who at the time was president of the Authors' and Publishers' Association.

Anthony Eden had for nearly ten years devoted himself almost entirely to the study of foreign affairs. Taken from Eton at eighteen to the World War, he had served for four years with distinction in the 60th Rifles through many of the bloodiest battles, and risen to the position of Brigade-Major, with the Military Cross. Shortly after entering the House of Commons in 1925, he became Parliamentary Private Secretary to Austen Chamberlain at the Foreign Office during Mr. Baldwin's second Administration. In the MacDonald-Baldwin Coalition of 1931 he was appointed Under-Secretary of State and served under the new Foreign Secretary, Sir John Simon. The duties of an Under-Secretary are often changed, but his responsibilities are always limited. He has to serve his chief in carrying out the policy settled in the Cabinet, of which he is not a member and to which he has no access. Only in an extreme case where conscience and honour are involved is he justified in carrying any difference about foreign policy to the point of public controversy or resignation.

Eden had however during all these years obtained a wide view of the foreign scene, and he was intimately acquainted with the life and thought of the great department upon which so much depends. Sir John Simon's conduct of foreign affairs was not in 1935 viewed with favour either by the Opposition or in influential circles of the Conservative Party. Eden, with all his knowledge and exceptional gifts, began therefore to acquire prominence. For this reason, after becoming Lord Privy Seal at the end of 1934, he had retained by the desire of the Cabinet an informal but close association with the Foreign Office, and thus had been invited to accompany his former chief, Sir John Simon, on the inopportune, but not unfruitful, visit to Berlin. The Foreign Secretary returned to London after the interview with Hitler, bringing with him the important news, already mentioned, that, according to Hitler, Germany *had now gained air parity with Britain*. Eden was sent on to Moscow, where he established contacts with Stalin which were to be revived with advantage after some years. On the homeward journey his aeroplane ran into a severe and prolonged

Anthony Eden, *was born on June 12, 1897, at Windlestone in Durham, to an excellent family. He studied at Eton and Oxford. In 1923, he was elected tp the Parliment as a candidate of the Conservative Party, and he collaborated closely with Foreign Secretary Austen Chamberlain (1926-1929). A skillful diplomat, he was Foreign Under-Secretary (1931-1933), and Minister for the League of Nations (1934). A staunch opposer of dictatorships, he became Foreign Secretary in December 1935, but resigned in February 1938 after economic sanctions against Italy failed to produce any result. At the outbreak of World War II, Neville Chamberlain appointed him Dominion Secretary (1939), while Churchill assigned him again to the Foreign Office (1940-1945). Designated as Churchill's successor, with the victory of the Conservative Party he served again as Foreign Secretary (1951-1955) and as Prime Minister from April 1955. In November 1956, he promoted an Anglo-French expedition to Egypt to impede the nationalisation of the Suez Sanal, but Soviet and American opposition caused the initiative to fail. Eden resigned in 1957. He was created Earl of Avon in July 1961, and died at Alvediston, Wiltshire, in 1977.*

storm, and when after a dangerous flight they landed he was almost in a state of collapse. The doctors declared that he was not fit to go with Simon to the Stresa Conference, and indeed for several months he was an invalid.

In spite of my differences with the Government, I was in close sympathy with their Foreign Secretary. He seemed to me the most resolute and courageous figure in the Administration, and although as a Private Secretary and later as an Under-Secretary of State in the Foreign Office he had had to adapt himself to many things I had attacked and still condemn, I felt sure his heart was in the right place and that he had the root of the matter in him. For his part, he made a point of inviting me to Foreign Office functions, and we corresponded freely. There was of course no impropriety in this practice, and Mr. Eden held to the well-established precedent whereby the Foreign Secretary is accustomed to keep in contact with the prominent political figures of the day on all broad international issues.

Late in the night of February 20 a telephone message reached me as I sat in my old room at Chartwell (as I often sit now) that Eden had resigned. I must confess that my heart sank, and for a while the dark waters of despair overwhelmed me. In a long life I have had many ups and downs. During all the war soon to come and in its darkest times I never had any trouble in sleeping. In the crisis of 1940, when so much responsibility lay upon me, and also at many very anxious, awkward moments in the following five years, I could always flop into bed and go to sleep after the day's work was done—subject of course to any emergency call. I slept sound and awoke refreshed, and had no feelings except appetite to grapple with whatever the morning's boxes might bring. But now on this night of February 20, 1938, and on this occasion only, sleep deserted me. From midnight till dawn I lay in my bed consumed by emotions of sorrow and fear. There seemed one strong young figure standing up against long, dismal, drawling tides of drift and surrender, of wrong measurements and feeble impulses. My conduct of affairs would have been different from his in various ways; but he seemed to me at this moment to embody the life-hope of the British nation, the grand old British race that had done so much for men, and had yet some more to give. Now he was gone. I watched the daylight slowly creep in through the windows, and saw before me in mental gaze the vision of Death.

MOLOTOV

"I have never seen a human being who more perfectly represented the modern conception of a robot."

The figure whom Stalin had now moved to the pulpit of Soviet foreign policy deserves some description, not available to the British or French Governments at the time. Vyacheslav Molotov was a man of outstanding ability and cold-blooded ruthlessness. He had survived the fearful hazards and ordeals to which all the Bolshevik leaders had been subjected in the years of triumphant revolution. He had lived and thrived in a society where ever-varying intrigue was accompanied by the constant menace of personal liquidation. His cannon-ball head, black moustache, and comprehending eyes, his slab face, his verbal adroitness and imperturbable demeanour, were appropriate manifestations of his qualities and skill. He was above all men fitted to be the agent and instrument of the policy of an incalculable machine. I have only met him on equal terms, in parleys where sometimes a strain of humour appeared, or at banquets where he genially proposed a long succession of conventional and meaningless toasts. I have

never seen a human being who more perfectly represented the modern conception of a robot. And yet with all this there was an apparently reasonable and keenly-polished diplomatist. What he was to his inferiors I cannot tell. What he was to the Japanese Ambassador during the years when after the Teheran Conference Stalin had promised to attack Japan once the German Army was beaten can be deduced from his recorded conversations. One delicate, searching, awkward interview after another was conducted with perfect poise, impenetrable purpose, and bland, official correctitude. Never a chink was opened. Never a needless jar was made. His smile of Siberian winter, his carefully-measured and often wise words, his affable demeanour, combined to make him the perfect agent of Soviet policy in a deadly world.

Correspondence with him upon disputed matters was always useless, and, if pushed far, ended in lies and insults, of which this work will presently contain some examples. Only once did I seem to get a natural, human reaction. This was in the spring of 1942, when he alighted in Britain on his way back from the United States. We had signed the Anglo-Soviet Treaty, and he was about to make his dangerous flight home. At the garden gate of Downing Street, which we used for secrecy, I gripped his arm and we looked each other in the face. Suddenly he appeared deeply moved. Inside the image there appeared the man. He responded with an equal pressure. Silently we wrung each other's hands. But then we were all together, and it was life or death for the lot. Havoc and ruin had been around him all his days, either impending on himself or dealt by him to others. Certainly in Molotov the Soviet machine had found a capable and in many ways a characteristic repre-

---

Vyacheslav Mikhailovich Scriabin, *a.k.a.* **Molotov** *(from molot, hammer), was born on March 9, 1890, in Kukarka, near Vologda, Russia. A member of the composer Scriabin's family, he joined the Bolshevik Party at 16. Exiled and deported several times, he started his collaboration with Stalin even before the Revolution of October 1917, in which he played an important role. A member of the Central Committee (1921) and of the Politburo (1926), Molotov was always loyal to Stalin. He was head of the Council of People's Commissars from 1930 until 1941. On May 5, 1939, he was appointed Foreign Minister, and in the attempt to bring about a rapprochement with Nazi Germany, he signed the German-Soviet Non-Aggression Pact (August 23, 1939). He was an advocate of the Cold War, and although he was removed from his post as Foreign Secretary, he was still second only to Stalin in the Soviet hierarchy. After the dictator's death (1953), he was not able to assume the premiership and served again as Foreign Secretary. He was forced to leave office in 1956, during the Khrushchev era. He was Ambassador to Mongolia (1957-1960) and the Soviet delegate at the International Atomic Energy Agency (1960-1961). He died on November 8, 1986.*

sentative—always the faithful Party man and Communist disciple. How glad I am at the end of my life not to have had to endure the stresses which he has suffered; better never be born. In the conduct of foreign affairs Mazarin, Talleyrand, Metternich, would welcome him to their company, if there be another world to which Bolsheviks allow themselves to go.

Molotov did not arrive until May 20, and formal discussions began the following morning. On that day and at the two following meetings the Russians maintained their original position, and even brought up specifically the question of agreeing to the Russian occupation of Eastern Poland. This was rejected as in-

Moscow, May 31, 1939: Molotov, appointed Foreign Minister only a few days before, speaks from the rostrum of the Supreme Soviet.

Berlin, November 1940: Molotov talks to Hitler through an interpreter, Gustav Hilger.

compatible with the Anglo-Polish Agreement of August 1939. Molotov also put forward a case for the recognition in a secret agreement of Russia's claims on Roumania. This also was contrary to our understanding with the United States. The conversations at the Foreign Office, which Mr. Eden conducted, though most friendly, therefore moved towards a deadlock.

Apart from the question of the treaty, Molotov had come to London to learn our views upon the opening of a Second Front. On the morning of May 22 therefore I had a formal conversation with him.

Our Russian guests had expressed the wish to be lodged in the country outside London during their stay, and I therefore placed Chequers at their disposal. I remained meanwhile at the Storey's Gate Annexe. However, I went down for two nights to Chequers. Here I had the advantage of having long private talks with Molotov and Ambassador Maisky, who was the best of interpreters, translating quickly and easily, and possessing a wide knowledge of affairs.

With the aid of good maps I tried to explain what we were doing, and the limitations and peculiar characteristics in the war capacity of an island Power. I also went at length into the technique of amphibious operations, and described the perils and difficulties of maintaining our life-line across the Atlantic in the face of U-boat attack. I think Molotov was impressed with all this, and realised that our problem was utterly different from that of a vast land Power. At any rate, we got closer together than at any other time.

The inveterate suspicion with which the Russians regarded foreigners was shown by some remarkable incidents during Molotov's stay at Chequers. On arrival they had asked at once for keys to all the bedrooms. These were provided with some difficulty, and thereafter our guests always kept their doors locked. When the staff at Chequers succeeded in getting in to make the beds they were disturbed to find pistols under the pillows. The three chief members of the mission were attended not only by

Soviet Foreign Minister Molotov shakes hands with his British counterpart, Eden, at Saki airport before the Yalta Conference (February 1945).

Moscow, April 1945: Tito, Stalin, and Molotov at the Kremlin to sign the pact of mutual assistance between the Soviet Union and Yugoslavia.

their own police officers, but by two women who looked after their clothes and tidied their rooms. When the Soviet envoys were absent in London these women kept constant guard over their masters' rooms, only coming down one at a time for their meals. We may claim, however, that presently they thawed a little, and even chatted in broken French and signs with the household staff.

Extraordinary precautions were taken for Molotov's personal safety. His room had been thoroughly searched by his police officers, every cupboard and piece of furniture and the walls and floors being meticulously examined by practised eyes. The bed was the object of particular attention; the mattresses were all prodded in case of infernal machines, and the sheets and blankets were rearranged by the Russians so as to leave an opening in the middle of the bed out of which the occupant could spring at a moment's notice, instead of being tucked in. At night a revolver was laid out beside his dressing-gown and his dispatch case. It is always right, especially in time of war, to take precautions against danger, but every effort should be made to measure its reality. The simplest test is to ask oneself whether the other side have any interest in killing the person concerned. For myself, when I visited Moscow I put complete trust in Russian hospitality.

When Molotov returned to London after his American visit he was naturally full of plans for creating a Second Front by a cross-Channel operation in 1942. We ourselves were still actively studying this in conjunction with the American Staff, and nothing but difficulties had as yet emerged. There could be no harm in a public statement, which might make the Germans apprehensive and consequently hold as many of their troops in the West as possible. We therefore agreed with Molotov to the issue of a communiqué, which was published on June 11, containing the following sentence: "In the course of the conversations full understanding was reached with regard to the urgent tasks of creating a Second Front in Europe in 1942."

I felt it above all important that in this effort to mislead the enemy we should not mislead our Ally. At the time of drafting the communiqué therefore I handed Molotov personally in the Cabinet Room and in the presence of some of my colleagues an *aide-mémoire* which made it clear that while we were trying our best to make plans we were not committed to action and that we could give no promise. When subsequent reproaches were made by the Soviet Government, and when Stalin himself raised the point personally with me, we always produced the *aide-mémoire* and pointed to the words *"We can therefore give no promise"*.

AIDE-MÉMOIRE

We are making preparations for a landing on the Continent in August or September 1942. As already

February 3, 1945: Molotov greets Churchill at Saki airport before the Yalta Conference.

In Ulan Bator in 1959: although disgraced after Stalin's death, Molotov was not entirely deprived of power, and was appointed Ambassador to Mongolia (1957-1960).

explained, the main limiting factor to the size of the landing force is the availability of special landing-craft. Clearly however it would not further either the Russian cause or that of the Allies as a whole if, for the sake of action at any price, we embarked on some operation which ended in disaster and gave the enemy an opportunity for glorification at our discomfiture. It is impossible to say in advance whether the situation will be such as to make this operation feasible when the time comes. *We can therefore give no promise in the matter*, but provided that it appears sound and sensible we shall not hesitate to put our plans into effect.

Molotov sailed off into the air on his somewhat dangerous homeward flight, apparently well satisfied with the results of his mission. Certainly an atmosphere of friendliness had been created between us. He had been deeply interested in his visit to Washington. There was the Twenty Years Anglo-Russian Treaty, upon which high hopes were at that time set by all.

ROMMEL

"His ardour and daring inflicted grievous disasters upon us, but he deserves the salute which I made him."

A new figure sprang upon the world stage— a German warrior who will hold his place in their military annals. Erwin Rommel was born at Heidenheim, in Wurtemberg, in November 1891. He was a delicate boy, and was educated at home till, at the age of nine, he joined the local Government school, of which his father was headmaster. In 1910 he was an officer cadet in the Wurtemberg Regiment. When he did his training at the military school at Danzig his instructors reported that he was physically small, but strong. Mentally he was not remarkable. He fought in the First World War in the Argonne, in Roumania, and in Italy, being twice wounded and awarded the highest classes of the Iron Cross and of the order Pour le Mérite. Between the two wars he served as a regimental officer and on the Staff. On the outbreak of the Second World War he was appointed commandant of the Fuehrer's field headquarters in the Polish campaign, and was then given command of the 7th Panzer Division of the XVth Corps. This division, nicknamed "the Phantoms", formed the spearhead of the German breakthrough across the Meuse. He narrowly escaped capture when the British counter-attacked at Arras on May 21, 1940. Thereafter he led his division through La Bassée towards Lille. If this thrust had had a little more success, or perhaps not been restrained by orders from the High Command, it might have cut off a large part of British Army, including the 3rd Division, commanded by General Montgomery. His was the spearhead which crossed the Somme and advanced on the Seine in the direction of Rouen, rolling up the French left wing and capturing numerous French and British forces around St. Valery. His division was the first to reach the Channel, and entered Cherbourg just after our final evacuation, where Rommel took the surrender of the port and 30,000 French prisoners.

These many services and distinctions led to his appointment early in 1941 to command the

Erwin Rommel *was born on November 15, 1891, in Heidenheim, in Württemberg. He attended the military academy in Danzig, and during World War I received Germany's highest military decoration. After the war, he left the army and joined the National Socialist Party. When Hitler rose to power (1933), he re-entered the army with the rank of major. He conducted himself brilliantly during the French campaign of 1940, and gained great popularity. Hitler appointed him commander of the Afrika Korps (February 1941), and in February 1942 he launched the offensive that led to El Alamein. Promoted to marshal, in October he was forced to retreat. He led the German forces in northern Italy (March-November 1943) and, from January 1944, in the sector between Holland and the Loire. Realizing that Germany would not be able to win the war, he became involved in a plot against Hitler, in which he did not take active part because of an injury (July 17, 1944). Hitler ordered him to commit suicide, which he did on October 14, 1944, in Ulm, and then gave him the honor of a solemn state funeral.*

German troops sent to Libya. On February 12 he arrived with his personal staff at Tripoli to campaign with the ally against whom he had formerly won distinction. At that time Italian hopes were limited to holding Tripolitania, and Rommel took charge of the growing German contingent under Italian command. He strove immediately to enforce an offensive campaign. When early in April the Italian Commander-in-Chief tried to persuade him that the German Afrika Korps should not advance without his permission Rommel protested that "as German general he had to issue orders in accordance with what the situation demanded". Any reservations because of the supply problem were, he declared, "unfounded". He demanded and obtained complete freedom of action.

Throughout the African campaign Rommel proved himself a master in handling mobile formations, especially in regrouping rapidly after an operation and following up success. He was a splendid military gambler, dominating the problems of supply and scornful of opposition. At first the German High Command, having let him loose, were astonished by his successes, and were inclined to hold him back. His ardour and daring inflicted grievous disasters upon us, but he deserves the salute which I made him—and not without some reproaches from the public—in the House of Commons in January 1942, when I said of him, "We have a very daring and skilful opponent against us, and, may I say across the havoc of war, a great general." He also deserves our respect because,

An official photograph of Rommel in May 1941, soon after he was decorated with the Savoy military order.

June 1942: Rommel and Italian General Azzi discuss the movement of troops in front of Tobruk.

although a loyal German soldier, he came to hate Hitler and all his works, and took part in the conspiracy of 1944 to rescue Germany by displacing the maniac and tyrant. For this he paid the forfeit of his life. In the sombre wars of modern democracy chivalry finds no place. Dull butcheries on a gigantic scale and mass effects overwhelm all detached sentiment. Still, I do not regret or retract the tribute I paid to Rommel, unfashionable though it was judged.

When Rommel took up his command in late January he had been displeased with the defences he found, and his energy improved them greatly. Along the coast there was a line of concrete works with all-round defence, many mines and difficult obstacles of various patterns, especially below high-water mark. Fixed guns pointed seawards, and field artillery cov-

ered the beaches. While there was no complete second line of defence, villages in rear were strongly fortified. Rommel was not content with the progress made, and had more time been left him our task would have been harder. Our opening bombardment by sea and air did not destroy many of the concrete works, but by stunning their defenders reduced their fire and also upset their Radar.

The German warning system had been completely paralysed. From Calais to Guernsey the Germans had no fewer than one hundred and twenty major pieces of Radar equipment for finding our convoys and directing the fire of their shore batteries. These were grouped in forty-seven stations. We discovered them all, and attacked them so successfully with rocket-firing aircraft that on the night before D Day not one in six

July 2, 1941: Rommel
speaks to a group of
German and Italian sol-
diers on the Egyptian
front.

was working. The serviceable ones were deceived by the device of tin-foil strips known as "Window", which simulated a convoy heading east of Fécamp, and they thus failed to detect the real landings. One piece of equipment near Caen managed to keep going and discovered the approach of the British force, but its reports were ignored by the plotting centre as they were not corroborated by any of the other stations. Nor was this the only menace which was overcome. Encouraged by their success two years before in concealing the passage up the Channel of the *Scharnhorst* and *Gneisenau*, the enemy had built many more jamming stations for thwarting both the ships which directed our night fighters and the Radar beams upon which many of our forces depended for an accurate landfall. But they too were discovered, and Bomber Command made some highly concentrated raids upon them. All were obliterated, and our radio and Radar aids were secure. It may be mentioned that all the Allied effort in the radio war for D Day was British.

It is indeed remarkable that the vast, long-planned assault fell on the enemy as a surprise both in time and place. The German High Command was told that the weather would be too rough that day for amphibious operations, and had received no recent air reports of the assembly of our thousands of ships along the English shore. Early on June 5 Rommel left his headquarters to visit Hitler at Berchtesgaden, and was in Germany when the blow fell. There had been much argument about which front the Allies would attack. Rundstedt had consistently believed that our main blow would be launched across the Straits of Dover, as that was the short-

305

Rommel with Marshal Albert Kesserling in northern Africa in May 1942.

Hitler and Rommel during a meeting in the bunker at Obersalzburg.

est sea route and gave the best access to the heart of Germany. Rommel for long agreed with him. Hitler and his staff however appear to have had reports indicating that Normandy would be the principal battleground. Even after we had landed uncertainties continued. Hitler lost a whole critical day in making up his mind to release the two nearest Panzer divisions to reinforce the front. The German Intelligence Service grossly overestimated the number of divisions and the amount of suitable shipping available in England. On their showing there were ample resources for a second big landing, so Normandy

might be only a preliminary and subsidiary one. On June 19 Rommel reported to von Rundstedt, ". . .a large-scale landing is to be expected on the Channel front on both sides of Cap Gris Nez or between the Somme and Le Havre," and he repeated the warning a week later. Thus it was not until the third week in July, six weeks after D Day, that reserves from the Fifteenth Army were sent south from Pas de Calais to join the battle. Our deception measures both before and after D Day had aimed at creating this confused thinking. Their success was admirable and had far-reaching results on the battle.

ALEXANDER

"Under any heavy fire men were glad to follow exactly in his footsteps."

Alexander decorates a Polish soldier of the Eighth Army during the Italian campaign.

Sicily, August 1943: Alexander examines some old Italian rifles; on his right is General Bernard Freyburg.

Central Italy, September 9, 1944: Alexander during the advance, between general Oliver Leese (on the right) and general John Harding (on the left).

No troops in our control could reach Rangoon in time to save it. But if we could not send an army we could at any rate send a man. While the correspondence which darkens these pages was proceeding it was resolved to send General Alexander by air to the doomed capital. To save time he was to fly direct over large stretches of enemy territory. After he had been made fully acquainted with all the facts of the situation by the Chiefs of Staff and by the War Office, and a few hours before his departure, he dined at the Annexe with me and my wife. I remember the evening well, for never have I taken the responsibility for sending a general on a more forlorn hope. Alexander was, as usual, calm and good-humoured. He said he was delighted to go. In the First Great War in years of fighting as a regimental officer with the Guards Division he was reputed to bear a charmed life, and under any heavy fire men were glad to follow exactly in his footsteps. Confidence spread around him, whether as a lieutenant or in supreme command. He was the last British commander

at Dunkirk. Nothing ever disturbed or rattled him, and duty was a full satisfaction in itself, especially if it seemed perilous and hard. But all this was combined with so gay and easy a manner that the pleasure and honour of his friendship were prized by all those who enjoyed it, among whom I could count myself. For this reason I must admit that at our dinner I found it difficult to emulate his composure.

In this his first experience of independent command, though it ended in stark defeat, he showed all those qualities of military skill, imperturbability, and wise judgment that brought him later into the first rank of Allied war leaders. The road to India was barred.

Harold Rupert Alexander *was born on December 10, 1891 in County Tyrone, in Ulster. Commander of the First British Army Corps at the beginning of World War II, he brilliantly conducted the evacuation of British troops at Dunkirk (1940). Sent to Burma in the spring of 1942, he led the retreat of Anglo-Indian troops before the Japanese. He then commanded the British troops in northern Africa, alongside Commander in Chief Eisenhower, and played a crucial role in the victory at Tunis, for which he received the title Earl of Tunis. In the Italian campaign (July 1943-April 1945), he commanded the XV group of armies through a cautious yet relentless advance; he created a sensation with his proclamation to Italian partisans (November 13, 1943) inviting them to demobilise because the offensive would not end that winter. Promoted to marshal (November 1944), he commanded all operations in the Mediterranean until the end of the war. Later, he was Governor of Canada (1945-1952), and Defence Secretary under Churchill (1952-1954). He died in Slough on June 16, 1969.*

MONTGOMERY

"He accurately predicted Rommel's next attack, and explained his plans to meet it. All of which proved true and sound."

It appeared that the War Cabinet had already assembled at 11.15 p.m. on August 7 to deal with my telegrams of that day, which had just been decoded. Discussion was still proceeding upon them when a secretary came in with my new messages, stating that Gott was dead, and secondly asking that General Montgomery should be sent out at once. I have been told this was an acute moment for our friends in Downing Street. However, as I have several times observed, they had been through much and took it doggedly. They sat till nearly dawn, agreed in all essentials to what I had proposed, and gave the necessary orders about Montgomery.

When sending my message to the Cabinet telling them of Gott's death I had asked that General Eisenhower should not be told that we had proposed to give him Montgomery in place of Alexander. But this was too late: he had been told already. The further change of plan involved a consequent dislocation of a vexatious kind in the preparation of "Torch". Alexander had been chosen to command the British First Army in that great enterprise. He had already started to work with General Eisenhower. They were getting on splendidly together, as they always did. Now Alexander had been taken from him for the Middle East. Ismay was sent to convey the news and my apologies to Eisenhower for this break in continuity and disturbance of contacts which the hard necessity of war compelled. Ismay dilated upon Montgomery's brilliant qualities as a commander in the field. Montgomery arrived at Eisenhower's headquarters almost immediately, and all the civilities of a meeting of this kind between the commanders of armies of different nations woven into a single enterprise had been discharged. The very next morning, the 8th, Eisenhower had to be informed that Montgomery must fly that day to Cairo to command the Eighth Army. This task also fell to Ismay. Eisenhower was a broad-minded man, practical, serviceable, dealing with events as they came in cool selflessness. He naturally however felt disconcerted by the two changes in two days in this vital post in the vast operation confided to him. He was now to welcome a third British Commander. Can we wonder that he asked Ismay, "Are the British really taking 'Torch' seriously?" Nevertheless the death of Gott was a war fact which a good soldier understood. General Anderson was appointed to fill the vacancy, and Montgomery started for the airfield with Ismay, who thus had an hour or more to give him the background of these sudden changes.

A story—alas, not authenticated—has been

Bernard Law Montgomery *was born on November 17, 1887, in Kensington (London). The son of a Protestant pastor, he attended Sandhurst academy, and fought on the French front during World War I. He became general in 1937, and commanded the Third British Division in the French campaign (1940). From 1940 until 1942, he commanded an army corps at home, and in August 1942 he led the Eighth Army in northern Africa. He won the decisive battle against Rommel (October 23-November 3, 1942) and was named Viscount of El Alamein. He collaborated with Eisenhower in the preparation for the landings in Sicily (July 1943) and Normandy, where he commanded ground troops (June-August 1944). He liberated the Scheldt estuary (October-November 1944), the Ruhr and northern Germany (March 24-April 1945). After the war, he commanded British occupation troops in Germany (1945-1946), was made Chief of General Staff of the British Army (1945-1948), and finally became Deputy Commander of NATO Forces in Europe (1951-1958). He died in Alton, Hampshire, on March 25, 1976.*

Northern Africa, October 1942: Montgomery during an inspection at one of the El Alamein sectors a few days before the decisive battle in which he defeated Rommel.

Northern Africa, August 1942: Montgomery with his tank crew, shortly after being appointed commander of the Eighth Army.

told of this conversation. Montgomery spoke of the trials and hazards of a soldier's career. He gave his whole life to his profession, and lived long years of study and self-restraint. Presently fortune smiled, there came a gleam of success, he gained advancement, opportunity presented itself, he had a great command. He won a victory, he became world-famous, his name was on every lip. Then the luck changed. At one stroke all his life's work flashed away, perhaps through no fault of his own, and he was flung into the endless catalogue of military failures. "But," expostulated Ismay, "you ought not to take it so badly as all that. A very fine army is gathering in the Middle East. It may well be that you are not going to disaster." "What!" cried Montgomery, sitting up in the car. "What do you mean? I was talking about Rommel!"

On August 19 I paid another visit to the Desert Front. I drove with Alexander in his car out from Cairo past the Pyramids, about 130 miles through the desert to the sea at Abusir. I was cheered by all he told me. As the shadows lengthened we reached Montgomery's headquarters at Burg-el-Arab. Here the afterwards

famous caravan was drawn up amid the sanddunes by the sparkling waves. The General gave me his own wagon, divided between office and bedroom. After our long drive we all had a delicious bathe. "All the armies are bathing now at this hour all along the coast," said Montgomery as we stood in our towels. He waved his arm to the westward. Three hundred yards away about a thousand of our men were

July 1943: Montgomery follows landing operations in Sicily from shipboard.

disporting themselves on the beach. Although I knew the answer, I asked, "Why do the War Office go to the expense of sending out white bathing drawers for the troops? Surely this economy should be made." They were in fact tanned and burnt to the darkest brown everywhere except where they wore their short pants.

How fashions change! When I marched to Omdurman forty-four years before the theory was that the African sun must at all costs be kept away from the skin. The rules were strict. Special spine-pads were buttoned on to the back of all our khaki coats. It was a military offence to appear without a pith helmet. We were advised to wear thick underclothing, following Arab custom en-joined by a thousand years of experience. Yet now half-way through the twentieth century many of the white soldiers went about their daily toil hatless and naked except for the equal of a loin cloth. Apparently it did them no harm. Though the process of changing from white to bronze took several weeks and gradual application, sunstroke and heatstroke were rare. I wonder how the doctors explain all this.

After we had dressed for dinner—my zip hardly takes a minute to put on—we gathered in Montgomery's map wagon. There he gave us a masterly exposition of the situation, showing that in a few days he had firmly gripped the whole problem. He accurately predicted Rommel's next attack, and explained his plans to meet it. All of which proved true and sound. He then described his plans for taking the offensive himself. He must however have six weeks to get the Eighth Army into order. He would re-form the divisions as integral tactical units. We must wait till the new divisions had taken their place at the front and until the Sherman tanks were broken in. Then there would be three Army Corps, each under an experienced officer, whom he and Alexander knew well. Above all the artillery would be used as had never been possible before in the Desert. He spoke of the end of September. I was disappointed at the date, but even this was dependent upon Rommel. Our information showed that a blow from him was imminent. I was myself already fully informed, and was well content that he should try a wide turning movement round our Desert Flank in order to reach Cairo, and that a manœuvre battle should be fought on his communications.

At this time I thought much of Napoleon's defeat in 1814. He too was poised to strike at the communications, but the Allies marched straight on into an almost open Paris. I thought it of the highest importance that Cairo should be

September 1943: Mont-
gomery and General
Mark Clark visit Allied
positions in the region
around Salerno.

defended by every able-bodied man in uniform not required for the Eighth Army. Thus alone would the field army have full manœvring freedom and be able to take risks in letting its flank be turned before striking. It was with great pleasure that I found we were all in agreement. Although I was always impatient for offensive action on our part at the earliest moment, I welcomed the prospect of Rommel breaking his teeth upon us before our main attack was launched. But should we have time to organise the defence of Cairo? Many signs pointed to the audacious commander who faced us only a dozen miles away striking his supreme blow before the end of August. Any day indeed, my friends said, he might make his bid for contin-

ued mastery. A fortnight or three weeks' delay would be all to our good.

On August 20, we went into his sweltering mess tent, and were offered a luncheon, far more magnificent than the one I had eaten on the Scarpe. This was an August noonday in the desert. The set piece of the meal was a scalding broth of tinned New Zealand oysters, to which I could do no more than was civil. Presently Montgomery, who had left us some time before, drove up. Freyburg went out to salute him, and told him his place had been kept and that he was expected to luncheon. But "Monty", as he was already called, had, it appeared, made it a rule not to accept hospitality from any of his subordinate commanders. So he sat outside in

313

Germany, March 1945: Churchill and Montgomery, who had just liberated the Ruhr.

This 1954 photograph shows Montgomery in the room of his country house where he kept war relics and memorabilia.

his car eating an austere sandwich and drinking his lemonade with all formalities. Napoleon also might have stood aloof in the interests of discipline. *Dur aux grands* was one of his maxims. But he would certainly have had an excellent roast chicken, served him from his own *fourgon*. Marlborough would have entered and quaffed the good wine with his officers—Cromwell, I think, too. The technique varies, and the results seem to have been good in all these cases.

We spent all the afternoon among the Army, and it was past seven when we got back to the caravan and the pleasant waves of its beach. I

was so uplifted by all I had seen that I was not at all tired and sat up late talking. Before Montgomery went to bed at ten o'clock, in accordance with his routine, he asked me to write something in his personal diary. I did so now and on several other occasions during the long war. Here is what I wrote this time:

"May the anniversary of Blenheim, which marks the opening of the new Command, bring to the Commander-in-Chief of the Eighth Army and his troops the fame and fortune they will surely deserve."

MARSHALL

"He was a statesman with a penetrating and commanding view of the whole scene."

Early the next day, May 26, General Marshall, the C.I.G.S., Ismay, and the rest of my party took off from the Potomac River in the flying-boat. The President came to see us off.

As soon as we were in the air I addressed myself to the Russian communiqué. As I found it very hard to make head or tail of the bundle of drafts, with all our emendations in the President's scrawls and mine, I sent it along to General Marshall, who two hours later presented me with a typed fair copy. I was immensely impressed with this document, which exactly expressed what the President and I wanted, and did so with a clarity and comprehension not only of the military but of the political issues involved. It excited my admiration. Hitherto I had thought of Marshall as a rugged soldier and a magnificent organiser and builder of armies—the American Carnot. But now I saw that he was a statesman with a penetrating and commanding view of the whole scene. I was delighted with his draft, and also that the task was done. I wrote to the President that it could not be better, and asked him to send it off with any alterations he might wish, without further reference to me. We landed to refuel at Botwood, in Newfoundland, and from there Marshall's draft and my letter were flown back to Washington. The President did not alter a word.

The selection of a Supreme Commander for "Overlord", our cross-Channel entry into Europe in 1944, was urgent. This of course affected in the most direct manner the military conduct of the war, and raised a number of personal issues of importance and delicacy. At the Quebec Conference I had agreed with the President that "Overlord" should fall to an American officer, and had so informed General Brooke, to whom I had previously offered the task. I understood from the President that he would choose General Marshall, and this was entirely satisfactory to us. However, in the interval between Quebec and our meeting in Cairo I became conscious that the President had not finally made up his mind about Marshall. None of the other arrangements could of course be made before the main decision had been taken. Meanwhile rumour became rife in the American Press, and there was the prospect of Parliamentary reactions in London. Admiral Leahy in his book mentions some of the American cross-currents. "The public," he writes, "assumed that Roosevelt would name Marshall as Supreme Commander. There was vehement objection to such a move in the Press. Opponents charged that Marshall was being given 'Dutch promotion'; that Roosevelt planned to take him out of a big job and put him into a small job; that it was a plot against Marshall. At the other extreme there were reports that the American Joint Chiefs considered the post of Supreme Command promotion and were jealous of Marshall."

This question was discussed between us at some length. I was anxious to emphasise the status of General Marshall in every way, pro-

George Catlett Marshall *was born in Uniontown, Pennsylvania, on December 31, 1880. He attended Virginia Military Institute, and fought on the French front in World War I. Between 1924 and 1927, he commanded a regiment stationed in China. He then taught at the infantry school at Fort Benning, Georgia. On September 1, 1939, Roosevelt appointed him Army Chief of Staff, an office that he held until the end of the war. In January 1947, Truman nominated him as Secretary of State. Believing that the Far East was lost to democracy, he focussed on Europe instead and advanced the economic plan that bears his name (1948-1952), which consisted of aid to 16 European countries: (85% of the relief was donated, while the remaining part was considered a long-term loan). For this initiative he received the 1953 Nobel Peace Prize. He resigned in 1949 and became president of the American Red Cross, but at the outbreak of the Korean War (1950), he was recalled as Defence Secretary (1950-1951). Marshall died on October 16, 1959, in Washington, D.C..*

vided that the authority of the Joint and Combined Chiefs of Staff was not impaired.

In all our many talks at Cairo the President never referred to the vital and urgent issue of the command of "Overlord", and I was under the impression that our original arrangement and agreement held good. But on the day before his departure from Cairo he told me his final decision. We were driving in his motor-car from Cairo to the Pyramids. He then said, almost casually, that he could not spare General Marshall, whose great influence at the head of military affairs and of the war direction, under the President, was invaluable, and indispens-

able to the successful conduct of the war. He therefore proposed to nominate Eisenhower to "Overlord", and asked me for my opinion. I said it was for him to decide, but that we had also the warmest regard for General Eisenhower, and would trust our fortunes to his direction with hearty goodwill.

Up to this time I had thought Eisenhower was to go to Washington as Military Chief of Staff, while Marshall commanded "Overlord". Eisenhower had heard of this too, and was very unhappy at the prospect of leaving the Mediterranean for Washington. Now it was all settled: Eisenhower for "Overlord", Marshall to

Southern Italy, February 13, 1943: from left to right, Generals W. G. Livesay, George Marshall, Joseph T. McNarney, Mark Clark, and Lucian Truscott examine the plan of action.

Great Britain, April 16, 1942: Marshall and Churchill in an armoured vehicle during an inspection of newly created units.

Italy, February 1945: General John K. Cannon talks with George Marshall.

stay at Washington, and a British commander for the Mediterranean.

The full story of the President's long delay and hesitations and of his final decision is referred to by Mr. Hopkins' biographer, who says that Roosevelt made the decision on Sunday, December 5, "against the almost impassioned advice of Hopkins and Stimson, against the known preference of both Stalin and Churchill, against his own proclaimed inclination." Then Mr. Sherwood quotes the following extract from a note which he had from General Marshall after the war. "If I recall," said Marshall, "the President stated, in completing our conversation, 'I feel I could not sleep at night with you out of the country.'" There can be little doubt that the President felt that the command only of "Overlord" was not sufficient to justify General Marshall's departure from Washington.

MARLBOROUGH

EISENHOWER

"He considered that Sicily should only be attacked if our purpose was to clear the Mediterranean sea-route."

On June 21, when we were alone together after lunch, Harry Hopkins said to me, "There are a couple of American officers the President would like you to meet, as they are very highly thought of in the Army, by Marshall, and by him." At five o'clock therefore Major-Generals Eisenhower and Clark were brought to my air-cooled room. I was immediately impressed by these remarkable but hitherto unknown men. They had both come from the President, whom they had just seen for the first time. We talked almost entirely about the major cross-Channel invasion in 1943, "Round-up" as it was then called, on which their thoughts had evidently been concentrated. We had a most agreeable discussion, lasting for over an hour. In order to convince them of my personal interest in the project I gave them a copy of the paper I had written for the Chiefs of Staff on June 15, two days before I started, in which I had set forth my first thoughts of the method and scale of such an operation. At any rate, they seemed much pleased with the spirit of the document. At that time I thought of the spring or summer of 1943 as the date for the

attempt. I felt sure that these officers were intended to play a great part in it, and that was the reason why they had been sent to make my acquaintance. Thus began a friendship which across all the ups and downs of war I have preserved with deep satisfaction to this day.

General Eisenhower considered that Sicily should only be attacked if our purpose was to clear the Mediterranean sea-route. If our real purpose was to invade and defeat Italy he thought that our proper initial objectives were Sardinia and Corsica, "since these islands lie on the flank of the long Italian boot and would force a very much greater dispersion of enemy strength in Italy than the mere occupation of Sicily, which lies off the mountainous toe of

Dwigt David Eisenhower *was born in Denison, Texas, on October 14, 1890, to an indigent family. In 1911, he entered the military academy at West Point, and he attained the rank of general in 1941. He was sent to Panama (1922-1924), and was later General MacArthur's Chief of Staff (1933-1935). In December 1941, he was called to Washington as Deputy Chief of Operation Projects, and he played an important role in planning the invasion of Europe. He led the landing in northern Africa (November 1942), the invasion of Tunisia, and the landing in Sicily. From November 1943, he headed the Allied forces in Europe, conducting the landing in Normandy and the invasion of Germany. After the war, he was Army Chief of Staff, and finally retired in 1948. Recalled by Truman, he was appointed head of the armies of NATO, but resigned from this office in 1952, turning to politics as a Republican presidential candidate. He won those elections, and was re-elected in 1956. He supported the Cold War and fought against racial segregation. He retired to private life and died in Washington, on March 28, 1969.*

the peninsula." This was no doubt a military opinion of high authority, though one I could not share. But political forces play their part, and the capture of Sicily and the direct invasion of Italy were to bring about results of a far more swift and far-reaching character.

The capture of Sicily was an undertaking of the first magnitude. Although eclipsed by events in Normandy, its importance and its difficulties should not be underrated. The landing was based on the experience gained in North Africa, and those who planned "Overlord" learned much from "Husky". In the initial assault nearly 3,000 ships and landing-craft took part, carrying between them 160,000 men,

14,000 vehicles, 600 tanks, and 1,800 guns. These forces had to be collected, trained, equipped, and eventually embarked, with all the vast impedimenta of amphibious warfare, at widely dispersed bases in the Mediterranean, in Great Britain, and in the United States. Detailed planning was required from subordinate commanders whose headquarters were separated by thousands of miles. All these plans had to be welded together by the Supreme Commander at Algiers. Here a special Allied Staff controlled and co-ordinated all preparations. As the plan developed many problems arose which could only be solved by the Combined Chiefs of Staff. Finally the convoys had to be assem-

Northern Africa, May 4, 1943: Eisenhower boards a British ship three months before the landing in Sicily. The American general, shown in a much more official photograph on the previous page, would have preferred landing in Sardinia and Corsica.

Eisenhower and Clark.

During the preparations for the landing in Normandy.

Great Britain, June 6, 1944: Eisenhower with U.S. paratroopers, shortly before the flight that will drop them in Normandy.

Eisenhower salutes infantrymen embarking for Normandy.

322

French front, November 1944: Eisenhower and Churchill, between Generals Brooke (on the left) and Tedder.

New York, June 1945: the triumphal homecoming parade on Fifth Avenue for Eisenhower; sitting next to him is New York Mayor Fiorello La Guardia. Seven years later, the American general was elected President of the United States.

bled, escorted across the oceans and through the narrow seas, and concentrated in the battle area at the right time.

Planning at General Eisenhower's headquarters had begun in February. It now became necessary to appoint his principal subordinates.

In all wars where allies are fighting together the control of strategy usually rests in the main with whoever holds the larger forces. This may be modified by political considerations or the relative war effort in other theatres, but the principle that the more powerful army must rule is sound. For reasons of policy we had hitherto yielded the command and direction of the campaign in North-West Africa to the United States. At the beginning they were preponderant in

numbers and influence. In the months that had passed since "Torch" began the arrival of the victorious Eighth Army from the Desert and the building up in Tunisia of the British First Army had given us the proportion there of eleven British divisions to four American. Nevertheless I strictly adhered to the theme that "Torch" was an American expedition, and in every way supported General Eisenhower's position as Supreme Commander. It was however understood in practice that General Alexander as Eisenhower's Deputy had the full operational command. It was in these circumstances that the victory of Tunis was gained and the general picture presented to the American public and to the world as an overriding United States enterprise.

CREDITS

The text in this book has been selected from the following pages of the paperback edition of *The Second World War*, published in six volumes by Houghton Mifflin Company.

The Battles

The Attack on Poland
Volume I, chapter XXIV, pp. 396-399

The Invasion of France
Volume II, chapter II, pp. 30-31, 35-36, 38-40

Dunkirk
Volume II, chapters IV and V, pp. 74-78, 84-86, 90-92

The Battle of Britain
Volume II, chapter XVI, pp. 281-282, 291-293, 297

War against Greece
Volume II, chapter XXVII, pp. 470-472, 486, 481-482

The Battle of the Atlantic
Volume III, chapter VII, pp. 98-99, 109-110

The Attack on the USSR
Volume III, chapters XXI and XXV, pp. 337-338, 419

Cyrenaica
Volume IV, chapter II, pp. 30-31

U-boats
Volume IV, chapter VII, pp. 95-97

The Battle of Midway
Volume IV, chapter XIV, pp. 221-224, 226

Malta and the Convoys
Volume IV, chapter XVII, pp. 265-271
El Alamein
Volume IV, chapter XXXIII, pp. 530-531, 536-539

The Caucasus and Stalingrad
Volume IV, chapter XXXII, pp. 522-525

The Battle of Tunis
Volume IV, chapter XLII, pp. 690, 692-693, 698

The Landing in Sicily
Volume V, chapter II, pp. 30-31, 35-39

The Landing at Salerno
Volume V, chapter VII, pp. 124-125, 133, 136-137

The Battle of Anzio
Volume V, chapter XXVII, pp. 425-426, 428-431, 433-434, 437

Cassino
Volume V, chapters XXVII, XXVIII, and XXXIV, pp. 428-429, 442-444, 448, 450-451, 528-531, 536-539

The Landing in Normandy
Volume VI, chapter II, pp. 15-18, 20-21, 25, 28, 30-33

The End of the Campaign in Italy
Volume VI, chapter XXXI, pp. 454-456, 458

The Atomic Bomb
Volume VI, chapter XXXVII, pp. 551-553

The Leaders

Churchill
Vol. I, chap. XXXVIII, pp. 599, 601
Vol. II, chap. I, pp. 17, 20-21, 24
Vol. IV, chap. IV, pp. 54; chap. V, pp. 78-79, 80

Hitler
Vol. I, chap. IV, pp. 47-51; chap. XV, pp. 232-234; chap. XXVI, pp. 429-430
Vol. II, chap. XXIX, pp. 509-511
Vol. III, chap. XX, p. 329
Vol. V, chap. III, pp. 48-50
Vol. VI, chap. XXXII, pp. 463-464

Mussolini
Vol. II, chap. VI, pp. 105-108; chap. XXXI, pp. 547-549
Vol. V, chap. III, pp. 40, 45-48; chap. XI, p. 170
Vol. VI, chap. XXXI, pp. 460-461

Chamberlain
Vol. I, chap. XII, pp. 189-200; chap. XXXVIII, pp. 596-598

Roosevelt
Vol. III, chap. XXXV, pp. 587-588; chap. XXXVI, pp. 604-605, 617
Vol. IV, chap. XXXVIII, pp.621-622
Vol. VI, chap. XXVIII, pp. 412-417

Stalin
Vol. III, chap. XX, p. 328
Vol. IV, chap. XXVII, pp. 429-435, chap. XXVIII, pp. 436-440, 443

De Gaulle
Vol. II, chap. X, p. 189; chap. XXVI, pp. 449-451
Vol. IV, chap. XXXVIII, p. 611
Vol. V, chap. XXV, pp. 400-402

Chiang Kai-shek
Vol. V, chap. XVIII, pp. 289-291

Tito
Vol. VI, chap. VI, pp. 79-84

Truman
Vol. VI, chap. XXVIII, pp. 418-419; chap. XXXVIII, pp. 546-548

Ribbentrop
Vol. I, chap. XII, pp. 200-201; chap. XV, pp. 243-244

Hess
Vol. III, chap. III, pp. 43-45, 47-49

Ciano
Vol. I, chap. XIX, pp. 305-306
Vol. II, chap. VI, pp. 115-116; chap. XXXI, p. 546

Eden
Vol. I, chap. VIII, pp. 118-119; chap. XIV, pp. 218-219, 231

Molotov
Vol. I, chap. XX, pp. 330-331
Vol. IV, chap. XIX, pp. 296-297, 300-301, 304-305

Rommel
Vol. III, chap. XI, pp. 175-177
Vol. VI, chap. I, pp. 9-10

Alexander
Vol. IV, chap. IX, pp. 146-147, 151

Montgomery
Vol. IV, chap. XXVI, pp. 419-420; chap. XXIX, pp. 462-465

Marshall
Vol. IV, chap. XLV, pp. 726-727
Vol. V, chap. XVII, pp. 267-268; chap. XXIII, pp. 369-370

Eisenhower
Vol. IV, chap. XXII, p. 345
Vol. V, chap. II, pp. 23-24